SENSE OF WONDER

MY LIFE IN COMIC FANDOM
—THE WHOLE STORY

BILL SCHELLY

North Atlantic Books
Berkeley, California

Part 1 of this book was published in 2001 by TwoMorrows Publishing and is presented here in slightly revised form. Part 2 is entirely new, written for this edition. The person identified as "Mario Vitale" in this book asked that his real name not be used due to privacy concerns. Captain America frontispiece is courtesy of the Jack Kirby Estate and Michael Allred. The cover photo is the author's senior high school photograph. Uncredited photos are courtesy of Bill Schelly.

Published by   Cover design by Jasmine Hromjak
North Atlantic Books   Book design by Happenstance Type-O-Rama
Berkeley, California   Printed in the United States of America

Sense of Wonder: My Life in Comic Fandom—The Whole Story is sponsored and published by the Society for the Study of Native Arts and Sciences (dba North Atlantic Books), an educational nonprofit based in Berkeley, California, that collaborates with partners to develop cross-cultural perspectives, nurture holistic views of art, science, the humanities, and healing, and seed personal and global transformation by publishing work on the relationship of body, spirit, and nature.

North Atlantic Books' publications are available through most bookstores. For further information, visit our website at www.northatlanticbooks.com or call 800-733-3000.

Library of Congress Cataloging-in-Publication Data

Names: Schelly, William, 1951- author.
Title: Sense of wonder : my life in comic fandom—the whole story / Bill
    Schelly.
Description: Berkeley, California : North Atlantic Books, [2018] | "Part 1 of
    this book was published in 2001 by TwoMorrows Publishing, and is presented
    here in slightly revised form. Part 2 is entirely new, written for this
    edition."—ECIP galley | Includes index.
Identifiers: LCCN 2017048122 | ISBN 9781623171513 (paperback)
Subjects: LCSH: Comic books, strips, etc.—United States—History. | Schelly,
    William, 1951- | Comic book fans—United States—Biography. | Gay
    men—United States—Biography. | BISAC: LITERARY CRITICISM / Comics &
    Graphic Novels. | SOCIAL SCIENCE / Popular Culture.
Classification: LCC PN6725 .S374 2018 | DDC 741.5973—dc23
LC record available at https://lccn.loc.gov/2017048122

1 2 3 4 5 6 7 8 9 KPC 22 21 20 19 18

Printed on recycled paper.

North Atlantic Books is committed to the protection of our environment. We partner with FSC-certified printers using soy-based inks and print on recycled paper whenever possible.

To Jaimeson and Tara

CONTENTS

ACKNOWLEDGMENTS   IX

INTRODUCTION   1

PART 1

1—MORE POWERFUL THAN A LOCOMOTIVE   7

2—FAMILY MATTERS   15

3—THE DAY IT ALL CLICKED   23

4—WELCOME TO FANDOMLAND   37

5—I YAM WHAT I YAM   59

6—ENTER: MARSHALL LANZ   81

7—*SENSE OF WONDER*: THE BIRTH OF THE FANZINE   95

8—COLORING OUTSIDE THE LINES   105

9—FULL-THROTTLE FANAC   121

10—STRANGER IN A STRANGE LAND   133

11—CONFESSIONS OF A FANZINE EDITOR   151

12—BLAME IT ON THE BOSSA NOVA   163

13—A SUCCESSOR FOR *ALTER EGO*?   181

14—THE LIFE YOU SAVE MAY BE YOUR OWN   195

15—SECRET IDENTITY NO MORE   207

16—THE PULSING HEART OF FANDOM   215

17—THE FAN SITTING TWO ROWS BACK   231

PART 2

18—BREAKING UP IS HARD TO DO   241

19—GIVING VOICE TO SILENT FILMS   255

20—SUPER UPS, SUPER DOWNS, SUPER COMICS   267

21—PUTTING DOWN ROOTS   287

22—BATMAN BROUGHT ME BACK   297

23—*THE GOLDEN AGE OF COMIC FANDOM*   317

24—HAMSTER PRESS   329

25—THE ART OF BIOGRAPHY   347

26—JAIMESON'S JOURNEY   367

27—FANDOM'S FIFTIETH BIRTHDAY   383

28—MAD ABOUT HARVEY   391

29—LOVE STREET   405

INDEX   410

ABOUT THE AUTHOR   420

OTHER BOOKS BY BILL SCHELLY   421

ACKNOWLEDGMENTS

The list of people who contributed to this book in one way or another is long, and it's even longer when I include those who inspired me in the process.

For artwork and photographs that appear herein, I'm grateful to Michael Allred, David Armstrong, E. B. Boatner, Tina Bradley, Aaron Caplan, Peter Carlsson, Bob Cosgrove, Steve Ditko, Michael Dooley, Rod Dyke, Jeff Gelb, Adam Haney, Anita Hoyle, Alan Hutchinson, J. Michael Kaluta, Batton Lash, David Lofvers, Russ Maheras, Raymond Miller, Keeli McCarthy, John Morrow, Nils Osmar, Perry Plush, Doug Potter, Jeanne Russell, Rob Salkowitz, Bob Sanborn, Gary Sassaman, Jim Shooter, Howard Siegel, Larry Summers, Dann Thomas, and Bill G. Wilson.

For other contributions of various kinds, I thank Barbara Barker, Howard Cruse, Jackie Estrada, Scott Fresina, Carl Gafford, Gary Groth, Merlin Haas, R. C. Harvey, Jeffrey Kipper, Greg Koudoulian, Paul Levitz, Andy Mangels, George R. R. Martin, Tom Robbins, Roy Thomas, Carol Tilley, and Michael Uslan.

My posthumous thanks go to Ken Barr, C. C. Beck, D. Bruce Berry, Otto Binder, Landon Chesney, Allen DeShong, Will Eisner, Will Elder, John Fantucchio, Dick Giordano, Richard "Grass" Green, Don Greene, Stan Henry, Rand Holmes, Bob Kane, Gil Kane, Jack Kirby, Joe Kubert, Harvey Kurtzman, Marshall Lanz, Don Newton, Julius Schwartz, Gary Speer, Rick Sprague, Don Thompson, Dick Trageser, and Biljo White.

For inspiring and supporting me, I must extend my love and appreciation to my children, Jaimeson and Tara, my brother Steve Schelly, and my extended family, which includes Renie (Maureen) Jones and her siblings, Robert and Andrea (and Andrea's husband Terry). I also thank Andrea's daughter, Jules Jones, whose significant other is Sam Akina; they're filmmakers with significant credits on Imdb. Then there's Renie's mother, Rita, who is ninety-two, and Sam and Jules's daughter, Tesla, who passed her first birthday not long ago. The Seymour family includes Stephanie; her husband, Steve; her mother, Jane; her daughter, Luna; and her siblings, Greg and Kristen, along with assorted aunts, uncles, cousins, and spouses.

Finally, thanks to the good people at North Atlantic Books who believed in this extended version of *Sense of Wonder* and who helped me every step of the way.

INTRODUCTION

In 2001, I wrote a book titled *Sense of Wonder: A Life in Comic Fandom.* It quickly sold out, and in the ensuing years, at signings in bookstores and other venues, people told me it was their favorite of all my books. They said things like, "I could really relate to it," "I'm not much into comic books, but it reminded me of [fill in the blank]," and "When I reached the end, I wondered what happened next."

This got me thinking. The book's story ended shortly after I turned twenty-one, when I had no idea what the future held. Now, forty-four years later, I know what came next, and it struck me how the more recent decades of my life have answered many of the questions that filled me as a youth. In particular, I used to wonder how I would find a way to express my inner creativity as an artist or writer. As it turned out, I did become a writer, although the way I got from there to here is much different from what I imagined as a boy, a teenager, and a young man. How that happened makes up part 2 of this expanded edition of *Sense of Wonder.* In my story, you might find some things we have in common and perhaps even some insight into how you might move forward on your own path. I find that inspiration comes from the unlikeliest of sources, so in your case, why not from my story?

Comic fandom is interesting because the sequential art medium itself is an endless source of fascination, but what's equally interesting is the way early fandom was a mix of all kinds of people. When you were corresponding with someone through that archaic method now known as snail mail, you didn't know if the person on the other end was black, or in a wheelchair, or a stutterer, or anyone ostracized for a myriad of reasons in white-bread America of the 1960s. The interests you had in common were all that mattered. Even when the grass-roots fandom movement progressed to the point where fans gathered for meetings and conventions, the love of a shared hobby was more important than any human differences.

However, it's important to remember that there are some differences—such as a nonconforming sexual orientation or gender identity—that aren't readily detectable in person. In the 1960s, the closet reigned supreme for homosexuals and others not on the societally sanctioned end of the Kinsey scale. If "coming out" as an adult comic book reader was difficult before the rise of nerd culture, coming out as gay was difficult to the power of ten. To a lot of people, being gay meant you were an untouchable. If you weren't heterosexual, you were considered, at the least, mentally ill.

I know because I'm gay and always have been. This means that along with all the other challenges one encounters in life, I've had one more: how to deal with this difference within myself and what it means for my life. How could I tell my parents and siblings, and what would they think when they found out? Did it mean I wouldn't have a spouse or partner in life? Did it mean I wouldn't have children? These are not small concerns. My sexual orientation raised other questions: how did being gay relate to my love of comic art? Did comic books mean something different to me from what they meant to a straight person? What did it mean to be a homosexual in comic fandom?

When I decided to write this expanded version of *Sense of Wonder*, I realized it was impossible to tell my complete story without being frank about my sexuality. (Of course, my friends and family have known about it for decades.) Who you are as a person goes deeper than your sexual orientation or gender identity, but there's no denying the life-shaping force of one's sexuality. Thanks to a lot of activists over the years, being gay has much less of a stigma now than it did in 1966. One thing I know for sure: I wasn't the only comics fan with a minority sexual identity. Fandom reflected the larger society, so every kind of human being was a part of that group. And aren't all of us different anyway? Don't all of us feel left out sometimes? Don't a lot of us feel like our dreams might not come true?

For me, the way forward took me through a hobby that told stories of heroic super-beings, intrepid reporters, enterprising ducks, worthless playboys, and a whole lot more. This is the true story of a boy whose whole world was altered forever at the age of eight, when his sense of wonder was awakened in the pages of a simple, four-color comic book. It's the story of how that hobby led, in the unlikeliest of ways, to the writing career he always wanted.

So if you're among the frustrated, there's a message here for you—a message of hope—which is all I had for a long time.

—BILL SCHELLY
SEATTLE, WASHINGTON

The most beautiful thing we can experience is the mysterious. It is the source of all true art and science. He to whom this emotion is a stranger, who can no longer pause to wonder and stand rapt in awe, is as good as dead.

—ALBERT EINSTEIN

The author in 1972. Photo: Anita Holye.

PART 1

Top: The young Schelly family ca. 1953. Joanne and Carl, with me and Steve.

Left: The Schelly clan several years later, with third brother Dave.

Above: The author at about eight years old.

1.

MORE POWERFUL THAN A LOCOMOTIVE

Why was it that no matter how early we got up on the first day of a Schelly family vacation trip, we were always behind schedule?

My tall father, Carl, led the way along the sidewalk. "There's the terminal entrance—hurry!" he said. I was too young to discern the inherent irony in such a thing as a "terminal entrance." We headed toward the blackened granite edifice of the Pittsburgh railroad depot known as Penn Station.

My mother, Joanne, fussed to keep us in line. "C'mon, Bill! You too, David! Where's Steve?"

We were jazzed on kid adrenaline, taking two steps for every stride of Dad's long legs. A porter wearing a snappy-looking uniform pushed a dolly full of our luggage behind us.

We entered the darkened interior of the massive building. The amplified metallic voice on the public address system twanged with the reverberation born of marble floors and walls. It sounded like the voice of destiny with nasal congestion.

Columbus ... Indianapolis ... Chicago.

To my eight-year-old consciousness, these destinations conjured up images as exotic as Singapore and Rangoon. I had butterflies in the pit of my stomach.

I was nearly hairless unless you counted my quarter-inch crew cut of bristling scalp stubble. With my blond hair and fair skin, I looked like a little bald man. My brothers Steve (ten years old) and Dave (age five) were similarly shorn.

Travel wasn't exactly an informal occasion in 1960. Mom wore a dress, a hat, and heels, and we boys mustered out in neat pants and shirts. Dad was dressed for the office in suit and tie because he had to stay behind for work; he'd fly out to join us in Oregon in a week.

"Your train is a few minutes late, so we're here in plenty of time," he told Mom as he scanned the big board marked "Arrivals and Departures." They visibly relaxed. Dad showed the porter the tickets with our seat assignments and slipped him a coin. The man wheeled our baggage through the swinging doors to the loading platform.

Amid the bustle, the wafting cigarette smoke, and the echoing announcements, a colorful display caught our attention as we made our way toward the waiting area: the terminal newsstand. Within the churchlike surroundings—vaulted windows and wooden pews—the newsstand was like a stained-glass window, with its glossy paper covers and pulpy newsprint emblazoned with four-color printing. It was well-stocked with all manner of ephemeral reading matter: newspapers, magazines, paperbacks, puzzle books, and, of course, comic books. The newsie also sold smoking products. His stand reeked of tobacco.

Dad turned to us. "Would each of you boys like a comic book to read on the train?"

My brothers were quick in making their reading choices. Steve grabbed a western-themed comic, probably featuring Walt Disney's Davy Crockett; he had only recently given up his coonskin cap. Dave went for an issue of *Looney Tunes* with Sylvester and Tweety.

My eyes were like pinballs, bouncing around the colorful display, checking out various possibilities. *Our Fighting Forces*? No. *My Greatest Adventure*? I don't think so. *Young Romance*? No! No! No!

Then something familiar attracted my attention. My eyes landed on a comic book featuring a character I couldn't help but recognize, even if I hadn't read his comic book adventures before: Superman. The logo in bold yellow and red block letters spelled out the title: *Giant Superman Annual* #1. The subtitle read: *An all-star collection of the greatest super-stories ever published!*

DC Comics' house advertisement for *Giant Superman Annual* #1 (June 1960). Characters ™ and © DC Comics.

My choice was made. I pulled the comic book out and handed it up to Dad. He tossed a dime onto the counter, but the clerk said, "That one's a quarter."

Dad frowned. "A quarter?" He withdrew the dime and handed the comic book back to me. "You'd better put this one back, son. Find one for ten cents."

I had sensed something more substantial about the *feel* of this comic book than the others ones on the stand. I said, "Look, Dad. This one is extra thick, see? I can read it for a long time."

"The ones I got for your brothers cost a dime," Dad said. "They won't like it if I spend more on you."

I looked up into his eyes looming high above me. "*Please* can I have this one? It has everything about Superman." I was working him, playing on our unspoken understanding that I was his favorite.

He sighed, then shared a smile with the clerk as he tossed down the larger coin. "Okay ... but don't tell your brothers."

"I won't. Thanks, Dad."

I struggled to contain my excitement. Until now I had only been looking forward to a train trip. Now I would have the extra bonus of an excursion into the Superman mythos. I joined my family on the wooden pews. The bustling milieu around me no longer held any appeal.

Giant Superman Annual #1 is the first comic book I remember picking out for myself. If I'd seen any before then, they hadn't made any particular impression on me—but this one certainly did. Maybe it was the solid, foursquare look of the cover, with Superman's heavily muscled frame facing directly forward as he burst a chain by expanding his chest. The cover symmetry was further enhanced by two rows of five panels on either side of the Man of Steel, each depicting an important supporting character: Lois Lane, Jimmy Olsen, Jor-El, et al. This was clearly a special comic book.

Quivering with anticipation, I opened the cover and read the title of the opening tale: "Superman's First Exploit." What was an *exploit*, I wondered? Well, I thought I could probably figure the word out from the way it was used in the story.

"Bill!" Mom's voice penetrated my bubble of concentration. "Put that down."

"What? This comic book? But ..."

"If you read it all now, you won't have anything left to read on the train."

I sighed and let the book fall shut. Ugh. Back to boring reality. It wasn't too bad, though. We didn't have long to wait. The public address system emitted a series of nasal barks. The word "Chicago" was comprehensible among them. It was time. We moved through the wide doors to the loading platform.

In 1960, steam trains were a thing of the past. We were traveling in a sleek, state-of-the-art diesel train. The smell of oil and air brakes charged the platform area with a special pungency. Amid the commotion of boarding passengers, we said our goodbyes to Dad, and my parents kissed. We mounted the steps, waved, and were swallowed by the train.

As soon as we found our seats, I again opened my comic book and began reading "Superman's First Exploit." It began at the offices of the *Daily Planet* newspaper, where Superman worked in his guise as reporter Clark Kent. The paper was sponsoring a contest to see which reader could remember the earliest feat performed by Superman after he'd arrived on earth in a tiny rocket as a tot fleeing the exploding planet Krypton. At the story's climax, Superman himself was asked to try to remember his own first feat, which must have occurred when he was a small child.

One image grabbed me: a dramatic close-up of Superman's face in deep shadows. The overhead caption read, "And the mighty mind of Superman reaches back, back to his

Key panel from "Superman's First Exploit." Superman ™ and © DC Comics.

infancy on the planet Krypton!" Superman said, "I remember —on Krypton, my father Jor-El warning of doom …" This was heavy stuff for a third grader. One phrase especially intrigued me, and I read it again: *The mighty mind of Superman.* I tried to imagine what it would be like to have a mighty mind. What would that mean? I understood super-strength, but a super-*mind?*

"Bill. What are you doing?"

"Reading."

"Don't read that whole comic book before the train even leaves the station," Mom commanded.

"Aw, *Moooommmm,*" I moaned, letting the book fall shut again.

The conductor pulled up his step stool and shut the door. The train jerked—jostled—stopped—then groaned into motion. The clack-clacking of the metal wheels on the tracks began. Slowly gaining speed, the train pulled out of the confines of the depot and headed on its route through the industrial part of town and points west.

I barely noticed. I was completely, totally, 100 percent absorbed in the colorful comic book on my lap. As I read the annual, the first of its kind from National Periodical Publications (now known as DC Comics), I was taking a crash course in Superman 101. I learned about his origin, his friends, his cousin, and his pets.

My first exposure to the working world was the portrayal of the *Daily Planet* offices. Characters ™ and © DC Comics.

Splash panel for the story introducing Supergirl, who turned out to be the Man of Steel's cousin (from *Action Comics* #252). Characters ™ and © DC Comics.

Most of all, I learned about his *powers.*

Superman's awesome strength was shown right up front on that memorable cover. I would soon realize that his strength was so great that its outer limit had never been determined. My favorite power was his ability to fly. Flying is a "dream power." When we do it in our dreams—and who of us hasn't?—it seems perfectly logical that we're able to cast off gravity's bonds. His X-ray vision, the ability to see through solid walls (unless they were made of lead), conjured up the capacity to know everyone's secrets. And the Man of Steel's invulnerability was something a kid could keenly appreciate. No matter what the school bully threw at you, it would bounce off.

"Superman's First Exploit" took place mostly in the offices of the *Daily Planet*, the leading newspaper in Metropolis, U.S.A. It gave me an early glimpse into the milieu of adults at work.

The concept of having a secret identity especially captured my imagination. No one suspected that under his mild-mannered exterior, Clark Kent was actually a being of untold power and glamour—a hero for all to admire. My daydreams came alive with fantasies of having my own powers that I had to conceal from the world, lest criminals harm my loved ones.

Some of the stories took me by surprise because they packed an emotional wallop. When Superman discovered that his romance with Lori Lemaris was doomed because she was revealed to be a mermaid (in "The Girl from Superman's Past!"), a feeling of intense regret washed over me. In "The Supergirl from Krypton!", when Superman learned that his cousin, Kara, had also miraculously survived the destruction of his birth planet—meaning not only that he wasn't alone, but he had a *family*—I was deeply moved.

That day on the train, I experienced a sense of wonder: the power of an imaginative universe to enthrall.

2.

FAMILY MATTERS

It was only natural that trains loomed large in our lives. Dad worked for the Northern Pacific Railroad, whose tagline was "the Main Street to the Northwest." He was the top man in the Pittsburgh office, which was an odd city for him to be located in because the NP didn't run farther east than Chicago. His job as general agent was to see that the railroad got its fair share of the freight traffic moving westward from the Windy City. The position had a good deal of responsibility but didn't pay a lot. Money was always tight in the Schelly family.

When it came to train travel, however, we had a special advantage. Dad's company discount made tickets inexpensive, allowing us to spend money on an upgrade of our accommodations. Instead of traveling by standard coach, we had private rooms, two compartments with two sleeping berths each, which could be connected by opening folding doors between them. This made travel a breeze.

I guess trains were more than just a job to my dad, because his first major gift to us was the Lionel train set he gave us for Christmas. All kids loved trains in those days, the same way they love computer games today.

By the time Mom, my brothers, and I changed from the Pennsylvania Railroad to a Northern Pacific train in Chicago, I must have read my *Superman Annual* #1 four or five times. My imagination danced with dynamic images as we sped past the endless wheat fields of North Dakota.

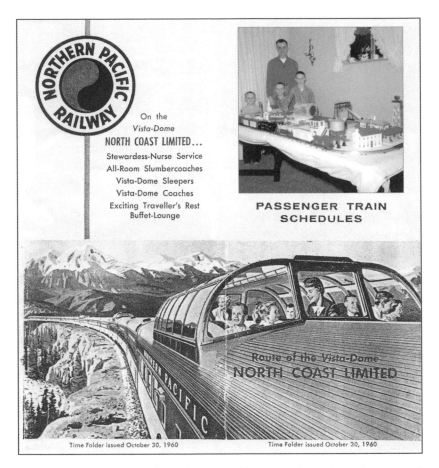

Top: The Schelly family train (Lionel) set up at Christmas 1958, not long after we moved to Pittsburgh. Dad with the three boys: Dave, me, and Steve. **Bottom:** Front of a Northern Pacific train schedule issued in 1960, the year *Giant Superman Annual* #1 was published.

For a kid, a cross-country train trip is an exciting adventure. As long as we didn't disturb the adults, we could explore all the passenger cars, including the Vista Dome with its panoramic view. We wanted to poke and pry into every part of the train—even the porters' stations, which were supposed to be off limits to us. My most indelible memory, however, is of the times when I simply curled up in my bunk and was gently rocked to sleep by the rhythmic gallop of the wheels on the metal tracks.

The term "nuclear family" could have been invented to describe the Schelly clan. Dad was the proton, Mom was the neutron, and my brothers and I were the electrons, spinning around them in our individual orbits.

We had been displaced from our original home in the Pacific Northwest like pawns on a chessboard when the railroad decided to move us to San Francisco in 1953 and then to Pittsburgh three years later. To serve a greater corporate purpose, we were plopped down thousands of miles from friends and relatives, faced with the task of building a whole new life from scratch. Dad had to work extra hours to get a grip on the railroad marketplace in his new territory, leaving Mom to take care of the home front on her own.

Although we were all newcomers in a strange town, we didn't exactly pull together and become closer through sharing the experience. Our family dynamics didn't allow us to benefit from this sort of challenge. Like a lot of families, we had difficulty communicating with each other. All of us seemed to have expectations of the others that we were ill-equipped to articulate or fulfill. It was like a car engine with spark plugs whose firing order was out of whack. Result? A bumpy ride.

Dad was an old-fashioned man whose worldview was mainly shaped by the Great Depression. A deep fear of unemployment haunted him, and he worshipped at the altar of job security. As a husband and father, he expected his word to carry the force of law in the family, and everyone else's role was to obey. When we didn't or couldn't fall exactly into line, he grew frustrated and, eventually, bitter.

My folks were brought up believing that duty and obligation to the family and the community were paramount. The needs of the individual, especially emotional needs, were of secondary importance. I suppose this is partly a result of the lingering social ethic that was so important during World War II. Neither the Schellys nor the Winns (my mother's family) had ever felt secure in their place on the social ladder, so they paid special attention to what the neighbors would think.

Dad was born on April 4, 1912 (a week before the Titanic began its doomed voyage), the only child of Charles and Helena Schelly, German immigrants who had settled in Ritzville, Washington, around 1900. (Helena was actually born in Ukraine.) Although my father was named Carl, his mother called him "Artie" (after his middle name, Arthur) during World War I to avoid anti-German sentiment.

Mom (Joanne Winn) was born on December 5, 1927, the year of Charles Lindberg's historic transatlantic flight. Her parents, Russ and Gladys, were descendants of English farmers who had moved west looking for better land and ended up in tiny eastern Washington towns. Joanne was the third child in her family, preceded by two boys. She grew up to be a dark-haired beauty who must have had her share of suitors.

By the time the United States entered World War II, both families had moved to the larger town of Walla Walla, which took its name from an American Indian tribal name meaning "many rivers." The romance between Joanne and Carl was of the May-September variety, as the fifteen-year disparity in their birth dates attests. Mom's first fiancé had been killed in an explosion when his car collided with a gasoline truck. Dad had a modest job as a clerk for the railroad when they met. They got married in 1948 and moved into a cottage at 1331 Tillamook Lane, where they began their life together. That life involved having three children in fairly rapid succession.

Stephen, the first of three boys, was born in 1949. Next came me, William, in 1951, named after my mom's brother, an Air Force navigator killed in World War II. (On the verge of completing his required number of flights in the Pacific theater, he volunteered for one more—and never returned.) After moving to San Francisco so my dad could accept a job promotion, the Schellys added a third and last sibling, David, in 1954. Not long after we settled in our new home, the Northern Pacific offered another, even better opportunity: the post of general agent in their Pittsburgh office. As 1956 drew to a close, my mother found herself riding herd on three rambunctious young boys on the three-day train trip to Steel Town, U.S.A.—and doing it without my dad, who flew ahead separately.

Having grown up in small towns, my parents must have found San Francisco and Pittsburgh intimidating. Yet cope they did. In retrospect, Mom's determination to do what was necessary to get settled in an eastern metropolis seems almost heroic. She had to learn to drive the city's labyrinthine streets, enroll us in school, find doctors and dentists for us, and decorate and manage our new household on a paper thin budget. Financial pressures on our family were intense, though probably no more so than for others in our neighborhood.

We had no family members around to rely on for babysitting, emotional support, or the many other ways extended families can ease life's burdens for each other. It was the five of us, marching, marching, marching, because there was nothing else to be done. This didn't stop holes from forming in our hearts—the kind that can never really be filled.

I wasn't thinking about any of that as I pored over my copy of *Giant Superman Annual* #1, which lost none of its magic in successive readings during the three-day journey from Pittsburgh to Portland, Oregon. Even as we got off the train to excited chatter and Grandma Winn's kisses, my mind was buzzing with colorful images. I was too preoccupied, and too young, to appreciate how much this moment must have meant to Mom. For the Schelly boys, it represented the beginning of a new phase of our vacation that was just as exciting as the train ride had been.

Russ and Gladys Winn owned several acres of land in Albany, Oregon, a small lumber town south of Salem, which accommodated a rambling house, a barn with stables, peach and cherry orchards, and some wild fields where they could ride their horses. Compared to our urban quarter acre, their spread offered a tremendous variety of activities. It was like a giant playground.

My joy was further amplified when I discovered that reruns of the *Adventures of Superman* television show were being broadcast on a local station. In 1960, the Superman show had been canceled two years earlier. For whatever reason, I had never seen any of the show's first run, and none of the three channels in Pittsburgh were carrying the reruns.

Primed by that extraordinary annual, I was elated to finally have an opportunity to see the program. Comic books were one thing, but a live-action show with a "real" Superman was almost too good to be true. Thrills ran through my body as the stirring theme music played, and I was glued to the black-and-white image on the set. There he was, flying through space, busting through brick walls with his bare fists, using his X-ray vision and super-hearing. Lois Lane, Jimmy Olsen, and *Daily Planet* editor Perry White were all on hand, too. This was my idea of riveting entertainment.

I soon realized that the Man of Steel wasn't the only one to don tights and sally forth to save humanity. I'd been introduced to the character of Batman in "The Super-Key to Fort Superman," the last story in that marvelous annual. On a shopping trip to the local market, I managed to snag a copy of *Detective Comics* starring Batman and Robin.

Initially, Batman's dark blue and gray costume seemed wrong for a hero, until I realized that he was chocolate to Superman's vanilla. Despite his ominous appearance, I soon understood that he was as much a champion of justice as the Metropolis Marvel. Batman and Robin quickly captured my fancy as firmly as Superman had.

In his book *The Great Comic Book Heroes* (1965), Jules Feiffer wrote: "The super *grown-ups* were the ones I identified with. They were versions of me in the future. There was still time to prepare. But Robin the Boy Wonder was my own age. He had the build of a middleweight, the legs of a wrestler. He was obviously an 'A' student, the center of every circle, the one picked for greatness in the crowd—God, how I hated him."

Not me. I strongly identified with Robin. Being Batman seemed far, far beyond me. I could much more easily imagine myself as the Boy Wonder, that "laughing, young daredevil" who could crack a pun and a crook's jaw at the same time.

Batman and Robin had another specialty I loved: swinging by ropes. While it might not appear as glamorous as flying, it had the appeal of the possible. Kids love to swing on ropes, though none of us could do it with the flair and gravitational defiance of the Dynamic Duo. When those two took to their silken Bat-ropes, they flew on the wildest, most breathtaking trajectories imaginable.

Left: The Dynamic Duo (from *Batman* #153) fascinated me as much as Superman did because (seemingly) anyone could duplicate their feats, given the proper training. **Right:** Artist Dick Sprang (from *World's Finest* #112) had a way of drawing rope-swinging that was dynamic, to say the least! Batman, Robin ™ and © DC Comics.

Here was the great appeal of Batman and Robin: they had no super powers, making it easier for readers of their adventures to imagine becoming crime fighters in the real world.

I had no shame in running around my grandparents' acreage with a towel for a cape, fighting crime wherever it raised its evil head. In the berry patch … up the cherry tree … by the railroad tracks … or behind the barn. Frequently accompanied by my brother as my sidekick, I patrolled the orchards and fields on those sunny Oregon afternoons with various degrees of vigilance. Other kids could play war or cowboys and Indians; superhero was our game of choice.

Our vacation, of course, wasn't over when we finally waved good-bye to Nanny and Gramps. We still had a three-day trip to get back east to Pittsburgh. On the return journey, I became acquainted with lesser stars in the DC firmament, such as Green Arrow and his sidekick Speedy, Tommy Tomorrow, and J'onn J'onnz, the Manhunter from Mars. A whole new galaxy of the imagination opened up before me. I didn't understand all the words in the captions and balloons, or the syntax of the sequential art form, but I was a quick study. It wasn't long before I figured out what "invulnerable" meant, even if

I pronounced it "invurnable." My reading vocabulary grew rapidly because I was hungry to understand every word on those pages.

Most of all, I loved the visual side of comics: the colorful figures in dynamic action, the stylized settings, the explosions, and especially images of futuristic items like rocket ships and ultrascientific gadgets. The only other place to see those kinds of things was at the movies, generally in low-budget fare that tended to look "fakey" (in our parlance) in the days before computer graphics. Comic books could easily and convincingly portray anything the writer and artist imagined.

Suddenly I felt myself possessed with the urge to draw my new heroes. I wanted to do my own version of what I saw on the printed page. Fashioning images of flying men was the closest I could come to having those powers myself.

I had learned somewhere that the human body (the male, at least) is eight heads high. I began by drawing eight ovals on a yellow lined pad, then built the body around them. At the same time, I was straining to imitate the art styles in the comic books. My first subjects were Superman, Batman, and Robin. The initial result was predictably crude, but I wasn't one to be easily discouraged.

Over the years, I would gradually come to understand that the colorful characters whom I met on that 1960 vacation would be with me in one form or another for the rest of my life. Like the train that carried me across America, the hobby that grew out of my love of comics would be the vehicle that would take me to a new world of dreams and endeavors.

3.

THE DAY IT ALL CLICKED

The hills and dales of our neighborhood in Pittsburgh were ribboned with freshly asphalted streets, houses scattered among them in whorls and clusters. We lived in a close-in suburb called Whitehall, at 5111 Lantern Hill Drive. Our brand-new brick house was too small from the start. The three boys shared one large upstairs bedroom for a time, but three twin beds side by side wasn't a configuration that led to peaceful bedtimes. Before long, Steve graduated to his own small room, and my father had to give up his den.

My happiest memory of Lantern Hill Drive was the feeling of freedom I got on Saturday mornings. After watching cartoons on television—generally *Popeye* or *Ruff and Reddy*, or maybe the *Three Stooges*—I would throw open the garage door and the day would stretch before me. The sound of whirring lawn mowers up and down the block, the smell of freshly cut grass, the warmth of the sun on my face—I felt totally safe and happy. All was right with the world as I ventured into the seemingly limitless possibilities available to a kid on a beautiful Saturday.

Although the house was small, my parents made a good choice of neighborhoods. We had lots of kids to play with and places to play, especially a large wooded area that flanked Lantern Hill Drive and ran down into a shallow ravine. The nearest houses could be spied up by the water tower on the next hill, which seemed light-years away. In between was a wonderland of secret forts, well-worn and hidden pathways, creeks, thickets, and tall trees. On another nearby hill were two lightning rods that resembled bayoneted rifles aimed toward heaven. We gave them a wide berth.

Above: The house at 5111 Lantern Hill Drive, just before we moved. **Left:** Our first winter at Lantern Hill, January 1958. Note the lack of shrubs or awning. **Below:** Dave, Steve, and me in the backyard that same winter. The snowman was just part of a fort we built, which may be difficult to make out in this photo.

Western Pennsylvania has distinct seasons. In the summer, it's hot and humid, relieved occasionally by dramatic thunderstorms. Spring and autumn are long periods of transition. The winter brings snow that stays on the ground until March.

I loved the winters in Pittsburgh. We built snowmen and snow forts to battle rivals in riotous snowball melees. Our neighbor would spray water on his backyard tennis court to make a skating rink, and all the kids were welcome to use it. We never missed school because of heavy snow. Mom piled us in the Plymouth with the giant fins, and away we'd go. I don't remember us ever getting stuck.

My best friend on Lantern Hill Drive was D. J. Birch. He and I went to different schools—he parochial, and I public—but we were the same age and liked to do the same sorts of things: dam up the creek in the nearby woods, climb trees, throw rocks, ride bikes, and poke around the partly built houses in our neighborhood on weekends when the construction crews were away, looking for boards we could swipe. We longed to build a treehouse but had to settle for an earth-bound clubhouse instead. We used it as headquarters for our various and sundry adventures. Whenever we formed a new club, D. J. and I were the chief officers. The one thing we didn't have in common was comics. His parents, probably remembering the time in the mid-1950s when horror comics had been scapegoated, wouldn't let him read them.

Dave and I making kites on Easter, 1959.

Around this time, my interest in comic books had become a bit more than casual. What had begun as a continuation of that moment when Dad bought me *Superman Annual* #1 was growing into rabid interest. I clamored for more, and Dad occasionally picked up a comic for me on his way home from the office. He quickly learned that I wanted only those devoted to the adventures of costumed heroes—and I didn't want him to fold them in his pocket, either.

At this point, comics with the DC logo on them (so similar, in its double concentric circles, to the Northern Pacific emblem) were the whole ball game. I would read anything starring the Superman family (*Superman, Action, Adventure, Jimmy Olsen,* and *Lois Lane*) or Batman and Robin (*Batman, Detective Comics,* and *World's Finest,* where they teamed up with Superman). At times I deigned to sample other DC titles, like *Blackhawk, Flash, Green Lantern,* and *Justice League of America,* but in those early days I was most drawn to the simpler adventures of the Man of Steel and the Dynamic Duo.

Pete Ross accidentally discovers Superboy's secret identity in *Superboy* #90. Characters ™ and © DC Comics.

Mort Weisinger, who edited the Superman titles, found in me a highly receptive reader. I loved the carefully woven mythos that he and his writers concocted, especially the emphasis he placed on the relationship between Superman and his friends at the *Daily Planet*. I enjoyed seeing how Superman would squirm out of Lois Lane's traps that were intended to reveal his secret identity. I was fascinated by the fact that all these characters had their own personalized robotic impersonators (given to them by Supes, of course) who could fill in for them when they were otherwise indisposed. I daydreamed about having my own personal robot who could do my household chores or substitute for me at school.

In the pages of *Superboy*, I identified with teenage Clark Kent's only close friend, Pete Ross, who secretly knew his pal was Superboy. In "Pete Ross's Super-Secret!" Pete was on a camping trip with the Boy of Steel when an emergency arose. Just as Clark was changing to Superboy, lightning lit up the inside of their tent, showing him removing his shirt to reveal a big red *S*. This panel burned itself into my brain, not only because of its impact but because it was repeated in almost every subsequent tale featuring Pete. I wondered if *I* would be able to keep the secret as staunchly as did Pete.

I also wondered about an odd thrill that I got from this image. There was something about the intimacy of sharing a tent with Superboy, and inadvertently discovering his great secret, that felt strangely compelling. I noticed how handsome he was in this shot, with the lightning behind him a fitting referent for the jittery sensation in my stomach. I didn't know it when I was nine, but these were the stirrings of an incipient physical attraction to other boys. As a comics fan, it's interesting to me that this early intimation of what I would eventually recognize as homosexual feelings was first aroused by a story in a four-color comic book.

Such feelings didn't arise from reading the adventures of Batman and Robin. Anticomics crusader Dr. Frederic Wertham had claimed there was a gay subtext to the relationship of Bruce Wayne and Dick Grayson. (Actually, the word "gay" wasn't commonly used to refer to homosexuals until the end of the 1960s.) While I might have had a bit of a crush on Dick as Robin, their relationship seemed very much of the father-son variety to me. At this time, Batman often found himself coping with science-fictional threats—too often, for my tastes. I didn't care much for stories of strange alien menaces. What drew me to the stories was the simplistic, colorful artwork and the stories that emphasized the Caped Crusader's detective skills. Batman also had a cool secret fortress—the Bat-Cave—and a supporting cast of characters nearly as large as the Man of Steel's.

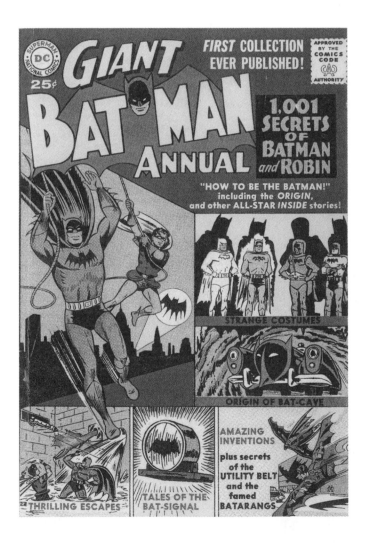

I was fascinated by schematics like this diagram of the Bat-Cave in *Batman Annual* #1. Batman ™ and © DC Comics.

I was hooked.

When it became feasible for me to go directly to the source, I spent every spare cent (other than the coins I kept aside for candy) on comic books. At the local shopping strip—that handy lineup of several stores in a row, serviced by a single large parking lot—there wasn't a newsstand as such. The proprietor of the Rexall drug store carried a small selection of comics behind the counter that he would allow us to examine while he stood by and watched. (He didn't want kids coming to his store to read comics for free off a rack.) It was in this stack that I was thunderstruck to discover a copy of *Batman Annual* #1. I was so ecstatic to find this collection of reprinted older stories (with its opening tale featuring the thrilling title "How to Be The Batman!") that I overexerted myself on the bike ride home and got a cramp in my side. I had to wait until it subsided before I could concentrate on my new comic book's wonders.

Soon I accumulated enough comic books to keep them together in what I started calling "my collection." This stack resided on the bottom shelf of the metal bookcase next to my bed. Within a couple of years, I had built up a substantial number of comics and was well on the way toward serious collecting.

I've often wondered about the collecting impulse. Some people don't have it, and some people do. Some people have it in spades. Comic book collectors have it in all suits. Part of it has to do with comics' serial numbering, allowing them to be collected sequentially. Almost from the beginning, I realized when I had missed an issue. Comics also lend themselves to being collected according to the publisher, the artist, the genre (e.g., western, war, horror, superhero), and many other categories. What made them supremely collectable by kids in the early 1960s was their friendly price, usually ten cents (increasing to twelve cents in late 1961), which was easily within reach. When a child decides to collect something, it's a way of expressing his or her individuality. "This," the child is saying, "is what I like."

Americans often prefer the new over the old. This was my reaction when a school was built near our house on Lantern Hill Drive. Spitler School (named after a well-meaning but poorly surnamed benefactor) was a cheaply constructed one-story affair that would, for at least a few years, seem nice before it deteriorated. I remember being happy to begin attending this elementary school in fourth grade not only because it was around the corner from our house, but also because it was *new*. Oh, Overlook Elementary had been all right for a place built in the 1910s of sturdy brick and granite, in the mold of the solid, traditional American schools of that era. But this was the 1960s, the eve of John Kennedy's New Frontier: time to shrug off the old and embrace a new, sleeker design for living, in everything from automobiles to appliances to architecture. If there was such a thing as a "new-school smell," Spitler had it. No scratches in the desktops, no gum underneath the chairs; just gleaming new aluminum molding around the windows, sparkling varnish on the wood surfaces, and virgin blackboards that had never known chalk.

At Spitler Elementary, I made my first attempts to write stories. My tendency toward mimicry led me to pen imitations of the Hardy Boys books that were among the first hardback books I read on my own. When my father showed off my early stories to a clerk in his office, the fellow kindly typed them up into a small booklet called *Mystery Tales about the Schellys* that Dad brought home for me. Each story (with titles like "The Mystery of the Peering Eyes" and "The Spook of Old Maclachlan's Farm") was a single typed page. In "The Ghost of Sleepy Hollow," the Schelly boys investigate a ghost sighting by Old Mister Brickner:

> The boys were exploring the valley when a terrible cry was heard and all of a sudden a ghost appeared. Two ladies passing by nearly fainted when they saw it. (One woman was known to have had a heart atack.) It turned out to be an old sheet that blew off a clothes line and got caught in a tree. Well that solves the mistery exclamed the boys in excitement.

Why was I drawn to writing? Where does the creative urge begin? From what recesses of my brain or soul did my desire to write originate?

Could it be nature—that is, was it genetic? Did creativity run in my family? In later years, I found out that a number of my forebears, especially on the Schelly side, exhibited creative abilities; at the time, though, Dad knew or said little about those who wrote poetry or played music, perhaps because none had made any sort of mark. They were not highly educated, nor did they have the luxury of much leisure time for frivolous pursuits. There were fields to be plowed, chores to be done.

Could it be nurture? Did my creative impulse come from the way I was parented? It's true that my father had a certain love of books and even had a few old tomes on a bookshelf in his den, things like a Mark Twain omnibus from the late 1800s, a collection of *Grimm's Fairy Tales,* and some of the poetry of Lewis Carroll. I examined those musty volumes, but I don't know that this in itself would have inspired me to make books of my own.

Maybe it comes from how our minds develop: the right brain/left brain theory. If this is true, the lobe that enables one to do abstruse math problems has got to be less developed in my cranium than the one that formulates words and patterns of color.

Personality type must also be considered. In my experience, most creative people are introverted or at least have an introverted side. Even the most raucous standup comedians claim to have been social rejects as youths. Celebrated actors are often shy when they're not on stage with a part to play.

This held true for me. From the get-go I had a reflective, analytical personality. Though I was a friendly child (or so Mom told me later, claiming that I'd talk to any stranger who came along), what I remember was my keen awareness of being internally rather than externally directed. Eventually the energy directed inward would need to find a way out again. For those with some sort of talent, that energy would be expressed creatively.

Hence, when I entered fourth grade at Spitler School, I decided it was time I became a real author. To me, that meant an author of *books*. A story on a sheet of paper was one thing, but a *book* was a solid, impressive achievement. If I could write one of those, then I would be somebody.

About the time the Schelly family left the Lantern Hill house, I received my first camera for my tenth birthday.

I took to folding several sheets of white paper in half, folding a sheet of colored paper in half on the outside for the cover, and stapling them into a booklike form. Next I would add the title in large block letters, and perhaps an illustration, to the cover. Then I would open it up, fold the cover back, and begin with chapter 1.

I rarely got beyond page three or four. I was in love with being a writer of books, but I had nothing to fill them with. The best I could come up with were imitations of other books I'd read. Originality would come later.

Dave and I shared a room, and we had a habit of talking to each other in bed at night before we fell asleep. Often this would consist of us exchanging ideas for building the perfect treehouse (our parents considered treehouses too dangerous) or soapbox racer (ditto), or some other scheme. One of those grand ideas was my plan to set up a neighborhood newsstand to sell books I had written and published. As I remember the idea, it was like a lemonade stand but with books. I would charge a nickel or a dime for my wares, thus earning extra money to buy ... *more comic books.*

In the next couple of years, my experiences with my peers at school became troubled. At the ages of nine and ten, children begin to form cliques and hierarchies. It was painfully obvious that I would be no athletic star. I wasn't one of the physically robust kids on the playground—in fact, I was clearly in the bottom half. I was an active kid and learned to swim at an early age, but I was never well coordinated. As early as fourth grade, you could tell who was popular. Among boys, it was usually the ones who were good at sports.

This fact had further implications. In our wolf pack, the dominant wolves had to demonstrate their power over the weaker members. This took the form of the ability—the street smarts—to taunt other kids and get one up on them, both verbally and physically. Thus began the teasing and bullying that would plague me during the ensuing school years, usually featuring that most dreaded of words, "sissy." (Or, later, "faggot.") This kind of treatment continued after we moved to a new house in a new neighborhood two years later.

I didn't understand—I still don't—why our society holds physical skill in higher regard than intellectual prowess. Isn't the mind as important as the body? Apparently not, for all our protestations to the contrary. Behavior doesn't lie.

Just as important as physical competence is a conformist physical appearance. Anyone who looks different from the herd—wearing thick glasses, dressing in less-than-stylish clothes, or having any sort of visible physical challenge, such as wearing a hearing aid—makes you a target as your age gets into double digits, and especially in early adolescence.

Another factor may have contributed to my lack of physical prowess compared to many of my classmates: I was a year younger than most of them, having started first grade when I was five. Research has shown that such early starters operate at a disadvantage all through school. Had I been the same age as most of my classmates, I could have given a better account of myself.

I did, however, discover an ability that would earn me a certain amount of respect among my peers, when an event occurred in my life that cemented my commitment to the world of the arts and imagination. It happened in one magic moment when I was in fifth grade at Julia Ward Howe Elementary in Mount Lebanon, another suburb a few miles from Whitehall.

Our house at 881 Lovingston Drive. My bedroom was on the upper right. While living there, I discovered comicdom and began publishing fanzines.

In the fall of 1961 we had moved from Lantern Hill to a larger house on Lovingston Drive. Dad was making a bit more money, and it was obvious that each of us three boys needed his own room. Plus, Dad wanted a den where he could fiddle with his stamp collection or read his hunting magazines in peace. The move was a big event in our lives.

Our new neighborhood was definitely an economic step up from Whitehall. Mount Lebanon was where the doctors, lawyers, and other professionals lived. The yards were larger and better kept, and the houses stood taller and were more spacious. It wasn't quite upper middle class, but it was the place to live if you seemed to be on the way to achieving that status. The schools, we were told, were more challenging there. Mount Lebanon boasted one of the top school districts in the country. We were a little intimidated when we reported to Howe Elementary, and there was a brief period of academic adjustment before school was smooth sailing again.

In my new school's art class, we were given the assignment to draw an image to represent the month of the year when we were born. Mine was November, so I drew a picture, largely in blues and greens, of an old man huddled before a campfire. Until this time, though I loved to draw and paint, I had showed no particular skill for either. I was never better than any of the other kids. But today as I was drawing my picture, I noticed something: my hand seemed to know how to move the pastel chalk on the page. Never before had I felt that sensation. Suddenly, I realized for the first time that *I could draw* ... and draw *well*. One day I didn't think I could, and the next it all clicked.

I felt a flush of energy zap through my body, almost like something had been channeled through me. Part of it was pride in my accomplishment, but there was something deeper—a sense of wonder that I had a special talent that set me apart from my peers. Comparing my drawing to the ones around me, it was obvious that mine had a kind of aesthetic organization of elements that was missing from the others. The teacher was impressed. I received an A on my project, and I continued to get top grades in art class thereafter.

Some of my classmates were likewise impressed. It was the kind of thing that generated an occasional compliment or garnered a certain amount of positive attention; not a lot, but a little. Art didn't cut any real ice when there were dodgeballs to be dodged, fly balls to be caught, or footballs to be thrown. But it did open up the possibility that I might one day make a career in the art field. What could have been more natural than for me to begin dreaming, from this day onward, of becoming a comic book artist?

4.

WELCOME TO FANDOMLAND

In Mount Lebanon, I never rode a bus to school. Howe Elementary was a mile from Lovingston Drive—just a long enough walk to get some fresh air and put color in my cheeks. When I graduated to Andrew W. Mellon Junior High in seventh grade, the walk was even longer.

I enjoyed those walks. Sometimes I was accompanied by a friend, but most of those walks were solitary treks up and down the rolling hills and sidewalks. That was my private time when my imagination would run free as I passed familiar stone walls, fences, hedges, and street signs. Every crack in the sidewalk became an old friend.

The route to the junior high wound through the rustic back end of a local cemetery and along a path through an adjacent patch of woods, eventually depositing me on the busy arterial street that led to the school. Many were my moody ruminations as I passed by hills dotted with tombstones marking the graves of people who, I imagined, might have been students like myself many years before. Though this portion of the walk was somewhat creepy, I found it strangely compelling. This was when I contemplated my own mortality for the first time.

Walking this path led to a major shift in my comic book reading habits. I began buying my comics at a new locale: a drugstore on the street approaching the junior high, right where I emerged daily from the woods. It was more convenient than biking down to the local shopping strip, and the selection of comics was more extensive.

This drugstore's wooden magazine racks were arranged in a U-shaped configuration. The familiar DC comics were given the most prominent display, but room was also allotted to other titles such as the Disney comics from Gold Key, and others from lesser publishers. Down below, lurking in the shadows in the bottom racks, were a number of comics that I remember eyeing dubiously. On or slightly after September 17, 1963 (I know because of the date stamp on the cover of my copy, which I still own), I spied a comic book featuring a weirdly named hero—Spider-Man—that caught my attention.

I held it hesitantly at first, not certain whether this pulpy-looking affair with its muted, moody colors and bizarre hero was something I might like. He was up against a villain called the Vulture, who looked different from the types of adversaries I was used to at DC. But at almost twelve years old I was ready to try something different from the somewhat sterile milieus of Superman and Batman.

At that age, I generally bought a comic based on the cover, so I'm assuming (rather than remembering) that I liked what I saw. I have vague memories of having seen a Human Torch–Spider-Man story in a friend's copy of *Strange Tales Annual* #2 a few months earlier, but there's no doubt that *Amazing Spider-Man* #7 was the first Marvel comic book I bought, as well as my first exposure to the art of Steve Ditko. His unique style of drawing faces, positioning the figures, and composing the panels impressed me from the start. His web-spinner hero was a remarkably elastic fellow who leaped, swung, and punched with a panache I'd never seen before. Ditko quickly became a personal favorite and, along with Jack Kirby (cocreator with Stan Lee of much of the Marvel universe), found a place among my personal top five artists, where he remains to this day. The Lee-Ditko Spider-Man drew me into the Marvel fold.

Amazing Spider-Man #7 (1963) was the first Marvel comic book I bought. ™ and
© Marvel Characters, Inc.

Excerpted panels from "The Return of the Vulture!" from *Amazing Spider-Man* #7. ™ and © Marvel Characters, Inc.

The visual storytelling and movement throughout "The Return of the Vulture!" were a revelation. The tale is a mixture of derring-do, utter mayhem, and laughs. This is one of the earliest issues to showcase Stan Lee and Steve Ditko's comedic ability, which became a high point of the series while Ditko was on board. The ending of the story, with Spidey at the *Daily Bugle* pasting J. Jonah Jameson's yapping jaw shut with webbing and then settling down on the floor for a sophisticated exchange with his girlfriend, Betty Brant, is superb.

By the time I finished the issue, I was completely won over. I couldn't believe how much I enjoyed it. I liked the humor, I liked the wild action, I responded to the personal touches Stan Lee put into the blurbs and letter column, and I especially liked Peter Parker being an average guy who is rejected by the in-crowd at school because he has brains. Now here was a comic book character with whom I could identify.

If this was Marvel, I wanted more. The next day, I returned to the same rack and bought *Fantastic Four* #21 ("The Hate Monger") and *Strange Tales* #115 ("The Origin of Doctor Strange!"). A turncoat from DC, I plunged into the Marvel universe and didn't read much else for the next few years. *Fantastic Four, Journey into Mystery* (with Thor), *Tales of Suspense* (with Iron Man), and *Amazing Spider-Man* became my comics of choice. When Lee and Kirby brought Captain America, a major hero of comics' Golden Age in the 1940s, into comics' Silver Age in the 1960s, he was a great addition to the Avengers and became a special favorite of mine. (I wanted Bucky to be revived too, but Lee hated boy sidekicks.) The fact that Marvel, unlike DC, published credits with each story made the creators of its comics seem more human and relatable, and it was easier to follow the work of my favorites. The self-proclaimed House of Ideas gave me a whole new world to explore, made even more cohesive by the fact that the heroes would frequently appear in each other's stories. Only when Batman was being returned to his roots as a "grim avenger of the night" in stories written by Dennis O'Neil and drawn by Neal Adams, several years later, was I was drawn back to DC.

So thoroughly did I internalize the Marvel ethos that it actually influenced my developing ideas and worldview. I quoted Doctor Strange (from the first *Spider-Man Annual*) to a school bully: "Fighting is the last resort of the ignorant," I told Butch Sanders.

"What a bunch of crap *that* is," he said, then punched me in the stomach. So much for the Zen of Stan Lee.

Still, Lee's humane, tolerant voice became a major one in my life, as I suspect it did for many other children of the baby boom. Stan never tried to do more than entertain us, but he did sometimes toss a kernel of his own philosophy into the mix.

When I walked home from school, I kept an eye peeled for the bullies who had decided to make my life miserable. I pretended to slink as silently as Spider-Man and to move through the shortcut in the woods protected by Doctor Strange's all-seeing Eye of Agamotto.

In the beginning of February 1964, when I was looking forward to the Beatles' first appearance on the *Ed Sullivan Show* on Sunday, I was shocked to discover a brand-new Marvel comic book on sale at my favorite drugstore. Unfortunately, I was flat broke, and there was only one copy of *Daredevil* #1 left. I begged the proprietor to hold it for me until I returned with twelve cents.

"I don't know," he said, shaking his head. "You might not come back, and I could lose a sale."

"I'll come back today. I promise!"

"But it's *snowing*."

"Can you hold it for me until tomorrow?"

"No, I couldn't do that. But maybe it'll still be here."

"Then I'll come back today. I'll go home now, get some money, and come right back."

He looked at me skeptically. "You'd do that? For a comic book?"

"Yeah. I really, really want that one."

He smiled at me. "Okay. If you'll do that, I'll hold it for you till six o'clock."

True to my word, I schlepped all the way home and back in heavy snow to pay my twelve cents for *Daredevil* #1.

Was I a true believer or *what*?

In the first half of 1964, puberty was hitting me like a ton of bricks. That's when I realized how much I wished I had a lock on my bedroom door. That's also when I began to understand that I was attracted to the male form.

Even at the age of nine or ten, I was drawn to the depictions of males in comic books who wore those tight, form-fitting costumes. Now I found myself paying close attention to the way Spider-Man's skintight costume fit him, especially in the crotch. A special page in the *Amazing Spider-Man Annual* #1 detailing the features of Spidey's costume was sexy as hell. Unlike the way other artists drew the male hero in tights, Ditko's handling of Spidey actually included a bulge where Peter Parker's male organs nestled. Yes, Peter Parker had a dick, and he had balls. (His bare feet and bare midriff shown as he was about to strip added to the hotness.)

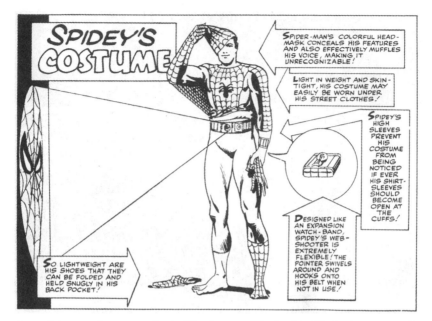

A panel that caught my attention in "The Secrets of Spider-Man!," a backup story in the *Amazing Spider-Man Annual* #1 (1964). ™ and © Marvel Characters, Inc.

Panel from "How Stan Lee and Steve Ditko Create Spider-Man!"

I also paid a lot of attention to another story in that Spidey annual: "How Stan Lee and Steve Ditko Create Spider-Man!," the humorous behind-the-scenes backup story. It showed Ditko in his studio, drawing and inking a page from a Spider-Man story on his tilted drawing board. It may have been the first time I realized that the artwork was drawn much larger than it appeared in the printed comic books. The words Lee gave Ditko as he penciled and inked were revelatory: "I might as well start roughing in the first panel ... I'm still tightening up the details here with a fine pen-point! ... Now I'll fill in the heavy black areas with my brush." It was like a mini-drawing lesson from Steve Ditko, and even though it was humorous, the story gave me an idea of what it was like being a comic book artist.

I was frustrated by the lack of anyone with whom to share my enthusiasm. I was basically alone with my hobby. A few neighbor kids (usually younger) had stacks of comics, and we would occasionally swap. Sometimes a school bazaar would have a table with some back issues. By the early 1960s comics were no longer the mass medium they'd been in the 1940s, when almost every young person read them, as well as older teens and those in the military. Since then, television had made major inroads, and the Comics Code (introduced in 1955) had removed any hints of sex and violence from the comics. Once a guy got into his teens, he tended to be secretive about liking comics. Comic books had become kiddie entertainment in the eyes of the masses, even though Stan Lee and company were doing their best to change that perception. How could I ever fill in the back issues of Marvel comics I had missed?

Nor was there any way for me to learn about comics of the past. The back cover of *Giant Superman Annual* #1 had provided tantalizing glimpses of the covers of *Action Comics* #1, *Superman* #1, and others from before World War II, but there weren't any books or magazines about the history of comics. I was solely dependent on the comic book letter columns that occasionally included factual tidbits about the comics published years ago, or the DC annuals with reproductions of old covers in color on the back. (Seeing the cover of *Superman* #1 reproduced on the back cover of that annual was like viewing the Holy Grail.)

I had no way to get in touch with other fans in my vicinity. I did notice that some DC Comics *(Flash, Justice League of America, Green Lantern)* were printing full addresses in the letter columns. Editor Julius "Julie" Schwartz made this unobtrusive change to facilitate contacts between fans, but the erudite commentators in those columns seemed far too imposing for me—a mere twelve-year-old—to contact. The same was true of the people who had letters published in Marvel's *Fantastic Four* Fan Page. I couldn't have held my own in a correspondence with them, and there was no hint that they could help me in my goal of filling in back issues. Besides, none of them seemed to live in Pittsburgh.

Then, by sheer chance, I met another comics fan. While perusing the comics rack at the drugstore in the spring of 1964, I was joined by a blond, freckle-faced youth who was also there to stock up on the latest issues. I recognized Richard Shields from school. We were the same age and had some of the same classes, but he ran in different circles from me, and I'd had no idea he collected comics too. I watched as he assembled a hefty stack of Marvel, DC, and Gold Key issues.

Richard had no qualms about buying and liking comics. "My older brother read 'em, and I do too," he said. We began commenting on our selections, and before I knew it I had a friend who shared my hobby.

Shields had amassed what to my eyes was a large collection of comics. He was mature for his age and had a paper route that gave him plenty of spending money, making him the envy of other kids, including me. My parents wouldn't let me have a paper route; they didn't want the neighbors thinking we needed the money. Hence, I sometimes resorted to shoplifting. I'm sure I wasn't the only kid who sneaked comic books out of a store under his coat. What was I to do? I felt guilty, but some things are just too compelling.

Richard and I began getting together on a regular basis to discuss comics, negotiate trades, and occasionally check out a far-flung newsstand on our bikes. A few months after we met, we found a curious item in an issue of *Justice League of America:* editor Schwartz had inserted a plug for some sort of magazine about collecting comic books. It didn't mention the price, but it gave an address where those interested could send for information. We both immediately sent away to Miami, Florida, to find out about something called *The Comicollector.*

I'll always remember the day when the envelope from an organization cryptically named "The SFCA" arrived at my house. Mom hadn't noticed that it was addressed to me, since the only mail I ever got was greeting cards from relatives on my birthday and holidays, and she opened it by mistake. She came into my room with a quizzical expression on her face.

"Bill, you got something odd in the mail," she said, handing the torn envelope and its contents to me. "What is it?" She stood there waiting for my reply.

I could hardly contain my excitement. It was three sheets of advertising. The first was for a "fanzine" called *The Rocket's Blast-Comicollector* (*RBCC* for short). The second was for the *RBCC Special* #1 featuring a long article on Timely (Marvel) Comics of the 1940s by someone named Raymond Miller. The third, which I found particularly intriguing, was for *Fighting Hero Comics* #10, starring a weird superhero called the Eye, Underworld Executioner, who had a huge eyeball for a head. SFCA, I discovered, stood for the Science Fiction and Comic Association.

"It's some stuff I sent away for," I explained. "For comic book collectors. You can order a magazine about comic books."

"How much does it cost?"

"Hmm … looks like a sample copy costs fifty cents."

Her eyebrows lifted. "That much? It sounds too expensive."

"I've got the money. I have over six dollars saved up."

She paused, then shrugged. "I guess it's all right. Let me see it when it comes. I want to make sure it isn't something dirty."

"*Mom!*"

I hopped on my bike and pedaled like mad over to Shields's house, where I discovered that he had not only received the three pages of information, but also a copy of *RBCC*. He had boldly included a dollar with his letter of inquiry. Shields was always rolling in dough.

"What's this?" I asked Shields, pointing to the sheet with the Eye character. "Some kind of comic book?"

"Yeah."

"Where do you buy it? I've never seen this character on the racks." I wondered if there were regional comic book companies that didn't distribute their wares in Pittsburgh.

"Idiot!" he said, laughing. "It's not like a regular comic book. You have to send away for it. It's probably printed like *RBCC*."

We looked through the copy of *RBCC*, which was duplicated by the same printing method our school teachers used for pop quizzes and worksheets. I didn't know the name of the process, but the print was purple. We were captivated by page after page of advertisements for old comic books, many dating back to the 1940s.

Shields let out a long whistle. "Look at this. Someone wants *fifteen bucks* for *Captain America* #1."

"That's nuts," I replied, shaking my head. "Who would pay that much?"

"I don't know, but a lot of the other old stuff is only three or four bucks. I think I'll get some of 'em, if I can figure out which ones are the best."

"That's too much for me, but here's a copy of *Spider-Man* #1 for a buck-fifty. I think I'll send for that."

Although the ads for much-sought-after back issues were fascinating, I was equally interested in the fanzines that promised information about comics of the past. Just the fact that you could buy a bunch of different *magazines about comics* excited me. What a momentous, mind-boggling development this was. My joy knew no bounds!

When I began receiving amateur magazines like *Alter Ego*, *Batmania*, and the *Yancy Street Journal*, they provided concrete evidence that there were people from all walks of life who appreciated comic books and strips. (The fanzines depicted here were published in late 1964 or early 1965.) All characters ™ and © their respective owners.

Without hesitation, I ordered several of the most promising fanzines, carefully taping quarters, nickels, and dimes to my letters and stuffing them into envelopes. The first ones I received after *RBCC* were *Yancy Street Journal* (devoted solely to Marvel comics), *Batmania* (dedicated to the Dynamic Duo), and *Fighting Hero Comics* (featuring a changing roster of amateur-created heroes such as the Eye, whose eyeball helmet was so visually arresting).

Soon I learned that the roots of comic fandom went back to the 1930s, when science fiction fans published amateur magazines that they circulated among themselves. They held conventions, gave awards, and did what they could to promote the science fiction field. One of these fanzines, *Fantasy Magazine,* was published by Julius Schwartz, who went on to become an editor for DC Comics in the 1940s. When Schwartz, who edited new versions of the Flash and Green Lantern in the late 1950s, began receiving letters from a serious-minded fan named Jerry Bails, he felt a kinship with Bails because of his own past as a science fiction fan.

Jerry G. Bails was a college professor who had grown up reading the adventures of the Justice Society of America in *All-Star Comics* in the 1940s. In 1960, Bails wanted to publish a newsletter to support the new version of the group, which was now called the Justice League of America. Schwartz encouraged Bails to publish the newsletter, and he promised to help by providing advance news of upcoming issues. The DC editor's decision to run full addresses in the letter columns of *The Flash, Green Lantern,* and other comic books under his purview had a major effect on the rapid growth of fandom by facilitating contacts among fans. Bails reconceived his newsletter as a fanzine called *Alter Ego,* and he enlisted a correspondent named Roy Thomas to help him fill its pages. The first issue, published on March 28, 1961, sparked the new fan movement, which spread like wildfire. Fans and collectors from all walks of life came together to share their appreciation for the superhero renaissance and for comic books in general.

After I received my first fanzines, I ordered a copy of *Who's Who in Comic Fandom,* published early in 1964 by Bails, which listed the names and addresses of some sixteen hundred active fans. These weren't a bunch of preadolescents; most were in high school or college, and a significant number were adults, like Bails and Thomas. Some had loyally followed comics for years on their own and didn't link up with other collectors until they learned about fandom through Bails and *Alter Ego* in 1961.

I was surprised and thrilled that supposedly sober and intelligent adults openly expressed their enthusiasm for comics. Bails was a professor of science and technology at Wayne State University. This was a strong message of validation. For the first time, I envisioned myself reading comics for the rest of my life.

The fandom phenomenon resulted from collectors' pent-up need to share information, trade and sell back issues, and express a wide range of opinions. Postage was cheap—four cents for a first-class letter—so just about anyone could afford to join in. Discovering the history of comics through fandom was exhilarating. I felt like Alice falling through a different rabbit hole—not to Wonderland but to Fandomland.

By the time I came along, six issues of *Alter Ego* had already been published. I ordered #7 and was introduced to the Marvel Family (Captain Marvel, Captain Marvel Jr., Mary Marvel, and the rest). I read editor Roy Thomas's article "One Man's Family" and a long letter from Marvel Family scripter Otto Binder over and over, and I yearned to peruse the adventures of the Marvel Family myself. Somewhere around this time I found out that Binder had written six of the nine stories in the *Giant Superman Annual* #1, which had had such a profound effect on me.

Shields was able to place orders right away for a number of rare old comic books. I benefited from his wealth because I was able to read and enjoy his acquisitions when they arrived from dealers around the country. Like me, he liked the Marvel Family and bought a selection of midrange issues of *Whiz Comics, Captain Marvel Adventures, Captain Marvel Junior, Master Comics,* and *Wow Comics.*

When we discovered the great EC comic books like *Tales from the Crypt* and *Weird Science* (which had ceased publication before we were in kindergarten), Shields went on a buying frenzy. We chortled with glee as we read the wonderful, gory, forbidden pre–Comics Code EC comics for the first time. This was our first inkling that comics of the past could be even more exciting than new ones.

Much as I enjoyed the old issues themselves, I was equally interested in the fanzines devoted to them. I didn't want to be a passive consumer; I wanted to be a participant. As an aspiring writer and artist, I soon began to think about publishing a fan magazine of my own.

"We could do one of these," I said to Shields one day, scant weeks after first seeing *RBCC*.

"What? Publish our own fanzine?"

"Sure. That would be so cool."

He immediately warmed to the idea. "Yeah. You're a good artist."

"And you could write about some of the old comics you've bought," I said. We were both seized with the urge to publish, but knowing my history, I suspect I was the main instigator of the idea.

Shields said, "Where could we get it printed?"

"I don't know. Let's ask our parents."

Soon we learned that Shields's father worked in a place that had a new type of machine called a Xerox copier. An average person could use this machine to photographically copy (sort of) an image and reprint it, rather than having to hire a professional printer. You could just slap your original copy face down on the window of a Xerox machine, press a button, and presto—instant copy on regular white paper. Mr. Shields kindly offered to print a limited number of copies of our publication if we kept the page count down.

I asked Shields, "What will we call it?"

"We can't name it after any particular superhero," he replied.

"Let's call it …" I was thinking fast. "How about … *Super-Heroes Anonymous*?" It sounded good to us. A new fanzine was born.

In truth, I'd had visions of being a publisher years earlier. Not long before I wrote *Mystery Tales about the Schellys* in third grade, I constructed a mockup of a newspaper for children that I called *Chit-Chat*. I still have a copy, which includes a Children's Dictionary page ("C—can, cook, cat, D—dog, dig, dark"), a connect-the-dots page, and so on. My new project, however, would be more than a mockup or a dream. It would be a real publication, sent to readers who paid real money for it.

Much as I loved *Alter Ego*, it was far more professional than anything we could produce. We chose as our models the funkier *Yancy Street Journal*, published by Marty Arbunich and Bill DuBay in San Francisco, and *Batmania*, produced by a talented artist with the odd name of Biljo White. Our magazine would consist of a cover, an editorial, pinup pages, short articles, a discussion column, a reproduction of the cover of a rare comic book, and our personal Want and Sale lists. None of the written pieces in that first issue (brief histories of Batman and Green Arrow, among other things) exceeded three hundred words in length.

The one original element in *Super-Heroes Anonymous* was the debut of a brand-new super hero ghoulishly named the Immortal Corpse. The idea had been born of a joke by my insouciant neighbor Norman Shor, who, when he heard the names of some of the other heroes I'd made up, began mocking me by proposing stupid

As early as seven years old, I was playing with the idea of publishing a magazine called *Chit-Chat* for the kids in the neighborhood.

heroes like the Idiot, the Fingernail, and the Corpse, the terrific hero who was already dead. "Real funny," I'd sneered, but later I found that I liked the idea of a hero who was dead but who came back to a kind of life to bring his "killer" to justice. Thus, I formulated the story of a mortician named Jon Walker who was gunned down and came back from the dead because of a strange chemical substance that had seeped into his wounds. He discovers that he is able to change his age at will, which effectively renders him immortal. I typed up his origin story ("Murder at Midnight!") and created a drawing of the character for our cover. It became my first piece of published fiction.

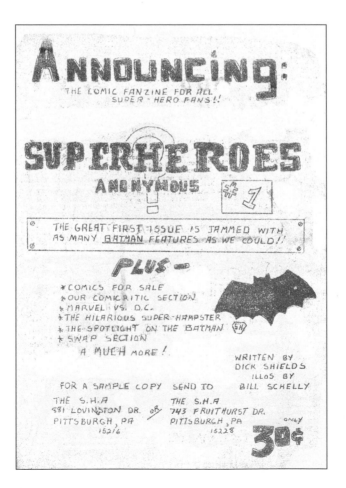

Fearlessly charging ahead, we paid our three dollars for a full-page display ad in *RBCC*. It appeared several weeks later, and before long I began receiving envelopes from around the country bearing coins. (Even with the tape removed, the coins stayed sticky.) I carefully made a list of our customers. It wasn't a long one. We received money for no more than twenty-five copies. By then, we had the twenty or so pages typed up, and I had both penciled and inked the artwork.

Predictably, I had to endure a grilling from my dad when he saw me working on the finished pages.

"What's all this?"

"Richard Shields and I are publishing a fanzine about comic books."

"What's a fanzine?"

When I explained what a fanzine was, he expressed concern that it might interfere with my schoolwork. "What about your grades?"

"They're fine."

"Well, if they drop, you'll have to stop this."

"Okay." I was confident they wouldn't.

"And it can't interfere with your household chores."

"It won't."

"Where will you get the money to print and mail it? How will you get it printed?"

My God, where was the entrepreneurial spirit in the Schelly family? Finally I'd answered his questions to his satisfaction. Shields gave the finished pages to his father to

Within weeks of discovering fandom, Richard Shields and I launched *Super-Heroes Anonymous* #1. The full-page advertisement, which appeared in *RBCC* #35, was met with a small but by no means discouraging response. The cover is reproduced as it appeared before printing. The Immortal Corpse ™ and © Bill Schelly.

be printed. We waited impatiently for him to bring the copies home from his office.

A few days later, Shields phoned. "They're here."

"How do they look?"

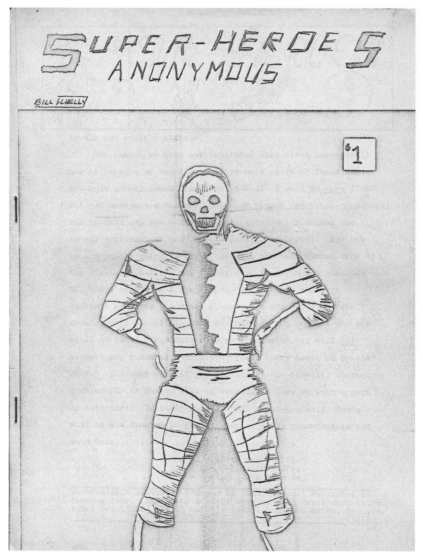

I was crestfallen when the primitive Xerox copy machine printed the cover illustration with the solid blacks completely washed out. It was the first of many printing snafus that dogged me through my years of amateur publishing.

"Well … pretty good. Except—um, you have to see them."

I rushed over to the Shields residence. Right away a problem was obvious. Early Xerox couldn't reproduce solid blacks, so all the areas in the artwork where the black area was thicker than a narrow line were completely washed out. Unfortunately, the front cover had been a figure of the Immortal Corpse standing against a solid black background.

I was bitterly disappointed, but at least the pages were all legible, and most of the other illustrations looked all right. Then and there, we collated and stapled the pages, addressed the copies, and applied the stamps.

Despite some misgivings, I couldn't help but feel a certain pride as I beheld the neat stack of copies.

"Where do we mail them? The post office?"

"Naw," Shields said. "Drop 'em in a mailbox on your way home. There's one on the corner."

"But when they fall into the box, they might get damaged."

He laughed. "What, you think if you take 'em to the post office, they aren't going to get thrown around? C'mon."

I followed his suggestion. On the way home, I carried the copies of *Super-Heroes Anonymous* #1 to the mailbox on the corner, opened its metal mouth, and shoved them in, five at a time. The moment gave me a tiny shiver. They weren't "mine" any more. I had released them to the wider world.

For better or worse, we were publishers.

5.

I YAM WHAT I YAM

No doubt about it: the rise of comic fandom was a genuine American grassroots movement. Entirely unplanned, it took hold in whatever fertile soil it could find. Fans emerged like so many wild mushrooms, popping up from sea to shining sea, from Peoria to Portland, from Nome to Norfolk. Linked by nothing faster than the plodding U.S. mails (in an era before long-distance telephoning was commonplace and the internet was science fiction), fans who were hungry for camaraderie spread the word quickly.

Viewed in its historical context, the emergence of a comic book subculture was no more than a blip on the seismic map of those years' events. The Cuban missile crisis, the assassination of President Kennedy, the civil rights movement, the Beatles, James Bond, the NASA space program—these made up the bill of the "really big show" that was the early 1960s. Still, the formation of an ongoing comic fandom was of earth-shattering importance for fans of that wonderful, bastard medium. 1965 was the year when everything jelled.

So many people got involved in such a short period of time that fandom's founders put together a booklet called the *Guidebook to Comic Fandom* to help newbies (sometimes called neofans) find their way. Dozens of new fanzines were published—so many that it was no longer feasible for anyone to buy them all. The circulation of *RBCC* soared to more than a thousand copies per issue, and these were undoubtedly shared among friends. The clamor began for a national comics convention. Stories about the movement started to appear in newspapers across the country.

Most of these articles focused on the high prices being paid for old comic books. The first bit of national media attention came in the *Newsweek* piece "Superfans and Batmaniacs," which appeared in early 1965. Comic fandom had taken hold—indeed, was spreading like crabgrass—and I was one of those blades of grass.

Had I been more socially adept in junior high, I might not have thrown myself into fandom with such gung-ho abandon. I did have a few friends at school, and I never sat alone in the lunchroom like the true pariahs. I harbored crushes on a number of girls, some of which were mutual. As time went on, I sported a semblance of a Beatle haircut and wore clothes that allowed me to generally avoid wholesale ridicule. But that was the extent of my social integration at Mellon Junior High.

I quickly found myself near the top of my classes academically because I was motivated not only by my desire to learn but also by a wish to please my teachers and parents. I was in all the accelerated courses from the beginning: advanced English, advanced algebra, special art. This didn't help me gain acceptance, though; quite the opposite. I was called "brain" and "teacher's pet." It was confusing. On the one hand, adults constantly preached the importance of education; on the other, anyone who was identified as anything resembling an intellectual was ostracized. Anyway, it wasn't that I was all that smart. I happened to enjoy most of my classes. Should I have feigned indifference? As that comic strip icon Popeye declared, "I yam what I yam and that's all that I yam."

Almost as easily as Richard Shields came into my life, he slipped out of it. We never had a fight or falling out. He was an athletic fellow, which naturally led him to make friends among the school jocks. He ended up joining the track team. Because of that, his paper route and school work, and the distance between our homes, we drifted apart. For the remainder of my first year in fandom, I was on my own.

RBCC was my guide. The covers highlighted heroes from the Golden Age of comics, and editor G. B. Love often ran historical pages inside the magazine about those champions from yesteryear. One could glean a tremendous amount of information merely by

RBCC #40 and #44 (both from 1965) with covers by Biljo White and John Fantucchio, two of fandom's top artists.

looking through the ads for old comics, pulp magazines, taped radio shows, and newspaper strips. Plus there were the blurbs for the proliferating number of amateur publications.

Those other fanzines offered much to absorb: articles on comics from the past and Raymond Miller's "Answer Man" columns in *Comic World*, complex think pieces about the comics medium in *Slam-Bang*, and a whole subuniverse of original heroes created by amateur writers and artists in the pages of *Star-Studded Comics*.

My fascination with Biljo White's striking underworld executioner was compounded when the professionally printed *The Eye* #1 arrived in my mailbox. Here was a hero (or antihero) who truly deserved his own comic book. When the editorial revealed that the character had sprung from a costume design created in the 1950s, I was delighted. Even heroes invented for the fanzines sometimes had complex histories like their mainstream counterparts.

To my pantheon of professional comics artist gods such as Jack Kirby and Steve Ditko I added a group of amateur demigods, including talented fan writers and artists Buddy Saunders, Jim Starlin, Alan Weiss, and Bill DuBay.

When I first saw a fanzine featuring the Eye, I wondered if there were regional comic book companies that didn't distribute to Pittsburgh. Many years later, I purchased the rights to this character and published new Eye adventures. The Eye ™ and © Bill Schelly.

The truth is, I *wasn't* alone. I had become a member of a brotherhood. After *Super-Heroes Anonymous* appeared, I began receiving mail from dealers, fanzine editors, writers, artists, and collectors. As I became more active and better known in fan circles, my mail grew from a trickle to a steady stream. Every day I rushed home from school to see what the postman had brought. Would a new issue of a favored fanzine await? More often than not, there was *something* for me—sometimes several items. Any day might be a mini-Christmas.

I quickly learned that the atmosphere in fandom was generally upbeat and supportive. Sure, a group largely made up of teenagers included some brash individuals. Some of the fanzine reviews could be harsh, but fandom wasn't plagued by feuds or rampant dishonesty. People got along and followed through on their promises. I trusted that if I sent twenty-five cents for a fanzine, I would receive that fanzine. It helped if the advertisement said "now out" or "ready to mail," so you knew you wouldn't have to wait for the fanzine to be finished or printed. The same was true if I sent a few dollars in cash to purchase some back issues. I always got either the comics or my money back. I read about a few instances of out-and-out thievery, but the thieves were quickly identified in print, and usually the post office was notified of their crimes. Serious mail-order theft was, as far as I know, kept at bay.

A question faced me: how would I fill the pages of the second issue of *Super-Heroes Anonymous,* now that I was its sole editor? (Did I even consider waiting until I had more to offer potential readers? Not for an instant. I was far too enamored of publishing.)

One could sense a superhero boom coming around the corner. The revivals and revisions of the heroes of the Golden Age of comics, starting in 1956 with the Flash, had snowballed into a number of new titles featuring costumed cavorters not just from DC and Marvel but also from most of the second-tier publishers. Archie Comics had Fly-Man and the Shadow, Charlton had Blue Beetle and Son of Vulcan, and Gold Key had Doctor Solar and the Phantom. By the end of the year, a new publisher named Tower Comics would enter the fray with a prefab super team known as T.H.U.N.D.E.R. Agents. Like most fans, I was caught up in the excitement. I wasn't one to linger on the sidelines. I *had* to be part of the parade.

I wrote to numerous fans whose writing and art I'd seen in the magazines I'd received thus far, asking for contributions. In some cases I enclosed a copy of *Super-Heroes Anonymous* #1 to prove that I was indeed a publisher. This might have been a mistake, crude as it was. Those who responded turned me down, citing prior commitments. Again the question: what would I put in *Super-Heroes Anonymous* #2? Luckily for me (and my readers) I received help from unexpected quarters.

Back when I was in third grade, Dick Trageser was the clerk working with my dad who'd typed up my early stories. I originally met him on a visit to the office with Dad when I was probably six years old. My earliest memories of Dick are of twinkling eyes, a broad smile, and a friendly demeanor.

Left: Dick Trageser at his desk in the Northern Pacific Railroad office in Pittsburgh, where he wrote the pulp-influenced tales of the Immortal Corpse. Above: Illustration by Alan Hutchinson is from the back cover of Bombshell #9 (1967). The Immortal Corpse ™ and © Bill Schelly

I'd had more occasions to visit with Dick over the years, and before long I discovered that he had been a comic book fan as a boy in the 1940s. This common interest added an important dimension to our friendship. He was the first person I met who had actively read comic books during their Golden Age. He was happy to regale me with stories of what it was like to collect and trade comics during World War II. Dick didn't seem at all astonished that comics were now worth sizable sums of money, and he regretted that he hadn't saved any of them after graduating from high school.

Dick had writing ambitions of his own. He'd picked up what he knew from reading a lot of hardboiled detective fiction, including popular authors Mickey Spillane and Raymond Chandler, in his youth. The Shadow was one of his favorite characters. Dick was the one who told me about the exciting adventures of old-time radio heroes.

Since I saw Dick as something of a mentor, and he had shown an interest in me, I made sure he got a copy of *Super-Heroes Anonymous* #1. To my great delight, he responded by writing an unsolicited story starring the Immortal Corpse, titled "The Ape." I could tell from the opening lines that Dick had perfectly grasped the character's noirish potential. It began:

> It was 3:00 a.m. when I finally stepped out into the night. The sprawling city slept under its glittering blanket of stars, while a cold wind swirled scraps of paper into the misty beams of the street lights. I shivered and drew my uniform collar up over my eyes as I walked north toward Main Street. Tonight was the night I had chosen to test my new powers. Tonight the Immortal Corpse would walk.

The story's climax packed a real punch:

> "Just lay the telegram on the table over there, kid," [Cabot] said as he turned his back to pick up a necktie.
>
> "I don't have a telegram," I said, concentrating my powers once more, and beginning to age at a rate of ten years a second. "I have come to take you to your grave."
>
> "What is this, a joke?" he snarled, whirling around with a pistol clenched in his hairy paw.
>
> "No," I croaked, shambling forward with my bony hands outstretched toward his neck. My face had become a grinning skull covered with drooping yellow skin. "It's no joke, Cabot. I am Death … *come to claim my own.*"

To me at the time, Dick Trageser was a man of towering talent. I immediately scheduled "The Ape" for my second issue. My impression that Dick had been published in some sort of detective magazines turned out to be wrong. The only place his work saw print was in my fanzines. I was happy to use anything he cared to write. Trageser authored a half-dozen stories over the next few years, most featuring the Corpse. It was Dick, not I, who made the character a success of sorts in my own small corner of fandom. (The character, sometimes written by others, went on to shamble through the pages of a number of fanzines beyond my own.)

Jack "King" Kirby, who cocreated many of the Marvel heroes of the 1960s, as well as Captain America in the 1940s, took the time to sketch Cap for a snot-nosed kid in Pittsburgh who wrote him a fan letter. ™ and © Marvel Characters, Inc.

I also had an assist from another unexpected direction on *Super-Heroes Anonymous* #2. Imagine my thrill when I opened a large mailing envelope in the spring of 1965 to find a beautiful sketch of Captain America drawn especially for me by Jack Kirby. At the time, I didn't realize how many Marvel comic book characters he had created or cocreated with Stan Lee. I did know from *The Rocket's Blast Special* #1 that Kirby had originated Captain America with Joe Simon. I had requested the sketch and was overwhelmed by his kindness. I immediately decided to use it for my cover.

As if this wasn't enough, I experienced similar exultation when—a few days later—I received a drawing of Doctor Strange by Steve Ditko, who had cocreated the hero with magical powers. It would serve nicely as a pinup page in that same issue. I was walking tall, publishing original work by both Kirby and Ditko in *SHA*.

Having been introduced to the Marvel Family in the pages of *Alter Ego*, I managed to scrape together a few dollars to purchase an issue of *Captain Marvel Adventures* from the 1940s. It was issue #91, dated December 1948, with stories written by Otto Binder and William Woolfolk, and art by C. C. Beck. I loved the slightly whimsical adventures of the original Captain Marvel, so different from the Marvel or DC style of the early 1960s. The article I wrote on this comic book, along with an editorial and letter column—yes, against all odds I did receive some letters in response to our premiere issue—would nearly fill out *Super-Heroes Anonymous* #2.

Captain Marvel Adventures #91 (1948). Captain Marvel ™ and © DC Comics.

The last major feature was a comics story I wrote and drew. I'd been working up to it for a long time but had never completed a strip starring any of my juvenile creations, probably because I lacked an audience and the inspiration. Also, they were all transparent imitations of Marvel or DC characters. Now, armed with a concept that I felt was sufficiently original and knowing it would be seen by others, I felt ready to try to weave my own form of comic book magic.

N

A drawing board and a T-square had been my big present last Christmas. Now I needed something to put it on. Dad and I found a table in the basement that was perfect for the job: sturdy and just the right size. It had belonged to his mother and had been in the Schelly family since the turn of the century. We put it in a corner in my bedroom and set up the board on top. I propped one end up with books so it tilted, approximating the slanted drawing board shown by Steve Ditko in the *Spider-Man Annual*. In the single drawer, I placed all my drawing equipment. I was ready to go.

I applied myself diligently and managed to finish the origin of a brand-new superhero called the Snow-Man, a scientist who gained immunity to cold and powers over frozen water molecules while performing experiments at the North Pole. "Meet the Snow-Man" was brief (seven pages) and immature in the extreme. Nevertheless, it was a beginning.

One more contributor stepped forward. In response to either the debut issue or an advertisement for #2, I received a superhero drawing by Jeff Gelb of Rochester, New York. It was accompanied by a brief note asking me what I thought of it and wondering if I would like him to contribute further artwork. I ran this illustration at the end of the letter column.

While my parents weren't exactly enthusiastic about my amateur publishing, they were at least moderately supportive over time. Mom even volunteered to type up the text pages for *SHA* #2. The Schelly family now owned a spanking-new Smith Corona portable typewriter, which aided me greatly in my publishing endeavors. Unfortunately, I no longer had access to a Xerox copier; I was forced to have my second issue printed at the Northern Pacific office on their ancient mimeograph machine. Dad brought home a stack of stencils and a stylus (a drawing implement) used to trace artwork onto them. I had to take it from there.

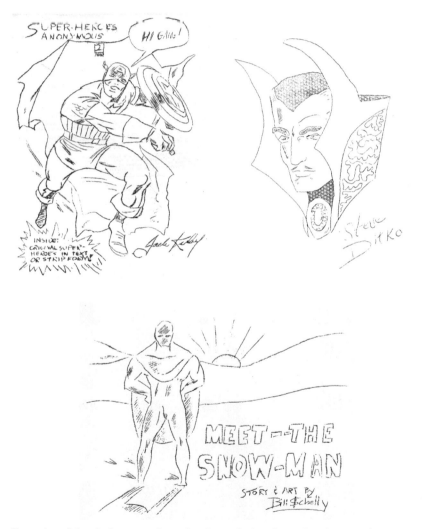

Examples of the chicken-scratch results obtained when I was forced to use the ancient Northern Pacific mimeograph machine for *Super-Heroes Anonymous* #2 (1965). The odd pattern in the "black areas" on Steve Ditko's Doctor Strange illustration occurred because I cut away the mimeo stencil entirely in those areas, and the pattern of the revolving drum of the machine emerged. "Meet the Snow-Man" was an embarrassment, but I had to start somewhere. Captain America and Doctor Strange ™ and © Marvel Characters, Inc.

Some fanzine publishers achieved marvelously subtle visuals in mimeo. I wasn't one of them. I was too young, too inexperienced, and too impatient. I did have an example of top-quality mimeograph printing in *Batmania,* but I was soon to discover that drawing on those stencils was tricky business. Unlike ditto printing, which was purple, mimeographed printing was black, as long as one coated the inside of the rotating drum (where one attached the stencil) with black ink. Unfortunately, the final printed art of the Snow-Man looked like a mass of chicken scratches because I hadn't pressed down hard enough on the stylus as I cut the stencils. I wasn't happy as I examined the printed pages when Dad brought them home. As with *SHA* #1, the final result fell *far* short of my vision, in this case due to my lack of understanding of the mimeo printing medium. (Printing snafus would dog me throughout my days as a fanzine publisher.) The typed pages came out readable, but the beautiful Kirby and Ditko art was poorly served by my ineptitude. The issue resembled a Bizarro World version of fanzine publishing, like looking through some sort of distorted glass.

The response to *Super-Heroes Anonymous* #2 was minimal. With a circulation of forty to fifty copies, and with such awful printing, it's no surprise that few were moved to write. The only letter I remember receiving sticks out in my memory for a good reason: it was from Steve Ditko, and he was mad as a hornet.

His letter, written in pencil on a single sheet of paper, said (more or less), "You should not have assumed that the drawing I sent you was for publication. You should have asked my permission. This isn't the first time I've been treated inconsiderately by members of fandom, which is why I've stopped sending out drawings to fans."

Ditko's rebuke stung. I had naively thought he would be pleased, but I got his point. Even at that age, I understood I had inadvertently done something wrong. I had "used" Ditko to sell my publication without his okay. I wrote a letter of apology to him, but he didn't respond. I felt especially bad because it was about this time that he did stop sending drawings to fanzine editors. (He had done several

Spider-Man and Doctor Strange drawings for fanzines up to that point; they had seen print in *Komik Heroz of the Future*, *The Comic Reader*, and *Alter Ego*, among others.)

N

Eighth grade at Mellon Junior High was a bad year for me. I experienced a resurgence of the bullying that had plagued me in the past.

Certain schoolmates decided that I deserved to be harassed, apparently because I was physically weak and an easy target, and perhaps because they sensed that I was gay (although I didn't act effeminate). One of my tormentors was the star player on the football team, Alan Walker. He and his toadies would wait for me after school, forcing me to employ various methods of evasion. Sometimes I would stay after school in the library until I was sure they had given up. Other times, I would slip out a side door and hope they wouldn't catch sight of me. I never told my parents about this recurring problem. Had I done so, they would have met with the school principal, the word would get out that I'd "squealed," and then my hazing would worsen.

One memorable day I either miscalculated or the guys who were after me figured out my method of evasion. They knew my normal route home and lay in wait in the woods near the cemetery. Their war whoop as they sprung from the bushes to attack is still one of the most frightening sounds I've ever heard.

I was lucky in the sense that they didn't actually gang up on me. Instead, one of them squared off against me, and the other two hovered nearby. With the desperation of a cornered animal (and, after all, I wasn't a *total* wimp), I gave a fair accounting of myself, getting in a few awkward punches here and there. But I took more than I gave, and when it wasn't fun anymore for my opponents, they left after some final sneering taunts.

Upon arriving home that day, somewhat bruised and battered, I found an envelope waiting for me on the kitchen table. Dodging Mom, who was busy in some other area of the house, I grabbed it and headed straight for my room. I shut the door, sprawled on the bed, and examined the envelope. I can still see it in my mind perfectly: it bore a return address from Columbia, Missouri.

I tore it open carefully and slid out a copy of *Batmania* #4 (1965). The cover by editor Biljo White featured the new, jazzy version of the Batmobile that had recently been introduced in the comics. I opened up the pages, and soon I had completely forgotten my troubles. I was home again in Fandomland.

◢

During the summer of 1965, I read all of the thirteen James Bond paperbacks that had been published so far. I loved them. Was it the "high-tension suspense, unexpected thrills, extraordinary danger" touted by the back covers of the inexpensive Signet editions? Was it their racy sex scenes? The exotic locales? All were important elements of 007's appeal.

I admired Ian Fleming, the author, at least as much as his charismatic creation. I liked his seemingly effortless way of setting a tale spinning and then taking the reader through a series of sensory and sensual situations, filtered through his unique point of view. It's a persona that's not easy to pin down. The word critics often used was "sardonic," which applies but does not go far enough; for, in Bond (Fleming's admitted alter ego), we also find an individual of quick emotion, even romanticism. Fleming the writer had the journalistic expertise to record the super-spy's experiences in such vivid terms that we can easily project ourselves into the protagonist's role. I discovered James Bond when I saw the film *Dr. No* in a theater in 1962, so I don't know why it took me so long to pick up one of the books. When I did, there was no end to my enthusiasm. I rushed out and spent all my meager savings on the entire run of paperbacks. Then I settled down to the most pleasurable communion with the written word of my life up till then.

I remember those summer days vividly. I slept in and then went downstairs to sip orange juice about the time Mom and my brothers gathered up towels, swimsuits, and goggles, and jumped in our car for a day at the country club pool, where we had a membership (paid for by Northern Pacific). Armed with a mammoth glass of instant iced tea and a plate piled high with buttered toast, I retreated to my room and got comfortable.

To mitigate the heat and humidity, I commandeered the family box fan (a twenty-four-inch affair) and kept it roaring on high all day. Then I curled up on the carpet in close proximity to its vibrating chassis, arranging myself on and around various pillows, and began reading.

What a deliciously languorous, carefree experience. I had nothing to do but delve into the virgin territory of a brand-new Bond tale, with all its familiar denizens: M, Miss Moneypenny, Bill Tanner, Bond's Scottish housekeeper May, and, of course, the spy with the thick black comma of hair on his forehead and a rather cruel mouth.

I wasn't an especially fast reader, but I recall deliberately taking my time with each book. Nevertheless, there were times when I would become so caught up in the narrative that I would find myself finishing a book in a single day, about when the Plymouth came lumbering into the garage in time for Mom to start fixing dinner.

That same summer I began drawing more comics stories, this time for other amateur publications. These early efforts were childish but readable. They were my baby steps in learning the syntax of comics: the close-up, the splash panel, the action shot, the super-villain. Each was no more than six or seven pages long, featuring "original" characters such as Pan, Master of Sound (a mythological concept probably inspired by Thor) and Star Brite (whose name sounded more like a floor wax than a superhero, and who resembled the Silver Surfer) for fanzines like *Fantasy Fandom Crossroads, Earthquake Comics,* and *Sanctum.*

This was also my introduction to working with ditto masters. They were so much easier to use than those waxy mimeograph stencils. Instead of having to cut through a stencil with a stylus to allow black ink to be forced through onto the surface of the paper, one merely drew or typed on the white top sheet of the ditto master, which had an underlying sheet coated with a thick purple substance, something like a sheet of carbon paper, lying face up. The impression of a pencil or typewriter would cause the purple to be transferred to the back of the top sheet, which would then be torn away from the carbon and placed onto the cylindrical drum of a spirit duplicator. Either by hand cranking or electrical motor, the drum rotated as paper was fed through, printing a purple image onto each sheet. The machine brushed a sheen of alcohol-laden spirit fluid against the ditto master, allowing a small portion of that purple to be transferred to each piece of paper. (As the fluid rapidly evaporated from the printed sheets, it gave them a sweet, almost intoxicating smell.) This method was easy to use, relatively clean, and inexpensive. In ditto, one could obtain a freewheeling, loose quality in printed artwork. It was one of the most informal printing mediums ever invented.

The process had another virtue: ditto masters were available in several colors other than purple. They came in red, blue, green, and black. By tracing various parts of a single drawing on first a purple master bottom sheet, then a red one, and then a blue one, a multihued effect could be created. If you wanted to save the master to print more, it was easy to remove it from the drum and reuse it later. Ditto was both user-friendly and viewer-friendly. Its only real drawback was that master units would eventually exhaust themselves, making the printing start to get lighter after two hundred copies or so. Also, I discovered later that the purple printing tended to fade over time.

I took to ditto like a fish to water. Luckily, I was on friendly terms with the school librarian. While helping her shelve books, I noticed that she was cranking a machine making copies of some worksheets. A closer look revealed that it was a ditto machine. When I asked if I might print up my own publication on it, she readily agreed. I immediately began preparing my next issue, which I christened with the new, more sophisticated title *Incognito* (in imitation of *Alter Ego*, no doubt). A new title felt like a fresh start, though I kept the original numbering, making it #3. In this issue, I was particularly proud of an ambitious, multipage feature titled "The Doctor Strange Story," which included some nice tracings of Ditko artwork, a checklist of all the Doctor Strange stories that had appeared in the back of *Strange Tales* thus far, and the longest prose article I had yet written. The result wasn't perfect, but it was much more satisfactory than the rotten mimeo mess that had preceded it. The contents were just about as poor, but the appearance was much improved. I loved being on the premises, watching, as the pages of my fanzine were printed. I even got to turn the crank myself on the later pages. When I'd typed and drawn on the ditto masters, I didn't know how effective they would look in print. My spine tingled as I watched the purple pages (with touches of red and green) appear before my eyes. They looked great!

By the time my fourteenth birthday rolled around, sex had become a major preoccupation of mine. I applied my artistic talent toward drawing Lois and Superman nude and having sex. Actually, I wasn't a good enough artist to do that from scratch, so I traced drawings from the comic book (pencils by Curt Swan), bending them to my purpose. My embarrassment knew no bounds when my father summoned me in hushed tones into his den and confronted me with these scandalous images. "Your mother was pretty upset when she found them," he said. "I know it's probably perfectly normal, but she doesn't understand, so you'd better knock it off. And if you don't, for God's sake make sure she doesn't find them again." As bad as this was, at least I hadn't drawn Superman having sex with Jimmy Olsen. That would have been a lot harder to explain.

This incident led Dad to give me a book called *For Boys Only* by Frank Howard Richardson, MD. It was a 1965 reissue of a book originally published in 1952. I was suitably flushed at this presentation. I already knew the basics of sex, although the book did fill in some information so that I had a somewhat clearer understanding. Of course, premarital sex was wrong, abortion made you a criminal and was dangerous, etc. The only reference to homosexuality was to child molesters. That some readers of this book might be gay or questioning their sexuality was obviously not something the author chose to discuss.

My artistic endeavors weren't limited to comic art. For Christmas I received a set of oil paints and an easel, and I became quite fascinated with the medium. Dad admired the paintings on canvas boards that I easily turned out. He could be supportive on occasion. It was only when I confessed that I wanted to pursue an art career "when I grow up" that he demurred.

"Art is a wonderful hobby, but you can't make a living with it," he'd tell me. "You should go into business or law. With the kind of good grades you're getting, you can be anything you want to be." Over time, this became a source of increasing conflict between us.

American television was becoming more adventurous in 1965 than it had been before. No longer were the schedules of the three networks so heavily larded with Westerns (although they were still around). Science fiction shows such as Irwin Allen's *Lost in Space* and *Voyage to the Bottom of the Sea* proved to be too juvenile for my tastes, but I was a fan of most of the spy shows, which were TV's attempt to cash in on the James Bond craze. My favorites were *The Man from U.N.C.L.E., Secret Agent,* and the spy comedy *Get Smart.*

After the announcement that a Batman television show would be a midseason replacement on ABC, probably every comics fan in the country was tuned in when it premiered. Perhaps this would be the occasion when all America would realize the potential of the Dynamic Duo, and acceptance of comics would become the norm. Maybe it would even usher in a surge in comic book sales. I'm sure I wasn't the only member of comicdom who had high hopes as I settled down in front of our new color TV set on January 12, 1966, to watch the first episode.

I experienced a sinking feeling as the program unfolded. Despite being pleased by the mere existence of the show—the fact that comic book characters were on the TV screen at all—my disappointment at the comedic treatment was immediate. Such dashed hopes! Instead of being an ambassador for comics, the show held them up to ridicule.

Soon it seemed the whole country was laughing, and it was laughing *at* comics, not *with* them.

Comics sales spiked during the show's brief period of meteoric popularity—especially those comics featuring the Caped Crusaders—but in the long run, it probably hurt the industry. Just as teenage and older readers were coming together in fandom to celebrate the medium's potential, the rug was pulled out from under us.

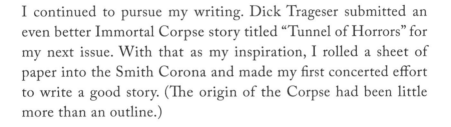

I continued to pursue my writing. Dick Trageser submitted an even better Immortal Corpse story titled "Tunnel of Horrors" for my next issue. With that as my inspiration, I rolled a sheet of paper into the Smith Corona and made my first concerted effort to write a good story. (The origin of the Corpse had been little more than an outline.)

After minor run-ins with school bullies, I yearned to add three (or more) inches of steel-like muscles to my arms. Instead, I created the dynamic muscleman Race Royal, shown here in a recreation of the concept drawing I did at the time (which has since been lost).

This new story starred a Doc Savage–like hero named Race Royal, Agent of B.A.D.G.E. (I never did work out what B.A.D.G.E. stood for; it was an acronym with no meaning.) "Race Royal on Chrona I—The Time World" begins:

> "I don't believe it!" drawled Shane Sherwood in utter amazement. "In all my days with B.A.D.G.E., I've never heard of such a thing!" He was referring to the blaring headline of the newspaper.
>
> It read "UFO SPOTTED IN UPPER ATMOSPHERE!" At that moment, the door flew open.
>
> A thundering voice pierced the dead silence. "Look Shane, I didn't join B.A.D.G.E. to sit around in an office." It was Race Royal. His handsome, rugged outline was indeed something to behold. He stood a sturdy six feet two inches tall, and it was sheer muscle. With his every movement, muscles yet unheard of rippled and flexed beneath his purple and gold outfit. "I want permission to investigate the UFO. They've predicted when and where it will land, and I want to be there to meet it."

As the story develops (and I use the word "story" loosely), the UFO aliens kidnap Royal and transport him to their planet, Chrona I, which is located (according to a disembodied voice) "in the 37th galaxy." It was the first part of what I envisioned as an exciting serialized saga, probably because I had no idea how to write a true short story, so I merely wrote the beginning of a longer one. Of course there were to be no further chapters of "Race Royal." Even for amateur fanzines, it was pretty bad.

Then there's the name itself: Race Royal. Was this some inchoate racist statement? I wouldn't blame anyone for thinking so, but I stole the name "Race" from the *Jonny Quest* TV series, which was produced by Hanna-Barbera Productions and was created and designed by comic book artist Doug Wildey. In the cartoon, which debuted in the 1964-65 television season, Jonny's companion and ally was an older soldier-of-fortune type named Race Bannon. Bannon provided the template and the first name for my character. Picking a last name was simply a matter of finding an alliterative surname to go with Race. It had nothing to do with me thinking there was something about being white that was kingly or ordained by God.

My interest in Race Royal was mainly focused on his nearly superhuman physique. I used to eyeball those Charles Atlas and Joe Weider muscle-building ads in the comics and fantasize about secretly working out for months, then surprising my foes with my newfound strength. In my mind's eye, I could see the astonishment on their faces as I sent them packing. However, I don't think I even went so far as to send in a dime for further information. Somehow I knew that revenge was an insufficient motive for the amount of work it would take to gain the physique of a Mr. America. (Maybe Bruce Wayne could do it, but not me.)

When it came time to publish *Incognito* #4, the friendly school librarian changed her mind about allowing me to use her ditto machine. "I thought you were going to print something *educational*," she sniffed. "Not a silly magazine about *comic books*." My protestations fell on deaf ears. I was forced to resort to using the Northern Pacific's godawful mimeograph again.

At least I could afford a photo-offset cover of Green Arrow and Speedy to accompany an article on them, and to print by Xerox a one-page comic strip by *Yancy Street Journal* coeditor Bill DuBay called "The Web." (I must have used the photocopier at the local library.) The rest of the issue was filled out by a letter from Roy Thomas, who had recently been hired as editorial assistant and writer at Marvel Comics. He described what has become known as the "Marvel method" of adding the dialogue and captions after the comic book is penciled. All in all, *Incognito* #4 wasn't much better than the previous three issues. I was getting nowhere.

Then an event took place that would do much to determine my course over the next couple of years. I received a letter from another Pittsburgh-based comics fan who would become my best friend in fandom.

6.

ENTER: MARSHALL LANZ

It began with five simple words scrawled on the bottom of an order for *Incognito* #4. Marshall Lanz, along with a pitiful few others, was responding to a small advertisement in *RBCC*. At the bottom of the sheet, below the taped coins, were the words, "We should get together sometime."

Lanz lived in Penn Hills, Pennsylvania. "Where's Penn Hills?" I asked Mom.

"It's a suburb of Pittsburgh."

"Is it a long way from Mount Lebanon?"

"It's on the other side of the city," she replied. "Why do you want to know?"

"Because a guy who ordered my fanzine lives there and wants to get together with me."

"It's too far away. There are plenty of kids your age to spend time with right here."

"But Mom, he's a comics fan. I don't know anyone in Mount Lebanon who buys fanzines like I do and collects old comics."

"What happened to Richard Shields?"

"He's busy with the track team."

"How old is this person?"

"I don't know …"

"—because you're *not* going to be meeting some older man, or …"

"He's probably right around my age."

She thought for a moment. "Write and find out more about him."

"Can I phone him?"

"I guess so, unless it's a toll call. It might be because Penn Hills is so far away."

I phoned Marshall Lanz—the same day I received his letter—and as Mom suspected, it *was* a toll call, a fact I kept to myself until later.

"Hello? Is this Marshall?"

"Yeah. Who's this?"

"Bill Schelly."

"Who?"

"You ordered my fanzine *Incognito*."

"Oh—*hi*."

"You suggested we get together, so I thought I'd call."

We quickly established that he had a large comic book collection, we were the same age, and we were both avid fanzine readers. When the subject of *Incognito* came up again, he asked, "Have you done a lot of fanzines?"

"A few. They're no big deal. What about you?"

"I've contributed to two or three," he said. "Only one that's any good."

"Which one?"

"Um ... *Alter Ego*."

I said, "*Alter Ego*? You contributed to *Alter Ego*?"

"Yeah, a Blackhawk cartoon. It'll be in the new issue, which is supposed to come out any time now."

"I ordered it."

"It's supposed to be on the last page. Actually I was shocked that Roy Thomas wanted to use it because it was just a doodle I sent him along with my order for that issue." It was Roy's last issue of *AE* before moving to New York City and working for Marvel.

I was impressed. "That's so cool. *Alter Ego* is the best."

"Yeah, I should have lots more in it next time," Lanz said, self-importantly. "I sent him a whole bunch of other stuff."

"I'll look for that Blackhawk thing," I said. (A month or so later, the fanzine arrived, and there was Marshall's cartoon on the last page of the issue.)

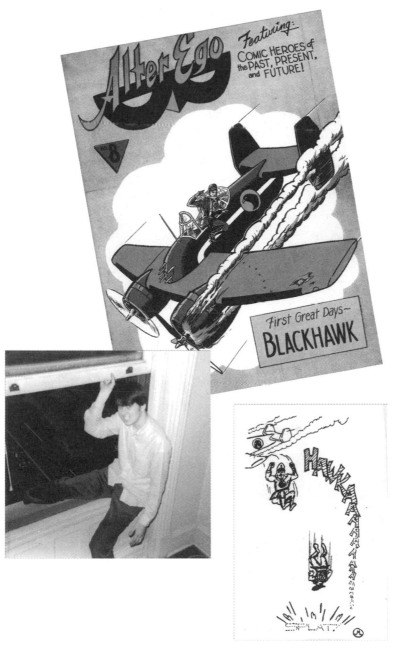

Marshall Lanz straddles a windowsill in the sixth-floor office of the Northern Pacific Railroad in downtown Pittsburgh. Is he about to imitate the Blackhawk cartoon he did for *Alter Ego*? The cartoon, a response to Biljo White's cover to *AE* #8, appeared on the final page of *AE* #9 in August 1965. Blackhawk ™ and © DC Comics.

"So—d'you want to get together?"

"Sure. Can you come over here, or should I visit you? My mom says Penn Hills is a long way from here."

"Why don't you come over here? If your mom can bring you over, I'll have mine drive you home."

It wasn't long before we finalized plans for the momentous meeting. I had to do some fast talking to get Mom to drive me what turned out to be about fifteen miles to the Lanz household. She finally agreed, if for no other reason than to check out Lanz's house and meet his mother.

We rang the doorbell of the modest brick house on Lindberg Avenue in Penn Hills, a nice, working-class neighborhood. The first thing I noticed about Lanz when the door swung open was his height. I wasn't short, but he must have been pushing six feet tall.

"Hi," he said, flashing a Pepsodent grin and flicking a crop of dark bangs from his eyes. "I'm Marshall."

I reached over and shook his hand. "I'm Bill."

A fiftyish woman with curly blond hair appeared behind him. "Hello, you must be Billy," she said to me, smiling.

"Bill."

She turned to my mother. "It's a pleasure to meet you, Mrs. Schelly. I'm Kay Lanz."

With that, Lanz gestured for me to follow him upstairs. "See you later," I said to my mom, leaving her to chat with Mrs. Lanz and to discuss the arrangements for my return home. From the window in Lanz's large room, I watched Mom drive away.

Lanz and I hit it off from the start. He obviously craved a comic-collecting buddy as much as I did. It was great fun to be able to chat about comics and fanzines. Like me, he had been involved in fandom for over a year and subscribed to most of the major fan publications. I'd brought some comics to trade, and I'm pretty sure we engineered a deal at that meeting. I discovered that Lanz's collection was quite a bit larger than my own. It was great to be able to look through bunches of back issues that I'd never seen before.

Marshall's and my school pictures in 1966. Lanz photo courtesy of Jeanne Russell.

I soon realized Marshall Lanz was an outrageous character. With that devilish smile and funny, puffy cheeks, he resembled nothing so much as a demented cherub. He had a cheerfully anarchistic take-no-prisoners attitude toward life, and for me he came to represent complete freedom from restraint and convention. He constantly incited me to color outside the lines.

Lanz exuded supreme self-confidence. He knew he was cool, and he knew he was a good artist. He expressed his opinions with the force of righteous conviction. Like many fourteen-year-olds, Lanz assumed an "I've got all the answers" pose. What made it all palatable was his sense of humor. I'd never met anybody who could be as funny—in a cuttingly sarcastic way—as Lanz. He had a quick mind and what I can only call charisma.

One of his favorite activities was making fun of some of the admittedly crude fanzines he received in the mail, such as one called *Comiclub*, which was not much worse than my own publications up to that point. Although he deigned to contribute some spot illustrations at the request of editor Gabe Eisenstein, Lanz had no end of fun ridiculing a truly awful comics story in the pages of *Comiclub* about a hero named Lightning Man. I joined right in with my own jabs at the feature's many ineptitudes. In this way, we developed a loopy comedy routine around this hapless character, which we elaborated over time. The riffs we did on Lightning Man were, in their way, probably the most creative thing Lanz and I ever did together. A sense of freewheeling fun became our *modus operandi.*

He could be tactful in certain respects, such as the supportive noises he made as he examined a stack of my drawings. His drawings employed a sort of neoprimitive style that had a certain appeal. If I found weaknesses in his work, for the most part I kept quiet about them (as I guess he did about mine) because our friendship was more important than pointing out artistic flaws. We managed to avoid the kind of brash honesty that could so easily have thrown our budding relationship off track. In time, Lanz would specialize in inking, developing a real facility with a brush and India ink.

He was an only child (or if he had an older sibling, that brother or sister had long since grown up and moved out). His mother waited on him hand and foot. For her, the sun rose and set on Marshall. She confided in me that her son was a genius, although he didn't apply himself in school.

Lanz was a little Caesar around the house, getting meals whenever he wanted them, being chauffeured around town, and being treated to trips to McDonald's for French fries at all hours. I soon became familiar with the routine: Lanz would make his request, and then Kay would flutter about saying she wasn't going to do what he asked, but eventually she always relented. I was envious of Marshall's power over his mother. My own mother wouldn't have stood for it for a second.

Kay Lanz was without a doubt the worst cook I've ever encountered. Here was a woman who would broil a nice cut of meat until it was tougher than shoe leather, and she had the unforgivable habit of using powdered potatoes rather than real ones—this at a time when the powdered variety tasted like paste. Still, I liked Mrs. Lanz a lot. She had a sweet, scatterbrained quality that was endearing, and she was unfailingly kind to me. Kay always called me "Billy," eventually referring to me as her "lost adopted son" (which didn't make a lot of sense, but I understood the gist of it).

Above, clockwise: Examples of the work of four of early comicdom's finest artists: Captain Ego by Biljo White, Xal-Kor the Human Cat by Richard "Grass" Green, the Cowl by Ronn Foss, and art from "One Summer Night" by Landon Chesney. Captain Ego ™ and © Bill Schelly and Roy Thomas. Xal-Kor ™ and © Bill Schelly. The Cowl ™ and © Mike Vosburg. "One Summer Night" © Bill Spicer.

While the geographical distance between us initially forced our visits to be few (and always at Marshall's place, for some reason), he and I bridged the gap by talking on the phone endlessly. Oddly, a phone call *to* him was a toll call, but a call *from* him was not. If I wanted to talk with him, I had to call him first. Then he would ring me back, and we could talk at length. (For the record, I wasn't attracted to Lanz in any way except as a friend. I always felt he was 100 percent heterosexual, and our focus was almost entirely on comic books, fandom, and making fun of the world around us.)

All the while, my comic book collection was steadily growing. It quickly filled the bottom two drawers of my dresser and began over-flowing into a series of cardboard boxes obtained from a local grocer. (Boxes and bags made especially for storing comics wouldn't become available until 1970.)

I collected fanzines right along with the comics. While they were inexpensive by today's standards, priced from twenty to fifty cents each, all cost more than a twelve-cent comic book, so I had to limit my purchases. I made sure I didn't miss any issues of *Star-Studded Comics, Batmania, Voice of Comicdom,* and *Fantasy Illustrated.* I bought my share of the humbler ditto fanzines, but I also found ways to obtain them without sending cash. I traded copies of *Incognito* for as many as I could. Another way to get a free fanzine was to contribute some art or writing, thus receiving a copy in payment. (Some fan editors even gave freebies to anyone who had a letter published in their pages.)

Just as I studied and imitated the work of professional comics art-ists, I keenly admired the artwork of a trio of gifted amateurs. I spent many hours poring over the comics stories and illustrations of Ronn Foss, Biljo White, and Richard "Grass" Green. I was interested in the way they handled anatomy, the storytelling techniques they used in their strips, their methods of shading, even their interpretations of facial expressions. Each had his own distinctive style. They weren't the only notable fan artists whose work I followed, of course. I loved the EC-flavored art of Landon Chesney, the anatomically impressive fig-ures rendered by Alan Weiss, and the neatly delineated stories and cartoons by Dave Herring. Talent, some of it nascent and some of it quite developed, abounded in comicdom from the beginning.

N

Shortly after meeting Lanz in the spring of 1966, I gained access to another ditto machine, this time in the basement of the local Presbyterian church. In an effort to make up for the printing flaws of my past publications, I decided to reprint some of the best features via spirit duplicator. This was *Incognito Extra* #1. As I began attaching my carefully prepared ditto masters to the drum and cranking the pages, I anticipated another excellent printing job like *Incognito* #3. This time, I would print on both sides of the page, rather than one side. It simply entailed taking the stack of copies of page 1 and, after turning them over, printing page two on the back. I was confident this would work out all right, but had made one important miscalculation: to save money, I had purchased paper of a slightly thinner grade than usual (sixteen-pound paper, versus the regular twenty-pound weight). The printing on side one looked fine, but when I printed on the back, the printing partially showed through to the other side, enough that it looked bad and made it harder to read. Not unusable, but far from ideal. I didn't notice this until I had printed up all the pages and was getting ready to leave. Again, printing problems! I lost my temper this time. After all that work! Good thing the church secretary wasn't there to hear the language I used in the basement that day.

I also reached a dead end with my next writing project. Having impressed myself with my literary efforts on "Race Royal," I decided to write a speculative novel about nuclear war with the working title *World War III*. The early chapters involved some counterspy espionage heavily influenced by Fleming's James Bond novels, and the next section was devoted to a portrayal of the postapocalyptic world, where orphans (like the children in the movie *Village of the Damned*) gained mind-control powers. Like my other early efforts, this one was left incomplete, although I did write about fifteen thousand words. I had no idea what direction the story would take or how it would end, so when my initial inspiration flagged, I set it aside.

As 1966 progressed and I began my sophomore year at Mount Lebanon High School, I noticed a subtle change in the advertisements in *RBCC*. A great number of old comics became available as a result of numerous newspaper articles about the high prices being commanded by comics from the 1940s. People who'd never thought much about the comics and pulp magazines in their attic had an incentive to dig them out and sell them. Where once such issues were hard to find for the average fan, thanks to *RBCC* now they were almost plentiful.

There were a number of comic book dealers, most notably Claude Held, Ken Mitchell, Bill Thailing, Phil Seuling, and the much-reviled Howard "tape is not a defect" Rogofsky. I overcame my reluctance to send money through the mail once I realized most dealers were reputable. On those occasions when I had a few extra dollars, I would buy a money order and send away for one or two reasonably priced comics. I owned one issue each of *Sub-Mariner, Daredevil,* and *Whiz Comics* from the late 1940s, but the most I ever spent was three dollars for a book. I could never afford to plunk down enough at one time to purchase any of the true rarities.

Lanz didn't have any key Golden Age comics either. There was no way for us to view the early classics of the field. Comic book conventions had begun in New York City in 1964, but we were not in a position to consider traveling to the Big Apple or Detroit fan gatherings where such rarities might be on display. Jerry Bails was selling photo sets of certain classic covers, but these were in black and white, as were his microfilm transfers of whole comics. Besides, we didn't have the wherewithal to buy a microfilm viewer. Fanzines often resorted to tracings of old covers.

The only comics reprint collection in print was Jules Feiffer's *The Great Comic Book Heroes,* which had been published by Crown Publishers the prior year. Somehow Feiffer was able to obtain permission to reprint classic stories of DC and Timely (Marvel) heroes from the early 1940s in full color, including Superman, Batman, Wonder Woman, Flash, Green Lantern, Hawkman, Captain America, the Human Torch, and Sub-Mariner, as well as sample episodes of Plastic Man and the Spirit. This book had a tremendous effect on me, not only because it gave me an opportunity to read a number of the best Golden Age stories but also because it validated my continuing interest in comics. It was as if the book said to adults, "It's okay to like comics." Considering that I courted ridicule every time I stepped up to the drugstore counter to buy the latest issues, I loved the fact that a respected writer like Feiffer was saying comics weren't only for kids. (With its twelve-dollar price tag, this hardback book was not being marketed to children.)

Then Lanz and I discovered that Raymond Miller, a fandom authority on the Golden Age who was well-known for his collection of comics from that era, lived not far from us. The man who had written so many articles and done so many character drawings on 1940s comics for *RBCC* lived in nearby Vandergrift, Pennsylvania. We wrote to him asking if we could visit. When he agreed, it wasn't long before we recruited Mrs. Lanz as our chauffeur. We showed up at Miller's door on Election Day of 1966.

Raymond Miller in his bedroom, 1966.

Miller lived in a small, older bungalow with his parents. He was in his middle or late thirties, slight of frame, and he wore wire-rim glasses. He welcomed us and ushered us to his bedroom, where he kept his impressive comic book collection.

He owned seven hundred comics published before 1946, not only from DC and Timely but also from Fox, Centaur, Fawcett, MLJ, and other smaller publishers. I'll always recall his shy, soft-spoken manner as he showed us many of his treasures. We felt truly awed by the beauty of those four-color rarities, which we were finally getting to see with our own eyes. We truly felt a sense of wonder. Many of the books came with a story, either about how it had found its way into Miller's hands or an explanation of a book's particular significance to collectors. It was a magical experience, holding those colorful marvels in our hands and gingerly opening a few (with his permission) to peer at the stories within.

Miller also owned a few pieces of original art, obtained either through trades or in recompense for letters published in DC comics edited by Julius Schwartz, who was rewarding the best letter writers with artwork. We marveled at the craftsmanship in pages drawn by Mike Sekowsky, an artist neither of us particularly liked until we saw those beautiful originals from *Justice League of America.* One of those Sekowsky pages made its way into my possession, the first such original I owned.

Lanz and I lit up when Miller pulled out a large stack of Spirit Sections that had been part of the *Pittsburgh Post-Gazette* in the 1940s. By this time, both of us were fans of Will Eisner's masked detective, having thoroughly enjoyed *The Spirit* #1, a twenty-five-cent book published by Harvey Comics in July that reprinted a bunch of his best stories. It seemed like everyone in fandom was raving about Eisner's amazing storytelling ability, which was originally shown off to such great advantage in the special comic book inserts that were included in Sunday newspapers in many major cities. Every week Eisner wrote and drew a complete seven-page Spirit story, usually set in the wonderfully noirish environs of the fictional Central City. Each tale was a gem, often taking the form of a little morality tale. These Spirit Sections were highly collectable because almost all of this great body of innovative work was unavailable in any other form. Luckily for us, Miller owned doubles of some of these sections and was willing to part with them for reasonable prices. Both Lanz and I walked out of there with some choice Eisner work.

Will Eisner's *The Spirit*, which appeared weekly in a special newspaper supplement during the 1940s and early 1950s, was an inspiration to just about every comics writer or artist who read it. Eisner demonstrated the importance of both good writing and visual storytelling skills. Yours truly was introduced to his work in two twenty-five-cent reprint specials from Harvey Comics in 1966. The Spirit ™ and © Will Eisner Studios.

Miller was obviously an introvert, but he was gracious and made us feel welcome. For his part, Lanz was polite, as he could be when the occasion warranted it. I think he liked Miller's lack of pretension. We were both totally blown away by the Golden Age comics he showed us.

1966 had been an eventful year for us, but it was only a prelude to what was to come. As the new year approached, our friendship and fanzine enterprises were about to shift into high gear.

7.

SENSE OF WONDER:
THE BIRTH OF THE FANZINE

In November 1966, I celebrated my fifteenth birthday. I also passed my second anniversary in comicdom. On one level, I had achieved a lot in those two years. I was an editor of magazines that were circulated all over the country. I'd published artwork by top industry professionals and corresponded with numerous collectors. I had also contributed to a handful of other similar publications. How many high school sophomores could make those claims?

On the other hand, I've always been realistic enough about my projects to see their flaws. I can't say I'm always totally objective about my creative efforts, but I've never suffered from extreme hubris. Some of my friends were impressed with *Super-Heroes Anonymous* and *Incognito,* but in my heart I knew they weren't all that good. Printing difficulties aside, the contents were weak, especially the text.

My next publication was a slim fanzine called *Fantasy Forum.* Why another new title? I guess I was trying to turn over a new leaf, and I figured a new title would help bury my less-than-stellar past. The format was similar to *Incognito:* editorial, brief opinion columns, pinups, and a story in either prose or comics form. One improvement was a cover featuring Plastic Man by a talented Florida-based newcomer named Alan Hutchinson. I had seen his beautifully detailed, finely crafted work in the pages of Gary Brown and Wayne DeWald's newszine *Comic Comments,* and I quickly enlisted his aid. The cover was printed photo-offset, and the interior was ditto.

The typing was a bit better, and the writing was marginally more intelligent. It contained a strip called "Vacation!" which was my take on the scary stories published by EC comics, and I thought it had turned out rather well. Admittedly, *Fantasy Forum* lacked good text features, apart from a new Immortal Corpse yarn by Trageser. This wasn't surprising because I didn't own many rare comics and had no other special knowledge to impart. I didn't want to do "shortie" articles a few hundred words long, like I'd mostly done in the past. About all I could do was offer my opinions—my analysis, if you will—of various current comic books.

Alan Hutchinson's playful cover for *Fantasy Forum* #1 (1966). Plastic Man ™ and © DC Comics.

My efforts to round up contributions from some of fandom's better writers met with no success. Highly regarded writers like Robert Jennings, Steve Perrin, and Rick Weingroff never answered my letters. The sample copies of *Incognito* were enough to discourage their participation, even if they had the time or inclination. It was a frustrating catch-22. Yet the publishing fever burned in me. I wasn't about to let anything stop me.

I gradually realized that I needed to go in the direction of *Star-Studded Comics,* a popular fanzine—what would now be called a small-press comic book—out of Texas that was entirely devoted to comic strips by fans. Unsophisticated though I was, I *could* write and draw. I was also assured of further prose from Dick Trageser. I could publish stories by others like me, or perhaps I could even attract work by top amateur comics creators like Ronn Foss and Buddy Saunders. After all, I wasn't publishing strictly to satisfy my writing ambitions. I also wanted to create comics. Thus, while putting out two issues of *Fantasy Forum* in the fall of 1966, I conceived my own version of *Star-Studded Comics.* At this moment, a letter arrived in my mailbox that had a major impact on me.

I had mailed out copies of *Forum* #1 gratis to several dozen prominent fans. Most didn't respond, as usual—they probably chucked it directly into the garbage. One who did take the time to write was Don Thompson.

Thompson, along with his wife, Maggie, published *Comic Art,* one of the most highly respected fanzines of the day. *Comic Art* had debuted about the same time as *Alter Ego* #1. Don was a reporter for the *Cleveland Press,* and his fanzine had the highest standards of journalism. It was produced for an older audience, mostly science fiction fans who also liked comics.

To put it mildly, Don didn't heap praise on me for my efforts. In fact, he didn't like *anything* about *Fantasy Forum:* the cover ("Why draw pro heroes when amateur efforts can't possibly compare?"); the comics story ("Trite, badly written, and badly drawn. If I want a story about a werewolf, there are any number of pre-Code comics I can read."); or the articles ("If you want to learn how to write, why don't you contribute to other fanzines first?") Don's letter hurt. No one likes to get raked over the coals, and I wasn't used to it.

When I showed the letter to Lanz, he sneered, "Aw, forget it. He doesn't know what he's talking about."

I wasn't so sure. Not that I agreed with everything Don said; I knew *Fantasy Forum* had been a step up for me and was as good as or better than a lot of amateur publications. Yet the more I thought about it, the more I had to admit that some of his criticisms made sense. At that moment, I made up my mind to do better.

Was I pissed off at Don Thompson? Initially, yes; but then I wasn't. I believed then, as I do now, that Thompson wasn't a mean-spirited guy. He was more curmudgeonly than most, but the main thing I took from his letter was that he *cared*—he wanted to make a difference. He certainly made a difference for me. I had been totally on my own, without a teacher or mentor to point out the weaknesses in my fanzines. In short, I needed guidance, even if it was just a kick in the pants. I'm glad it came from one of fandom's founders.

I vowed to produce something that would prove to Don Thompson and the rest of comicdom that Bill Schelly *could* contribute something worthwhile to fandom. I would take my time on the artwork. I would make sure the printing was as good as ditto could possibly be. And I would try harder to round up higher-quality features.

True to my pattern, this fresh start required a brand-new fanzine title. I wanted something that would remind readers why they loved comic books. Then it came to me: I would call it *Sense of Wonder*. The expression is probably centuries old. The earliest instance I've found of it was in a poem written in 1820. I chose it because I wanted this fanzine to evoke or at least pay homage to the thrill a reader feels when a new vista of the imagination opens up before him or her the way it did for me when I read my first comic book on that train trip back in 1960.

Now I had to come up with a publication worthy of that name. The omens were good. Dick Trageser wrote a terrifically moody, exciting Immortal Corpse story called "Skimmer's at the Museum!" which I sent off to Ronn Foss, who was then living in Florida. The story impressed Ronn, and he produced a superb cover that illustrated its climactic scene in a spooky wax museum. Doug Potter, a talented fan artist, and Sherman Howard, publisher of *Action Hero*, also agreed to contribute to this or the second issue.

Sense of Wonder #1 (May 1967). Ronn Foss's fine cover probably convinced other top fan writers and artists to contribute to the new fanzine. It illustrates a scene from Dick Trageser's Immortal Corpse story "Skimmer's at the Museum!" The Immortal Corpse ™ and © Bill Schelly.

Then I hunkered down to pour my all into a comics story that was inspired by the Spirit. I called my character Twylite, but he did resemble Will Eisner's character in appearance (slouch hat, domino mask, ordinary business suit and trench coat) if not in origin.

Always in the past I had been in too much of a hurry. I had never spent the necessary time on niceties like the lettering in captions and word balloons, nor had any of my prior illustrated stories had anything but the most primitive panel backgrounds. I set out to rectify these shortcomings with Twylite. Sitting at the drawing board in my bedroom, I took my time developing the plot. Instead of inventing it directly on the ditto masters as I went along, I patiently created rough layouts on typing paper. Instead of racing to the finish line, I put a great deal of thought into the panel-to-panel continuity and how to tell the story most effectively. I tried to use special touches rather than standard straight-ahead superhero action. It was my first serious attempt at a high-quality sequential art story, and I was pleased (and a little surprised) by how well it turned out.

✦

Understanding the lure of comic fandom—or *any* kind of fandom, from Star Trek to Doctor Who—might be difficult for those who don't feel its pull. Even those of us who have been a part of such a group don't often think about our reasons for joining in. We're doing what comes naturally to us.

What's the difference between one person who can casually enjoy reading science fiction books and another who makes science fiction the center of his or her universe? Where does hobbyism leave off and fanaticism begin?

The common wisdom holds that everyone needs a hobby. We all need an avocation—something totally different from what we do to fulfill our responsibilities. We all need to have fun. I'm not a psychologist, but I'm sure mental recreation is at least as important for our well-being as physical activity.

Is avidly following a favorite sports team a fandom-like activity? Perhaps in the broadest sense, but when I think of "fanac" (short for "fan activity") I tend to think of something more cultish in nature, and also more extreme.

Most often, fandom involves collecting the objects of our fascination. Rather than being spectators, comics fans become owners of each comic book they possess. Each book is a tangible object to read, reread, refer to, and collect. Sports fans may collect memorabilia, but they can't collect the actual games. And many comics fans want to do more than simply read and collect comics. They want to meet the writers and artists, write or draw their own stories, and gather with like-minded people at conventions. Fandom is a place where it's perfectly okay to be a fanatic.

Fans do come in different stripes. Some divide them into two groups: those who believe Fandom Is A Way of Life (abbreviated FIAWOL) and those who think Fandom Is Just A Goddam Hobby (FIJAGH). FIAWOL and FIJAGH are terms that were invented by science fiction fans long before comicdom came along. The same origin is true of most of the terms that make up the jargon comics fans use, including the word fanzine itself.

Many of the people in fandom are on the fringes of the American Dream for one reason or another. In a number of cases, those who make fandom a way of life are socially challenged in some fashion. There are those who are physically handicapped, like *RBCC* editor G. B. Love, who had cerebral palsy and had to start an enterprise of his own when no one would give him a job. Since comic fans mainly communicated through the written word, his difficulty with being verbally understood didn't prevent him from becoming a Big Name Fan and a central player in comicdom's Golden Age.

At its best, fandom was (and still is) a place where all sorts of people could be judged by their creativity and their minds, rather than their appearance. People with weight problems, speech impediments, chronic illnesses, or other physical challenges found that none of those factors presented a barrier to participating in fandom. One didn't have to dress well, drive a flashy car, or pony up a hefty sum to join. *Everyone* was welcome. A sort of basic egalitarianism has always been one of fandom's most laudable qualities.

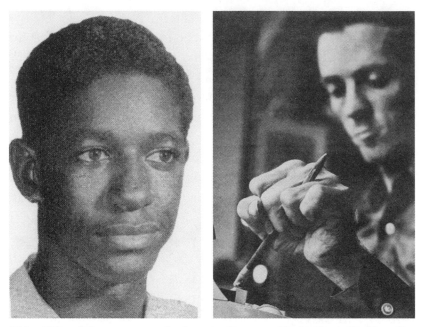

Richard "Grass" Green was a popular fan artist. Courtesy of Janice Green. Big Name Fan G. B. Love, publisher of *RBCC,* had to clutch a pencil to hit the keys of his typewriter due to his cerebral palsy. Courtesy of the *Miami Herald.*

In the midst of the civil rights movement in the 1960s, fandom was completely free of interracial tensions. Since fans rarely met each other in those early years, many had no idea that Grass Green was (in the parlance of the era) a Negro. Sherman and Wayne Howard, publishers of *Action Hero,* were also African Americans. So was Fred Jackson, a fan in the Detroit area who attended the Alley Tally Party in 1964, the first sizable gathering of comics fans in America. There were never any racist incidents among fans as far as I know.

True, there weren't many women in fandom, probably because comics were mostly geared toward the young male audience. But Maggie Thompson, copublisher of *Comic Art,* was a prominent fan, as was Margaret Gemignani of Rochester, New York. Coreen Casey, a fan who married Ronn Foss in 1965, became a well-known presence through their fanzine *Pandora.* Women were welcome, but they didn't arrive in substantial numbers until later.

Why do *adults* continue to collect and read comic books? After all, it's widely held that a time comes when one must "put away childish things."

Fandom founder Jerry G. Bails, PhD, addressed this issue when a stringer for *Newsweek* interviewed him in early 1965. "In my professional world, the amount of literature that I read is considerable," Bails said. "But I enjoy something that's a total break with that mundane world that doesn't place quite the same kind of demands on me. They say that men in our society frequently make a total break from their childhood. I see no reason, if you enjoy something as a youngster, why you should ever lose that enjoyment."

There's also the strong pull of nostalgia that causes people to want to collect comics. The same way people often remember what they were doing when they heard a favorite pop song in their youth, comics fans find themselves transported to the simpler days of their childhood when they reacquire the comics they read back then. Each comic book is like a little time machine.

Not to be minimized is the pop-culture component. Comics reflect the social milieu of their time: the fashions, the trends, and the politics. They are artifacts of the American scene. For instance, one way to understand the World War II era in the popular consciousness is to read the anti-Nazi and anti-Axis comics of the early 1940s.

Besides, comic books and especially comic strips had always been read and enjoyed by a large number of adults. Grown-up readers avidly followed classic newspaper strips like *Tarzan*, *Prince Valiant*, and *Terry and the Pirates*. During the war, comic books were one of the favorite forms of entertainment for GIs.

It's true that after the Comics Code arrived in 1955, comic books were sanitized in such a way as to lose a lot of older readers. However, as the 1960s progressed, more and more comics were being produced especially for the older reader. The popularity of Marvel Comics can partly be attributed to being aimed at a teenage and college-student readership.

Richard Kyle, one of fandom's most erudite writers, invented the terms "graphic story" and "graphic novel" in 1964 to refer to so-called "funny books" that weren't humorous at all. Kyle knew there was no particular reason why comic books couldn't be read and appreciated by adults in America, as they always had been in Europe and Japan. Fandom began promoting that idea, and gradually more and more material was produced for adults: in the fanzines, in various editions reprinting strips of the past like *The Spirit*, and in various black-and-white magazines *(Creepy, Eerie)* that began appearing on magazine stands. Before long, the roof would be blown off by a whole new type of adults-only comic book produced by the counterculture cartoonists who emerged in 1967 and 1968. Underground comix (spelled with the *x* to differentiate them from their mainstream counterparts) broke all the taboos and were produced *exclusively* for adults.

The truth is that the comics medium is adaptable to a wide variety of material geared toward any level of maturity. A broader recognition of comics' potential was dawning as the decade progressed. It was an exciting, hopeful time for comics fans.

8.

COLORING OUTSIDE THE LINES

At first, Marshall Lanz showed no interest in fanzine publishing. He didn't want to be bothered. About six months later, he changed his mind when he met a fan named David J. Esser.

Esser achieved overnight prominence in fandom when he took out a jumbo six-page advertisement in *RBCC* announcing a new comic book club to be run by him and his friend Walt Coddington. The club was called the DCTC (short for DC Trade Center) and was envisioned as a grand attempt to unify comics fans no matter where they lived.

Fandom already had the Academy of Comic Book Fans and Collectors, which Jerry G. Bails and Roy Thomas had established in 1963. But after the Academy signed up most of the active participants, it became bogged down in debates about its charter and its purpose in fandom. Along came David Esser in 1966 with his own idea for such an organization, and he was able to garner a certain amount of support due to growing dissatisfaction with the Academy and because he was willing to finance a lot of the spadework.

Esser lived not too far away from us, in Wexford, Pennsylvania, and he quickly lured Lanz and me by offering to let us use his brand-new ditto machine. He seemed intent on Lanz publishing a newsletter for DCTC members in western Pennsylvania, and he was willing to pay for supplies and postage to get him started. Lanz seemed fairly impressed with Esser at first, mainly because he had graduated from high school and had a job that paid him the princely sum of one hundred dollars a week. To us, Esser was a virtual tycoon.

Never let it be said that Marshall Lanz looked a gift horse in the mouth. In Esser, Lanz saw opportunity. He agreed to publish the newsletter, which only needed to be a few pages in length. It would be an easy way for him to dip his toe into the publishing pool. Lanz's initial goal was to entice the would-be kingpin to loan him that marvelous new ditto machine. It was on that machine that the first *DCTC Bulletin*, and all of Lanz's subsequent dittoed fanzines, were printed.

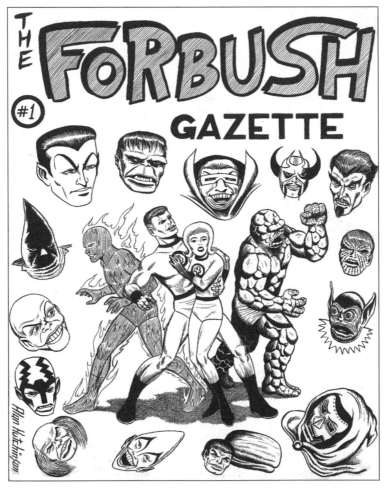

Cover of *The Irving Forbush Gazette* #1 (1967) by Alan Hutchinson. ™ and © Marvel Characters.

Yancy Street Journal had reached its end, and I had been planning my own zine dedicated exclusively to Marvel Comics. *The Irving Forbush Gazette* (named after Marvel Comics' mascot) was about half done when I invited Lanz to be coeditor. I had already pulled some of the contents together—including a superb cover of the Fantastic Four and their villains by workhorse Alan Hutchinson, and artwork by Jeff Gelb—and was soliciting fans' opinions of the art change on Spider-Man from Steve Ditko to John Romita. Once we set about finishing the first issue, I quickly realized we couldn't coedit the fanzine. My efforts to raise my standards were being frustrated by what I thought was a less exacting approach on Lanz's part. Now that he had an issue or two of the *Bulletin* under his belt, I was able to convince him that he could handle *Forbush* on his own while I concentrated my efforts on *Sense of Wonder*.

The distance between Penn Hills and Mount Lebanon was proving to be a real problem. My dad offered a solution. He gave me a key to the Northern Pacific Railroad office downtown, which was empty on the weekends. Lanz and I could meet there and use it as our "base of operations" whenever we wanted to get together. We could use the typewriters, and even some office supplies, as long as we cleaned up after ourselves and made sure to lock up. I would take the trolley downtown on a Saturday morning, spend some time at the office with Lanz, and then stay overnight at his house. Kay was always more than willing to drive me home the following day. As a result of this frequent in-person contact, Lanz and I produced a slew of fanzines in 1967.

The Northern Pacific office was located in the heart of the downtown area on the sixth floor of an aged office building called the Park Building. It was one of those musty old structures with a lobby of granite and marble, shiny brass doors on the elevators, spittoons, and a tobacco and gum stand in the lobby. The building was usually deserted on the weekends except for the janitor, whom we never saw. The only evidence of this phantom presence was the distant sound of footsteps echoing through the building via the huge open stairwell.

The NP office was small, just three rooms. In the largest room, there were two desks in close proximity, where we could both work at typewriters while facing each other. Our most basic activity was creating issues of our fanzines. Both of us would arrive loaded down with boxes of fresh ditto masters, articles, artwork, and comics.

The first order of business, after dropping off our stuff in the office, was making a circuit of all the used book and magazine stores downtown to forage for comics. We had read about bookstores that carried large selections of old comics, but we were never to find an equivalent (or anything close) to the Cherokee Bookstore in Hollywood or the Able-Man Book Store in Hamtramck, Michigan. We never found any valuable back issues, though we remained hopeful. Occasionally we would unearth some Big Daddy Roth hot-rod magazines (which ran comics features in some issues). If we found any old comic books at all, they were good for reading purposes only, since the top third of the cover was invariably torn off.

For freshly minted comics, we frequented a magazine and comic rack that I'll never forget. It was in the basement of the mammoth W. T. Grant store around the corner from the Park Building. That rack covered most of one long wall. The superhero explosion of the mid-1960s was abating by 1967, but there remained a sea of colorful titles to greet us. These were still the days when there were many western, war, romance, and hot-rod comics, and all found a place on Grant's generous shelf display. Naturally, we were on limited budgets and could only select our favorites. As I recall, Marvels were at the top of both our lists.

For food, we patronized a handy hamburger joint called Sandy's (a McDonald's imitator) for greasy cheeseburgers, mounds of salty fries, and massive sodas. Rather than eat on Sandy's tacky premises, we would return to the NP office. Lanz in particular seemed to subsist on junk food, and I happily wolfed down the stuff right along with him. Once finished, we would turn to the tasks of the day.

On one particular occasion, I remember watching in amazement as Lanz rolled a ditto master into a typewriter and began composing a fanzine editorial right on the master, without so much as using notes for reference.

"Aren't you going to write it out first?" I asked.

"Why?"

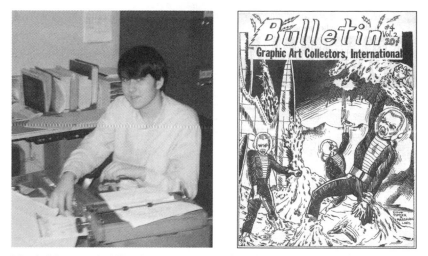

Marshall Lanz at the NP office. *The Bulletin* #4 (1967) was his first professionally printed fanzine.

"Well ... how can it be any good if you type it right on the master?"

Lanz flashed that Pepsodent grin. "It'll be *good*." He always put extra emphasis on the word *good*. It was his way of saying that his evaluation was final, period.

I sat there watching him, aghast. He started typing. And he kept on typing and filling up ditto masters in prodigious numbers over the next year. Lanz was a phenomenon. I think he surprised himself with how easily he churned out publications: *The Forbush Gazette, The Panel Art Examiner, The Graphic Art Collector*. When you had the "Marshall Lanz E-Z Method," it was easy as pie.

First: obtain a front cover drawn by a well-known fan, like Dave Herring or Doug Potter. Then send it off to be printed photo-offset. All Lanz zines at least had professionally printed covers—nothing cheap about them.

Second: beg, borrow, or steal an article from Raymond Miller or Larry Herndon or someone else with marquee value in fandom, and make it the cornerstone of your zine. Of course, you might want to cut it in half and print it in two successive issues, thus getting twice the advertising mileage out of it. Or print part of it, then drop the rest because your interest has moved on to something else.

Third, fill up the rest of the issue with a rambling, nonsensical editorial, a few pointless letters, and several pages of ads for other Lanz zines, Schelly zines, or anything else you care to plug. Throw in a pinup or two, and presto! Instant fanzine.

His record-keeping methods were, shall we say, a bit haphazard. Once when I was visiting him at home, I watched Lanz open up several envelopes containing orders for fanzines. He deftly pocketed the cash and coins, then tossed the envelopes into a box full of other letters and envelopes. His practice, I discovered, was to spend all the money as it came in ("I *need* it," he explained) and then, when it came time to print and mail his zines, hit his mother up for a trip to the stationery store, promising to pay her back later. I'd shake my head in wonder. However, I never heard of anyone claiming that Lanz was a crook, so I guess he came through in one form or another. But woe be unto those who sent in money for multiple-issue subscriptions. Lanz was constantly shifting plans about what he was going to publish next, so unwary fans who had ordered *Forbush* #2 would instead receive *The DCTC Bulletin* #4 or the *Flash Comics Special.*

Lanz was an irrepressible prankster. One of his favorite targets was Tony Rutherford, publisher of *Bombshell,* a popular lower-tier ditto fanzine. In his mind, Rutherford's "I am a Christian" stance was ludicrous, and he seized on any opportunity to make life miserable for poor Tony.

For some reason, Rutherford asked Lanz if he would be willing to ink a comics story on ditto masters titled "The Champions of Freedom" because another fan unexpectedly couldn't do it. The strip had already been penciled by Richard Buckler, a precocious young fan sensation out of Detroit whose work was highly regarded in our circles. It was a real coup for Tony to have this feature, but he needed someone to ink it quickly. He mailed the precious dittos to Lanz. I saw them when they arrived.

"These are great," I said, marveling at the detail and professional appearance of Buckler's work.

"Yeah," Lanz said casually. "I'll get to them later."

"But didn't Rutherford specifically ask you to rush?"

Lanz grinned. "Uh-huh." He tossed them off to one side of his huge desk.

Soon Marshall began receiving increasingly hysterical letters from Tony, begging him to finish the job. Lanz gloated over the letters, chuckling gleefully. I'm not exactly sure why he got such a kick out of this. Eventually he returned the masters after inking a few panels, but not before he had his fun.

One of Lanz's gags involved sending Tony an official-looking letter on Northern Pacific Railroad stationery informing him that the railroad had gained a right of way directly through his living room and ordering him to vacate the premises within forty-eight hours. We never did find out if little Tony shook fearfully in his shoes as the deadline approached, wondering when the railroad men were going to show up, or if he realized we were putting him on.

I wish I could say I was morally outraged by Lanz's behavior. While I took a dim view of withholding the Buckler story from Rutherford, I did enjoy a lot of his pranks. I laughed along with him as he made fun of Gabe Eisenstein of *Comiclub* in print or played mind games with Dave Esser. (Esser was forever trying to get his ditto machine back from Lanz.) I'm pretty sure I was the one who typed up that letter to Tony on the NP stationery. For the most part I was Lanz's willing acolyte. His iconoclastic attitude was contagious, and it was fun playing at being a troublemaker. That was something I could never do in my regular life; I didn't have the nerve.

I had my own projects that occupied most of my attention. After a great deal of patient work, *Sense of Wonder* #1 was printed on the captive ditto machine, and the result was a big leap forward for me. All my prior experience, coupled with my new resolve, really made a difference. The response was excellent, and I soon sold out the entire print run of a couple hundred copies. A surprising number of reorders and subscriptions began arriving in the mailbox at 881 Lovingston Drive. *Sense of Wonder* was the first thing I published that I thought was truly well done and that generated genuine interest from its readers.

Imagine: here was a venue in pre-internet times where a fifteen-year-old could publish his writing and art totally without any control or censorship. My parents never read my fanzines or had much of an idea what was in them. Not that the content was daring or in any way obscene; but I was my own boss, and as long as there were enough orders to pay for the printing and postage, nothing could stop me. Over time, I've realized that creating, editing, and publishing fanzines was the aspect of fandom I loved most.

Marshall Lanz, safecracker.

It was a heady experience. I didn't realize I was getting quite an education in running a small business once *Sense of Wonder* became a going concern. I learned strictly from trial and error. The bookkeeping alone was a huge job. I had to keep detailed records of names and addresses and which issues people had ordered in advance. Then there was the banking, the advertising, soliciting contributions, dealing with printers and the post office.

I believe publishing *Sense of Wonder* inculcated within me a sense of self-reliance that stood me in good stead as I later learned to handle the responsibility of college and eventually earning a living. It also spoiled me, because it took a real adjustment to work for other publishers in later years. Like most people who have called their own shots, it wasn't easy to give up those prerogatives.

As for why I was doggedly determined to continue publishing fanzines, it's clear in retrospect that it was more than a creative outlet. It was the way I demonstrated who I was and what I could do. As an editor and publisher, I had potency, which was reinforced every time someone sent me an order or a letter of comment. I was the kind of "somebody" in fandom that I never was in school or on the playing field.

𝙉

Lanz and I never failed to find ways to entertain ourselves on our weekend rendezvous. When there wasn't a publication to produce, we were writing letters of comment to our favorite fanzine editors, planning new practical jokes, or poking around the office itself—one day with startling results.

The railroad office's storage room was located about seventy-five feet down the hall from the main office, past the elevators and the restrooms. Although the Northern Pacific was a major railroad, its office wasn't large; hence the need for additional storage space. In that room, hidden wonders awaited.

The storage room was long and narrow, about fourteen feet by nine feet, with the door on one end and a window on the other. The ceiling was maybe ten feet high. Though the room was small, it was kept organized and served as a functional space. As you entered, there was a large wooden shelving unit along the left wall. The shelves held extra stock of forms, paper, stencils, manila folders, and other typical office supplies. Below the shelves at waist level was a long work table that jutted about two feet out from the wall. This was where the mimeograph machine sat. Along the right-hand wall was a tall metal cabinet that contained pens, pencils, tape, staples, and other tempting items. Unfortunately for us, this cabinet was kept locked on the weekends.

The room also had various miscellaneous items: a coat rack, NP calendars on the wall sporting that ubiquitous yin-yang symbol, a dusty old sink, and office files in labeled boxes. At the far end, a small amount of light filtered through a dirty window that faced a central air shaft.

After I saw the mimeograph machine, I understood why it did such a poor printing job on my fanzines. It was a minor miracle that Trageser could coax any readable copies out of that ancient relic. To add the ink, you had to use a messy brush to spread the viscous, gloppy stuff inside the drum, inevitably smearing your hand and forearm in the process. I've theorized since then that this machine in the NP storage room— rusted, cranky, and coated with many layers of dried ink—may have been one of the original mimeograph prototypes.

When Lanz first entered the storage room, his eyes lit up at the sight of shelves full of mimeo paper. Thus began our practice of appropriating reams of paper for our personal use. It didn't matter that mimeo paper was a little too abrasive for ditto printing; Lanz used it anyway. When I cautioned him, he'd flash that smile and say, "It's *free.*"

An unexpected attraction of the storage room was the stack of *Playboy* magazines that Dick kept there. Here was an opportunity to familiarize ourselves with Harvey Kurtzman's sexy *Little Annie Fanny* comics feature. Lanz told me, "The guy who writes these is the guy who created *Mad* magazine."

I became aware of *Mad* not long after I started reading comics. My brother Steve showed me the issue that came out after the close presidential election of 1960 that had two covers: one that congratulated John F. Kennedy as the winner, and when you turned it over, another congratulating Richard Nixon. But I was still a bit young for the satire in *Mad* magazine in 1960. What really turned me on to *Mad* were Steve's copies of a couple of the early *Mad* paperbacks, which I saw two or three years later. They contained reprints from the Kurtzman-written issues of the early 1950s. One was *The Mad Reader*, with "Superduperman!" Another was *The Brothers Mad*, with "Black & Blue Hawks!" and "Woman Wonder!" He gleefully showed me the bit in "Woman Wonder!" with her changing into her costume in her see-through plane. I guess we were our own Brothers *Mad*.

Panels from the Kurtzman-Elder "Woman Wonder!" that originally appeared in *Mad* #10 (1954). ™ and © William M. Gaines, Agent.

Little Anny Fanny painted by her cocreator, Will Elder. ™ and © Playboy.

What impressed me most was how funny those comics were, and equally, how they were so much wilder and sexier than anything in regular comic books in 1963. They amply demonstrated that there was great excitement to be had outside of what was considered polite or acceptable, and that somewhere in the world there were adults who could create funnier, more outlandish comics than I had ever dreamed possible. I didn't know who had written or drawn them because Kurtzman's name didn't appear in those printings, and the artists' names only appeared sometimes, but I loved the *Mad* comics reprinted in those books, and I bought copies for myself.

Lanz and I looked through all the *Playboy* issues on that shelf for the ones with *Little Annie Fanny,* and we traded them back and forth, chortling over the gags by Harvey Kurtzman and artist Will Elder. Comics artist Frank Frazetta, whose work adorned covers for James Warren's *Creepy* and *Eerie* magazines, "sat in" and finished a number of panels in those issues. His distinctive painting style stood out among the more cartoonish renderings of Kurtzman and Elder.

We spent time examining the nude pictorials. These paeans to heterosexual desire interested me because of their forbidden quality and because at fifteen, even a burgeoning gay boy could get excited looking at pictures of nekkid women. But they also made me uncomfortable because they reminded me of a side of myself that I couldn't share with Lanz or anybody else.

One day when I was in that storage room by myself, I discovered a drawer full of X-rated porn novels. They were typical of the cheaply printed prose books of that ilk, but as I checked them out, I was astonished to find that one was gay porn. My heart beating like a trip hammer, I checked to make sure the door to the storage room was locked, and I excitedly began reading. What an eye-opening experience it was! This was where I learned what such people did in bed. It's awful that it fell to a porn novel to explain those things to me, but there was no other source available. (Why did Trageser have a gay porn novel? I later found out that he had a little side business selling such material to others in the building or the area.)

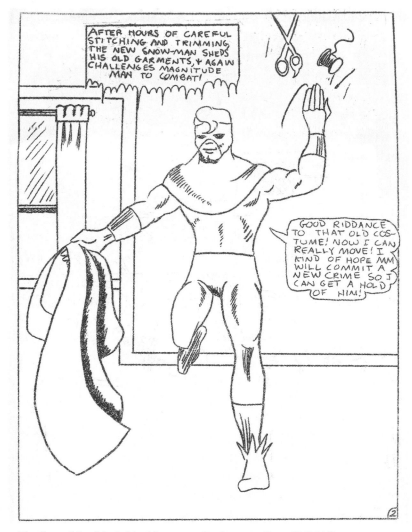

The Snow-Man "sheds his old garments" in *Incognito Extra* #1 (1966).

I did my best to conceal the forbidden feelings that were becoming more insistent as I entered high school. What I didn't realize was that it was beginning to show in some of my artwork, such as a comics story I had done in *Incognito* featuring my fairly ludicrous hero the Snow-Man. I thought the character needed a new, more dynamic costume, so in a story called "The Metamorphosis of the Snow-Man," I have him stripping off his former garb and saying, "I'm going to have to alter my costume! It's too hot and bulky! I can't move freely!" He proceeds to sew a new one that is much briefer and more revealing … and more *gay*. He thinks, "Now I can really move! I kind of hope Magnitude Man will commit a new crime so I can get a hold of him!" Indeed. In retrospect, it looks as if the Snow-Man himself was coming out of the closet. I wasn't aware of anything except that it was exciting drawing him in his tights, bare skin, and "fanciful" new booties. I don't know how it escaped notice, except that it's just this side of blatant.

I only found out later that comic fandom, like any other large group, had participants who were members of certain minority groups that weren't accepted by society at large. The general ambience in fandom was one of acceptance, since everyone's focus was on the hobby. Still, as far as I know there no comics fans who were out in fandom at that time. That sort of difference could and did remain under wraps. After all, sexual intimacy between people of the same gender was a criminal act, and gays were routinely harassed by the police, even in Greenwich Village, the epicenter of bohemia in the United States.

So I went through periods of denial that were made possible because I also felt attracted to girls. I hoped I could at least keep the inappropriate feelings at bay, but I was already losing the battle. It was a secret struggle in which I was entirely alone. About all I could do was hold on and hope that somehow it would work itself out. When it came to coloring outside the lines, I wasn't yet ready to use the pink crayons.

N

My friendship with Marshall Lanz revolved around discovering new and often forbidden ways of having fun. Occasionally these minor amusements were of a morally questionable nature or just plain wrong. Stealing paper to print our fanzines was theft, pure and simple. But other distinctions were less obvious. What, for example, was an acceptable prank, and when did it cross the line to become hurtful? What exactly was our responsibility to the fans who sent us money for fanzines? Marshall relished playing the role of rogue. As I dallied for a time in that sphere, I didn't realize it, but the seeds of my own ethical awareness were being planted.

9.

FULL-THROTTLE FANAC

"Did you hear that Jim Shooter, the kid who writes for DC Comics, lives in Pittsburgh?" No, I hadn't heard—until the fandom grapevine let me know.

The word was out that a mere fifteen-year-old was scripting the adventures of the Legion of Super-Heroes in *Adventure Comics* and had branched out into other Superman-family titles. It was hard to believe that someone my own age was selling scripts to a company that was, for all intents and purposes, a closed shop even to many seasoned professionals. What was Jim Shooter's secret? Was he some sort of *wunderkind*? Could he open the door at DC for me?

I pulled out the city telephone directory. The only listing under "Shooter" was for a Kenneth Shooter in Bethel Park. I dialed the number. A woman answered.

"Is Jim home?"

"Yes, one moment."

Bullseye.

When Jim got on the phone, I introduced myself and proceeded to explain something about comic fandom to him. I think it wasn't long before he realized that I was someone his age genuinely interested in the creative side of comics and in his working methods in particular. He agreed to get together, but he didn't have transportation. When I asked my mother if she would drive me over to pick Jim up for a visit, she agreed since Bethel Park was just two or three miles from Mount Lebanon.

The Shooter home was located in a modest residential neighborhood. It was a small brick house with a neat, well-kept appearance. Jim's mother, Eleanor, wasn't overly friendly, but we weren't there long. Mom ferried us back to Lovingston Drive and even fixed us lunch.

During our visit, Jim told me how he came to write for DC Comics. At the age of twelve he'd been in the hospital, and during his stay he began reading the well-worn comics available in the ward. After discovering the joys of Marvel comics by Stan Lee, Jack Kirby, and the others, he found the Superman family titles on hand to be unbelievably stodgy. Shortly thereafter, he wrote and drew a story for the weakest of the DC lot, which in his estimation was the Legion of Super-Heroes, a group of futuristic teens appearing in *Adventure Comics*. His secret was that he infused the feel of Marvel titles into his DC script. He sent it in, not knowing what to expect. Much to his surprise, DC editor Mort Weisinger wrote Jim asking for another. When that was done, Weisinger called him up and began sending him checks for his work. What sold Weisinger on his scripts, he believed, wasn't solely his writing ability. "What makes me valuable," Jim explained, "is that I send in my scripts all drawn up. It saves his artists a lot of time and trouble because they can follow my layouts."

He showed me several pages he had completed for his next assignment. Jim was a capable artist in his own right, and I could see how these pages would save Curt Swan or DC's other artists a great deal of time. Drawn in pencil on letter-sized pages, they were fairly detailed layouts. All the important figures were there, and basic backgrounds too. He was getting ten dollars per page, which added up to as much as two or three hundred dollars a month, given his rate of production. That was a lot of money for a sophomore in high school. Nearly all of it, he told me, went to his family. I don't recall the specifics, but his father, Kenneth, was a steel-mill worker and may have been on strike or laid off at the time.

Jim had never heard anything about comic fandom until I contacted him. I liked him. He was a polite, intelligent guy. He seemed to like me too. When I invited him to do a cover for *Sense of Wonder,* he accepted with alacrity. The first piece of artwork he did for me appeared on the cover of my second issue, depicting the Star Rangers feature I had drawn inside. He sketched out the idea right there, completing the pencils and inks at home later. I was impressed with his talent, though it was clear that he was stronger at layout than he was at finished art technique. That only stood to reason.

We decided to collaborate on a comics story. We invented a hero named Brimstone who gained his superpowers from a deal with the Devil. Shooter was to do all the script and artwork except for the lettering, which he asked me to handle. This ten-pager turned out to be the only complete strip he wrote for fandom.

Photograph that appeared in a Pittsburgh newspaper article profiling Jim Shooter, "boy wonder of comic book writers." Jim lived just a few miles from me.

Jim and I cocreated a character named Brimstone, who used Satan's power to fight for good. I finished the last eight pages of the strip from his script after we lost touch. Jim drew pages one and two himself, although I did the logo.

Jim was diplomatic about my work. He zeroed in on my weakest point: my uncertain grasp of human anatomy. He even loaned me a copy of a book on drawing the human figure (probably by George Bridgeman or Andrew Loomis), which helped me a lot.

There was really nothing he could do to help me break into DC. The fact is that Jim Shooter was an extraordinarily precocious comics talent, and I was nowhere near ready to produce anything that would satisfy Mort Weisinger or any other professional comics editor. I made some halfhearted stabs at plotting a Jimmy Olsen story, but it came to nothing.

In these early days of fandom, you could count the number of comic book conventions on one hand. The New York and Detroit comics conventions drew about a thousand fans each, and the regional cons in Dallas and St. Louis were just getting started. Other cities, including Pittsburgh, had not reached that point yet. Lanz and I decided to see if we could put on a modest event that would draw the local fans we had met plus a few attendees from the region.

As early as Lanz's *DCTC Bulletin* #1 (1966), it was obvious that some kind of fan meeting was in the air. In a blurb headlined, "Pittsburgh Con Now Being Planned by the DCTC for Next Summer," Lanz wrote, "We want all of you to make a special effort to come and see us for a few days. All of you are welcome. Dave [Esser] is even now making arrangements for cheap motels."

What could have been no more than a pipe dream wound up coming true, probably because the plan was scaled down to simple proportions. The Pittsburgh Mini-Con was held at Marshall's house on August 19, 1967. As far as I know, it was the first such gathering in the city. In attendance were Bill G. Wilson, editor of *The Collector;* Larry Walczak, editor of *Comic Feature* and *Blackjack;* Dennis Palumbo, an aspiring writer; and Chuck Rogers, who published *Fantasy Fandom Crossroads* and contributed artwork to dozens of ditto fanzines of the day. Rogers had driven all the way from Norfolk, Virginia, and Walczak had made the journey from Erie, Pennsylvania, 130 miles north of Pittsburgh. In all, there were about ten teenagers in attendance at the Lanz home. Our "Pro Guest of Honor" was Jim Shooter, of course—whom Lanz was dying to meet. (Jim and I had gotten in touch a few weeks earlier.) This was the only time he ever visited the house on Lindberg Avenue.

No special agenda was necessary. Put ten comics fans together and they will do what comes naturally until forced to stop: gab about comics, haggle over sales or trades, and admire each other's comics treasures. Everyone paid special attention to the few pages of original comic art that were on hand. The only break was for dinner, a weenie roast on the back patio.

The highlight was the production of a team fanzine to commemorate the event. We all jammed into Lanz's office to write and draw the zine. Bill Wilson worked on an illustration; Dennis Palumbo used Lanz's typewriter to write a brief text feature. The others were similarly occupied. My contribution was a caricature of us crowded into a small room producing that publication. Everyone watched as Jim Shooter created a beautiful pencil drawing of Iron Man smashing through a brick wall. (Remember, he was still working exclusively for DC Comics.) As far as I can recall, this special fanzine never saw print.

The mini-con was a fun, high-spirited affair, topped off with a visit from a disgruntled Dave Esser, still trying to wrest his precious ditto machine from Lanz's clutches. He didn't get it back that day, though eventually Mrs. Lanz interceded on his behalf. By then it didn't matter, because Marshall had moved on to using professional printers for entire issues.

⚡

Shortly after the mini-con, *Sense of Wonder* #2 was ready to go to press. I was pleased with the letters of comment I had received on the first issue. Floridian Gary Brown wrote, "I can honestly say that

I enjoyed the entire zine, cover to cover. No doubt, the best thing you've put out yet."

Oklahoman Matt Waldroop wrote, "*Sense of Wonder* was worth every cent of the price. Your Twylite was superb and certainly a good work of art. The better of the two texts was Dick Trageser's Immortal Corpse yarn. It really had me going."

Tom Fisher, who would collaborate with Raymond Miller on an important article in a later issue, commented, "Your splash panel for the Immortal Corpse text story [was] one of the high points of the issue. Excellent, Bill. Your use of shading, proportioning, and the background detail you provide, are all very good."

Nearly all of the letters I received were positive. My hard work (and that of Ronn Foss, Dick Trageser, and others) had paid off. Now, as I pulled the second issue together, I knew there was no going back. Each issue had to be as good as or better than the one before.

Since Dick's Corpse story had topped the readers' poll, I was happy when he came through with another in short order. "Wild, Wild West!" (which bore no connection to the popular TV series) was a change of pace; it took the envoy of death to a dude ranch to right injustice.

The comics story in the second issue was the first of a two-part Star Rangers script written under the pseudonym "Dennis Madison." The real author was Sherman Howard, brother of Wayne Howard. From their home in Cleveland, Ohio, they published the popular ditto fanzine *Action Hero*. Sherman was a talented writer, and by a tremendous coincidence he lived in the same college dorm as my next-door neighbor.

As for why Sherman used a pseudonym for Star Rangers, he said it was because it wasn't his best work, though he was still proud of it. Personally, I couldn't see any difference from his usual fine scripts, but I naturally went along with his request, although it hurt a little because I couldn't use his well-known name in my advertisements. I handled the art on this two-parter.

When I discovered that Jim Shooter was not only a talented writer but also an artist, I asked him to do a cover for *Sense of Wonder* #2. He provided an illustration using characters from that issue's lead story, "The Star Rangers," which was scripted by African American writer Sherman Howard.

With the front cover by Jim Shooter, a Manhunter text story by Mark Savage Jr., art by Doug Potter, and a letter column, I was confident I had managed to produce a worthy follow-up to the premiere issue. *SofW* #2 turned out to be my biggest-selling issue until I switched to photo-offset printing—so popular that I went back to press to fill another fifty orders. (The initial printing was done by Tony Rutherford, who took it upon himself to scratch out the occasional use of a "damn" or "hell." I didn't really care, because it was more important to me that the printing be done well, and he did a fine job in that department.)

The Pittsburgh Mini-Con and *Sense of Wonder* #2 weren't the only endeavors I tackled that summer. The most ambitious was the first novel that I actually completed. It was a spy thriller in the James Bond mold starring my own espionage agent, Richard Stern.

Having read and reread the Fleming Signet paperbacks until they were dog-eared and falling apart, I decided that I was ready to do my own version. After all, 007 wasn't the only super-spy around. There was also Donald Hamilton's Matt Helm. Nick Carter, formerly a hero of the dime novels, had returned in a series of newly commissioned adventures. *Man from U.N.C.L.E.* paperbacks began popping up on the racks. In a tongue-in-cheek, racy vein, Ted Mark's *Man from O.R.G.Y.* series came on the scene. Why not another?

I distinctly recall sitting down at my desk in front of the Smith Corona, telling myself to concentrate as hard as I could and do my best writing.

The Eyrie began with the suave, sophisticated Richard Stern deplaning in Washington, DC, ordering breakfast (with cynical comments on the poor quality of airport food, straight from Fleming), then taking a cab to the headquarters of Section B, a top-secret division of the CIA where he reported to his M-like boss, improbably named Mr. Shade. Eventually, Stern was on his way to Hawaii on the trail of a Nazi war criminal named Ernst Lichman in a plot that was much like those in the Fleming novels. There was a local operative, a sexy girl assistant, and a cover story that helped Stern penetrate the villain's lair on an island with a supposedly dormant volcano. Guess what happens at the climax.

In retrospect, the idea of a teenager living in a middle-class suburb presuming to write from the point of view of a jaded, thirty-five-year-old espionage agent is laughable. The result was, predictably, a pastiche of scenes and dialogue varying only slightly from ones found in Fleming's books. For example:

> With his portly figure, round head, and bizarre contact lenses, Ernst Lichman resembled a giant owl. "Welcome to my eyrie, Mr. Stern," he said in a sibilant voice filled with menace. "Are you an admirer of our avian friends?"
>
> Richard Stern let his eyes return to the view of hundreds of birds in the mammoth aviary.
>
> "Not until now, but I must admit they are extraordinary."
>
> "As am I," Lichman said, pursing his lips. "For example, I have discovered twenty-three new ways to kill a man in under thirty seconds."
>
> "Impressive," Stern replied. "I only know seventeen."

Still, *The Eyrie* did build up to several effective action sequences, and it was significant because I took it to its conclusion, thereby gaining much-needed experience in writing an ending. (I already had written plenty of beginnings.)

That same summer I found myself in considerably more demand as an artist or writer by editors of a slightly higher-quality bunch of fanzines. To some extent, the demand for my services was a reflection of my improving drawing skills or the reputation of *Sense of Wonder*, but I think a bigger reason is the howling vacuum that was created as dozens—maybe as many as a hundred—fanzines were launched in 1967. Fandom was growing by leaps and bounds.

My fan activity was at its peak at this time. I was contributing artwork, comic strips, and even some text features to quite a list of fanzines, which included *Action Hero, Bombshell, The DCTC Bulletin, Cloak and Dagger, The Collector, The Dangling Conversation, Differo, Earthquake Comics, Enterprise, The Irving Forbush Gazette, The Panel*

Art Examiner, Shroud, Voice of Comicdom, and *Wonderment.* I don't think I ever turned anyone down, flattered to be asked by the better zines and taking pity on the publishers of lesser ones, knowing that I was only in a slightly higher echelon myself. I worked at my drawing board late into the humid nights, listening to the Beatles' *Rubber Soul* and *Revolver* over and over.

Seminaked sword-and-sorcery heroes were becoming popular in fandom in 1967 when I drew this cover for *Cloak and Dagger* vol. 2 #1.

My junior year at Mount Lebanon High School began auspiciously when I was elected homeroom president. This was largely a token position, yet it felt good to be chosen by my peers for the job. Soon, however, I suspected that it had been a setup. Over the smallest incident in one of our meetings, certain members of the class turned against me and moved that I be impeached. The move narrowly failed, but I could hardly count it a victory. Something told me it was going to be another long school year.

Then one evening my parents greeted my brothers and me with serious faces. We were told to sit down and get ready for some big news: the Schelly family was going to move. The Northern Pacific Railroad had agreed to merge with the Great Northern, and my father was being transferred to a new post.

Where?

I didn't care where.

Hallelujah!

10.

STRANGER IN A STRANGE LAND

"This is it? This is the whole of downtown Lewiston?"

Mom, Steve, Dave, and I were standing on Main Street in Lewiston, Idaho, looking for a good place to have breakfast.

"I told you this is a small town," Mom replied.

"What's the population here?" I asked.

"About thirty thousand, if you count both Lewiston and Clarkston," she said.

I said, "Where *is* everyone?" The street was nearly deserted.

"It's still early," she said. "There ought to be a coffee shop around here somewhere."

We continued walking. "What's that funny smell?" Dave asked, crinkling his nose.

"Who farted?" Steve quipped.

Mom shot him a dirty look. "It must be the pulp mill. It isn't so bad."

"And everyone thinks the air in *Pittsburgh* stinks," I said sarcastically. In truth, the air in Pittsburgh by the late 1960s bore no noticeable traces of steel-mill pollution.

"I don't think we're going to find anything," Mom sighed. "Let's go back to the hotel and see if their restaurant is open."

We had arrived in Lewiston by prop jet the night before and were now ensconced in the once-lavish Lewis-Clark Hotel at the apex of Main Street. We found that the hotel's Tomahawk Room restaurant was open for breakfast.

As we ate, I reflected that the euphoria I'd experienced during the plane journey had been replaced by a sense of pronounced surreality. Still, I continued to welcome the change. All my embarrassments and mistakes, the rejections and growing pains, were now permanently consigned to the past. Like a Catholic after confession, my slate was wiped clean.

The others in my family, though resigned to the move, were less sanguine about it than I. Steve was in his senior year; now he would have to graduate with a class of strangers. Dave had been well-integrated into his circle of friends and activities in Pittsburgh, and he was upset about leaving them. Mom had finally, after much searching, found a good job to augment the family income; now she would have to begin looking again. Later I was to learn that Dad had the worst time of us all in making the adjustment.

Marshall Lanz had been depressed ever since I had broken the news of the move to him. I would miss him, although something told me our friendship had mostly run its course. During the last few months, we had perceptibly grown apart. The differences in our personalities were becoming more obvious. Marshall's parting gift to me was a copy of Robert A. Heinlein's *Stranger in a Strange Land*. The irony of reading this book at this juncture wasn't lost on me.

Located at the confluence of the Clearwater and Snake Rivers, Lewiston and its sister city, Clarkston, Washington, on the other side of the Snake River, were named after northwest explorers Meriwether Lewis and William Clark. During its Gold Rush days, Lewiston had been established as the capital of the Idaho territory, but that honor had long since been lost to Boise in a power grab that was still a subject of controversy and conjecture. In 1967, the town existed primarily to service the local Potlatch Forest Industries pulp mill and a couple of ammunition factories. One of them, we were told, produced the bullet that had killed President Kennedy.

Brother Dave took this photo of Steve, me, Mom, and Dad just before we left for the airport to travel to our new home in Lewiston, Idaho. I'm holding the copy of *Stranger in a Strange Land* given to me by Marshall Lanz, which I began reading on the plane. *Stranger in a Strange Land* © the Estate of Robert A. Heinlein.

Although I'd been born in an equally small town in eastern Washington, I had lived in Pittsburgh for almost as long as I could remember. I grew up in a suburb of one of the largest cities in the United States. I was an Easterner and a big-city kid. Although our parents had tried to prepare us for the change, we were unable to comprehend what living in a small town would be like.

Mom had flown out to Lewiston weeks earlier to find a house, and now we were waiting for the movers to arrive with our furniture and other belongings. That first day we were given a tour of what would be the Schelly family abode for the foreseeable future. Instead of the four-square, box-like structure of our house on Lovingston Drive, the house on Carol Drive in Lewiston was more agreeably designed, with a small foyer presenting stairs up to the main floor or down to the partly underground lower level. The outside was covered with aesthetically pleasing wood and brick, as opposed to the aluminum siding of our former home. All of us, including Dad, applauded Mom's house selection.

Our house at 2211 Carol Drive in Lewiston, Idaho.

Naturally, I was keenly interested in finding out what Lewiston High School was like. It proved to be a mixed revelation. From the outside, it looked all right. After seeing Main Street, I'd had visions of a little red schoolhouse, but the structure itself was fairly impressive: an old-style two-story brick building of sufficiently imposing proportions. While Mount Lebanon High School had a population of some two thousand students, Lewiston could boast about 1,200, but that was a sizable student body. So far, so good.

The school principal would not allow me to enter their advanced classes in English. Never mind that I had been enrolled in such courses since seventh grade and had done well in them. He claimed that, with the first quarter already over, it would be too much to expect me to get up to speed in those advanced classes. Mom, who knew the fellow from Walla Walla and didn't like him, was livid.

This didn't bother me much. In fact, I welcomed the chance to take it easy—until I entered that class, my first of the day. I felt like I had walked into a Li'l Abner comic strip.

For one thing, the fashions were a bit different from what I expected. The boys wore skintight jeans that only reached to their lower calves, with horizontally striped socks that made them look like clowns.

For another, the kids talked funny. They had a way of stretching out words that sounded idiotic to me. To me, the word "book" was a brief, one-syllable word. To them, it became "booooooook." The filler in the middle, where they stretched out the vowel with a twang, made them sound distinctly moronic, as if they had just come into town from the backwoods.

The schoolwork I was presented with in this eleventh-grade English class was laughable, about on a par with what I had been doing in seventh or eighth grade. Of course, some of the dramatic change could be attributed to moving from accelerated to "regular" English. This was clearly not a class for the college-bound. I began to wonder how I was going to fit into Lewiston High School. Despite my difficulties in Pittsburgh, I didn't feel like a fish out of water there (more like a fish in a barrel.) Here I wasn't sure how I was going to connect with these country folk.

Fortune smiled upon me when I trekked out to the art building for my next class. I was welcomed by Ernest ("Ernie") Harrison, an amiable instructor who seemed pleased as he looked through my portfolio. Some kids in the class crowded around to check out the capabilities of the new kid. That portfolio contained a number of assignments from my art classes—still-life sketches, charcoal portraits, landscapes in watercolor—plus a number of large pages of original art for a comics story.

One of the onlookers quickly voiced his approval. His name was Bob Sanborn, perhaps the most talented artist in the class. Bob looked like a robust version of Buddy Holly: horn-rimmed glasses, engaging smile, and an easy, confident manner. I liked him immediately. It took only a quick examination of his work to see that he was someone whose

Barbara Barker, 1968 senior photo

opinions about art meant something. Bob was especially adept at oil painting; our mutual admiration for the work of Frank Frazetta confirmed that we had common interests. While he didn't actually collect comics, Sanborn did read them occasionally and wasn't one to put them down. I felt as if I had already found a potential friend.

I also felt welcome in French class. The instructor, Madame Wilson, had a pleasant if formal approach to her job. She asked me about my background in front of the small class, and the other students seemed genuinely interested in my answers. I always dreaded

Bob Sanborn and Ernie Harrison. Bob, my best friend in high school, was a talented artist who especially admired the dynamic paintings of Frank Frazetta. Ernie was the amiable art instructor at Lewiston High School who helped me develop skill at painting and taught me how to use an airbrush. Photo from Lewiston High School yearbook.

being the center of attention, but I found this experience more tolerable than most. When I was assigned a seat, it wasn't long before I found myself *kibitzing* with my neighbor, a petite girl with big, expressive blue eyes and curly brown hair. Her name was Barbara Barker.

Barbara thought my impromptu cartoons making fun of the teacher's terrible hairpiece (which made her head look like a triangle) and absurdly large false eyelashes were hilarious, and she had her own variations on that theme that cracked me up. It's always flattering to have people laugh at one's jokes. She was also relatively new to Lewiston, having moved there the prior year from Missouri. Barbara didn't talk with that Lewiston twang. This second acceptance led me to entertain real optimism that things in this new school would work out after all.

In a flash it occurred to me that none of these people knew my history. I wasn't working against a long-held reputation as a nerd or a class brain. I was a completely unknown quantity. The principal had also decided that he would waive the physical education requirement for me (since I'd had so much of it in my two years in high school back east), so no one was likely to ostracize me for my lack of athletic prowess. Things were looking better and better.

With the arrival of our furniture, the Schelly family settled into the house at 2211 Carol Drive. As in Pittsburgh, I had a corner room in front over the garage. My drawing board and art equipment were set up much as before, and my comic book collection (which had survived the rigors of Atlas Van Lines) found a new home in the sizable closet.

High on my agenda was finding the best place to buy comics in Lewiston. My collecting goals had increased along with my allowance, and the thought of missing my favorites was unacceptable. In two or three days I found a drugstore near the high school, called the Eighth Street Drive-In, that carried a more or less complete selection. (Odd name, that, since it wasn't a drive-in in any way that I could tell.)

Three comic books on my buy list in 1968: *Captain America* #100, *Showcase* #76 with Bat Lash, and *Our Army at War* with Sgt. Rock, featuring work by some of my favorite artists (Jack Kirby, Nick Cardy, and Joe Kubert). ™ and © respective copyright holders.

With the end of the superhero boom, a number of comics publishers had retired their long-underwear characters, but DC and Marvel were in the process of expanding their lines. Marvel Comics was finally rewarding Captain America, Iron Man, Doctor Strange, and the Hulk with their own self-titled comic books. Carmine Infantino had taken over the helm at DC and was offering a remarkable variety of new titles, including innovative Westerns *(Bat Lash)*, spies *(Secret Six)*, cavemen *(Anthro)*, and new types of heroes from top creators like Steve Ditko (*The Creeper* and *Hawk and Dove*). This was also when I began to pay attention to Joe Kubert's artwork on Sgt. Rock in *Our Army at War*. Kubert's artwork had been too dark and impressionistic for me when I was younger, but now I found myself increasingly drawn to his mature, dark style that made the characters look more like real people. I could also appreciate stories set in something approximating the real world, albeit the world of World War II. I was old enough to enjoy Robert Kanigher's complex, multilayered tales of morality and mortality, with life lessons about how we as individuals are defined more by what we do than what we say.

I kept up with as many comic book titles as I could, although that was tough to do in a time of expansion at both DC and Marvel.

If the Drive-In was missing a title, I would walk a couple of blocks down Eighth Street to Shennimen's Market, where comics were also available. My reading and collecting addiction continued without missing a beat.

I found comic fandom to be as accessible as ever. The only small obstacle was getting the word out that my address had changed. I had already given my new address to the fanzines from which I had ongoing subscriptions, so little fell through the cracks. Despite good omens at school, it would take some time before I could get really comfortable there. In the meantime, I could have suffered from new-kid loneliness if it hadn't been for my friends in fandom.

Lanz and I exchanged some letters, but he wasn't the best at expressing himself in print. Much of his personal charm came through in his verbal quirks. He lobbied for a "tape-spondence" in which we would exchange audio tapes with each other. This was before cassette tapes were invented, but inexpensive tape recorders using three-inch reels were common. Because we planned to exchange tapes of this sort, I asked for and received a recorder that would handle larger five-inch reels for Christmas in 1967. In this way we shared not only our thoughts and jokes but also our favorite music. It was Lanz who introduced me to the Arlo Guthrie song "Alice's Restaurant."

I used a tape to let him know how much I had enjoyed *Stranger in a Strange Land*. I was just the right age, and this was the perfect time, for me to read that book. Although it was written in the late 1950s, Robert Heinlein's ideas of free love and communal living were particularly fitting for the time when I discovered it, just after the so-called Summer of Love. Maybe the most positive, optimistic period of the counterculture had peaked in San Francisco that summer, but the movement was only now reaching the hinterlands. The possibility of finding a way to live outside the dictates of the Establishment and the accepted norms of the past was highly appealing to me. Why did there need to be such barriers between all of us, when the human race was really all brothers and sisters? An intense idealism overwhelmed me as I finished the moving saga of Valentine Michael Smith. By the end of the book, I shed real tears—not for the death of its protagonist, but in a kind of cathartic release at experiencing a spiritual epiphany. I really "grokked" what Heinlein was saying, and I desperately wanted to find a way to make deep, truthful connections with others. I didn't want to travel the same path as my parents, for it hadn't seemed to take them to a good place.

As kids, we all coped with life in Lewiston in our different ways. Steve would soon be finishing high school and had already decided to enlist in the army after graduation. (By this time, the Vietnam war had escalated to major proportions, and enlisting was seen as a way to avoid going right to the front lines.) Dave was having trouble making friends at school, and he soon isolated himself in his room with his music and electric guitar. Eventually he formed a rock band named Ogre, which became his passion well into the 1970s. My dad was finding his job difficult because of resentment in the local office over the loss of the man he'd replaced, who had been there a long time. He also didn't like that my mother insisted on working and found a job as a secretary for a local attorney. Their marriage was showing the strain.

As always, my outlet was comicdom. I dove into its bracing waters with renewed commitment. *Sense of Wonder* #3 saw print shortly after the move to Idaho. The third issue continued to show incremental improvement, offering better-quality amateur writing and art by Larry Herndon (publisher of *Star-Studded Comics*), Sherman Howard (part 2 of the Star Rangers story), Mickey Schwaberow (whose *Magnum Opus* one-shot I admired), and a nice Flash Gordon back cover by Ronn Foss.

As the calendar turned over to 1968, I began to focus on my fanzine as never before. I wanted to find out how far my talent and drive would take me. These new issues, published in Idaho when I was a junior and senior in high school, were my glory days as a publisher of ditto fanzines. I was bringing everything I'd learned to bear in an effort to produce something of real quality.

My first project in the new year was completing the artwork for the ten-page Brimstone story that had been scripted by Jim Shooter. He had only drawn two or three pages before mysteriously cutting off contact with me. Had I offended him? Years later, Jim told me that Mort Weisinger found out that Jim was contributing to some fanzines and threatened to fire the young writer if he didn't stop. He'd never said anything against Weisinger to me; their working relationship was a lot bumpier than I'd realized.

Jim's excellent story and my creative ambition resulted in another quantum leap in my artistic progress. Instead of working merely on one panel, then the next, I began thinking in terms of the layout of the whole page. Richard Kyle's likening of the comics artist to a film director inspired me to experiment with viewing action from different camera angles, lending the story more variety than in my earlier efforts. Jim's urging that I improve my knowledge of human anatomy was beginning to pay dividends too.

I found the perfect printing facility in Lewiston. Harrington's Copy Center, located off Main Street, had a ditto machine on the premises that I could operate myself. The owner was the kindly Eva Harrington, a classy woman in her fifties who looked like Jessica Tandy in *The Birds*. Though she was more than a little amused by the nature of the material I was printing, she was unfailingly helpful. *Sense of Wonder* #3 and #4 printed up beautifully.

✄

My junior year at Lewiston High School unfolded with unexpected ease. The classes I was taking were a snap. I immediately began getting straight As (something I had never quite been able to achieve in hypercompetitive Mount Lebanon). My friendships with Bob Sanborn and Barbara Barker had grown to include their circles of friends. Eventually it hit home that I didn't have to worry about being a social pariah any more.

I noticed that some of the students didn't talk with that pronounced twang and that the school had its share of people like me who identified with the counterculture. Long hair and bell-bottom pants might have been slow to arrive in Lewiston, but they showed up in a big way in 1968.

A milestone in the evolution of my social life was learning to drive. The driving age for a daytime permit in Idaho was fourteen. I was already sixteen and had missed the sophomore driver's education class. Therefore, I was given a license with no formal driving training at all. I merely had to pass a written test.

Mom taught me to drive. There was no way my parents would let me take their banana-yellow Oldsmobile out onto the road, even in Lewiston's relatively low-key traffic, on the strength of my passing only a written test. It was a big car—a Delmont 88 model—that lumbered along, hogging the road. Dave and I nicknamed it the Whale.

Despite its size, the Whale was amazingly responsive due to its power steering. It could be sent lurching one way or another with the slightest jerk of a finger. The car was deceptively easy to drive, which gave the person behind the wheel a feeling of invincibility. More than once, when taking me out on a practice run, Mom gasped in sudden panic as I sent the Whale sailing down a narrow side street with cars parked on either side, as another car approached from the opposite direction. For me, an inch of clearance was as good as a yard, possessing as I did the bland confidence of youth.

I wasn't ready to give up the idea of having a girlfriend, despite my secret sexual desires. I was, I decided, bisexual. Girls continued to interest me. By spring of 1968 I had my first serious girlfriend, a cute, bubbly blonde named Mary. She was friendly and easy to talk to. We walked home from school together each day, but we didn't kiss until I took her out on a date in my parents' car. Finding a place to park with a nice view of the Clearwater River, we tentatively groped and slurped at each other, discovering what "real kissing" was all about.

One particular night while we were blissfully sitting in the car at our frequent vantage point, I mentioned that the clouds were really beautiful at sunset.

"Those aren't clouds," Mary pointed out, giggling. "That's pollution from the smokestacks at the pulp mill."

All I can say is, when one is in the throes of the hormonal surges of adolescence, even pollution can be romantic.

Though my contacts with Lanz tapered off, I began the period of my most voluminous correspondence. While I had exchanged letters with other fans in the past, most of them were in furtherance of my fanzine publishing plans: looking for contributions, writing letters of comment on the fanzines I received, and searching for back issues that I needed for my collection. Now my correspondence took on a different purpose: it served as a way to exchange ideas about all manner of topics, from politics to sex to social issues to popular music. These letters often ran to two or three pages of single-spaced typing, where I would pour out much that was going on inside me in a stream-of-consciousness way. My views on most topics were hopelessly naïve, but you have to start somewhere. It was a highly satisfying—and undoubtedly therapeutic—process.

One of my favorite correspondents was a college student in New Jersey named Dave Bibby. Because he was a few years older than I, perhaps nineteen or twenty, I saw him as a sort of big brother. Bibby had contributed to some of the top fanzines, but now it seemed his principal interest was rock music. As a result, I had the inside track on the cutting edge of college music. He alerted me to the latest trends in rock, from second-tier San Francisco groups like Quicksilver Messenger Service to British bands like Cream and a guitar visionary named Jimi Hendrix. I learned a lot from Bibby, and so did my younger brother.

Just as Dave Bibby introduced me to the broadening rock genre in 1968 through his album recommendations, Ronn Foss brought me an awareness of environmental and other social issues in his new fanzine *Pandora*. Although it was subtitled "the Romance of Adventure," *Pandora* offered a not-unsympathetic analysis of the Black Panthers by Ronn's wife Coreen, a slice-of-life piece about being an ambulance driver in San Francisco (Foss's current occupation), and several other pieces on science fiction books, amateur filmmaking, and the Society for Creative Anachronism. *Pandora* was created by comics fans, but it ran the gamut of Ronn and Coreen's interests.

This and other fanzines like it (notably *Sanctum* by Steve and Dave Johnson) were subtly preparing me for impending adulthood by expanding my view beyond high school and comic books.

I even began publishing a small letter-zine called *Asterisk* that I sent to my correspondents and other friends in fandom. That way, about thirty-five fans' letters were shared among the closed group. One issue had a long letter from Gene Klein, who soon would change his name to Gene Simmons and form the rock group Kiss. Others had letters from Dick Trageser, Ronn Foss, and a new correspondent named Mario Vitale. Mario became a subscriber to *Sense of Wonder* starting with #4, at the tender age of twelve years old. He lived in Providence, Rhode Island, an only child of Italian immigrants. We began a correspondence when he wrote a letter of comment on that issue. I almost always wrote back when someone commented at length on any of my fanzines. I found Mario to be intelligent, and he was interested in exchanging letters on an ongoing basis. At the time I had no idea he was four years younger than I. He could write intelligently about anything, it seemed: comics, yes, but like the fanzines of the late sixties, his interests also included science fiction, popular and classical music, movies, and the fine arts.

N

Although I still bought and read plenty of comic books in 1968, that year an event occurred that ignited my interest in cinema.

My parents had almost no interest in the arts or even in popular culture such as movies. Before I moved to Idaho, I'd probably only seen about a dozen movies in a theater. In my younger years, there was *The Absent-Minded Professor* and *The Shaggy Dog;* when I was older, I saw *A Hard Day's Night, The Birds,* and the James Bond movies. That was about it.

In those days, few old movies were shown on television. However, during the *NBC Saturday Night at the Movies* TV show, we were treated to many selections from the 20th Century Fox vault, including some of Marilyn Monroe's best early movies: *How to*

Marry a Millionaire, Gentlemen Prefer Blondes, Niagara, and *River of No Return.* Thus, the star I was most familiar with as a young teen was Monroe. I didn't respond to her sexuality; I enjoyed her ability as a comedienne and how she managed to go beyond normal sexual boundaries yet maintain a certain innocence. Otherwise, my viewing consisted mainly of Chiller Theater presentations of the classic Universal horror films: *Frankenstein, Bride of Frankenstein, Dracula, The Wolfman,* and so on. That was about the extent of my film awareness before our move to Idaho.

Then came *The Graduate*—the award-winning movie based on Charles Webb's novel of the same name—which arrived at the Liberty Theater in Lewiston in early 1968. After that, my eyes were opened, and I realized how creative and enjoyable motion pictures could be. It's hard to pinpoint why this movie was the turning point for me. I had no idea what to expect when my Mom and her best friend allowed me to accompany them to what was reputedly a racy movie.

I loved everything about it: the theme song ("The Sound of Silence") and other music by Simon and Garfunkel, the highly disciplined directing of Mike Nichols, and the performances of the actors, especially Dustin Hoffman as Benjamin Braddock and Anne Bancroft as Mrs. Robinson (who never had a first name). The outline is all there in Webb's short novel, but Nichols and screenwriters Calder Willingham and Buck Henry knew which parts to use and which to discard. There's the famous moment when Benjamin tells a family friend that he's "a little worried about my future," and the friend's advice is one word: "Plastics."

Doubtless the film resonated because I, too, would soon be a graduate, albeit the high-school kind; but I was definitely worried about my future. The real reason I fell under the spell of *The Graduate* had to do with the masterful filmmaking and storytelling, which, I was soon to understand, was a cousin of the graphic story. There could be voice-overs (captions), frames edited in brief staccato bits (like a series of tall, narrow panels in a comics story), and the intercutting of scenes, which could also be done in comics. Comics, in short, could be cinematic, and *The Graduate* was an example of the many ways a movie could be directed and edited to tell a story perfectly, highlight the key moments, and propel the narrative forward. Given the visual storytelling that both movies and comics shared, it's no surprise that I was drawn to cinema so strongly once I saw an example of moviemaking at its finest. Of course, I wasn't the only one who loved the movie; at one time it was the third-biggest moneymaker in cinema history.

With my interest in film on the rise, I used three books over the next year to learn more about the history of cinema and about one of its greatest directors. They were *Hollywood and the Academy Awards* by Nathalie Fredrik (Hollywood Awards Publications, 1968), a British book titled *The Films of Alfred Hitchcock* by George Perry (Dutton Vista 1965), and *Hitchcock/Truffaut* (Simon & Schuster 1967), in which film director François Truffaut interviews director Alfred Hitchcock about his films. The book on the Academy Awards gave me information about many of the important movies of the past and the actors who appeared in them. (Hm, I remember thinking, this Humphrey Bogart looks unusual and interesting.) The Hitchcock books further educated me on the grammar and syntax of cinema, for Alfred Hitchcock was one of its greatest masters. Around this time, I saw a theatrical rerelease of *Psycho* (which was too "hot" for broadcast television in 1968). As a result, perhaps my first mature piece of writing was an article on Hitchcock's career, which I began preparing for the next issue of *Sense of Wonder*. Meanwhile, armed with some knowledge, I was able to comb through *TV Guide* and circle the movies I wanted to see. I also made sure I made it to any promising new movies that came to town. My lifelong love affair with cinema had well and truly begun.

N

As my junior year chugged along to its conclusion, I had to start thinking in earnest about college. My art teacher, Mr. Harrison, who thought highly of my talent, suggested that I consider going to an art school where I could pursue my stated interest in commercial art. When I told my dad about this, he was taken aback.

"Has he got any idea what those schools cost?" he grumbled. "Does he think I'm made of money? He's got a lot of nerve filling your head full of those kind of ideas." Going to an art college in California, for example, was simply out of the question, financially speaking.

Besides, my parents wanted me to get a degree that I could "fall back on," and that meant a teaching degree. It would be okay if I studied art and English, as long as there was a certainty of a job after graduation. My father also expressed his wish that I should have a good liberal-arts education, rather than attending a commercial art school that might be, in effect, a trade school. I had no choice but to capitulate.

That being the case, it was a foregone conclusion that I would attend the University of Idaho. My father earned a modest income, but we weren't poor enough for me to qualify for need-based scholarships. I applied for some academic scholarships, but I didn't get any of them, despite my honor-roll grades. Therefore, the University of Idaho in Moscow was the best school we could afford. It was reasonably priced for Idaho residents, and it was thirty miles from Lewiston—far enough away to preclude surprise parental visits, but close enough for easy bus trips home for holidays and special occasions. All in all, everyone concerned found it to be an acceptable alternative.

11.

CONFESSIONS OF A FANZINE EDITOR

It's one thing to print up a fanzine, advertise it, and mail out the copies. By 1968, I had this process down cold. It's quite another to master the combination of ethical and aesthetic judgments that are, shall we say, the higher responsibilities of an editor/publisher. In this area, I still had much to learn. I prided myself on not making the same mistake twice, but there were times when it seemed like I was constantly reeling from blunder to blunder. The production of *Sense of Wonder* #5, right before the beginning of my senior year, was maybe the worst disaster in my amateur publishing experience.

The fanzine itself came together with more than the usual ease. Noted science fiction and comics artist D. Bruce Berry sent in a nice illustration that served as the cover, and Dave Bibby's report on the 1968 New York comics convention was the lead-off feature. British correspondent Anthony Roche came through with a prose story, and I penned a dialogue between a right-winger and a left-winger who meet on a park bench one day. The feature I had the most invested in personally was a comics story called "Heisenberg Alley."

Tom Fisher and I had been regular correspondents for some time. Both of us were ardent admirers of the work of Will Eisner on *The Spirit*. Although the Spirit was nominally a costumed hero because he wore a domino mask, Eisner actually devoted most of his seven-page self-contained stories to short tales of a more universal nature. They were stories steeped in urban atmosphere that delved into the tragedies and triumphs of the human condition.

Tom informed me that he had an idea for a comics story in the Eisner mold. Though he had never written a comics script before, he wanted to give it a try. Would I be interested in illustrating it for *Sense of Wonder*? I responded enthusiastically, and over the summer I adapted Tom's charming script into what I felt was an effective comic strip.

"Heisenberg Alley" was the story of two tenement children who are given a "magic pen" by a derelict scientist. The children don't know that the pen is actually an invention called a "cybernetic encephelo-probe" that derives its power from a computer. When one draws with the pen, the mind sees the drawings as real objects. As the story develops, the children are able to use the pen's powers of illusion to help the police capture a gang of criminals. Fisher's story had excellent characterization, atmosphere, pathos, and a gentle conclusion that was genuinely touching.

Splash panel of "Heisenberg Alley" from *Sense of Wonder* #5 (1968). Though I had the best of intentions, scripter Thomas Fisher was so incensed by my edits that he never wrote to me again.

The only thing about the script that I felt betrayed Tom's lack of experience was the number of words he expected to appear in the captions and (to a lesser extent) the word balloons. Maybe he had been reading a lot of *Crime Does Not Pay* comics from the late 1940s, which were without equal in their wordiness. Or maybe he was taking his cues from certain stories for EC horror and science fiction comic books written by Al Feldstein in the early 1950s, which also poured on the words.

My solution was to carefully compress the material in a number of the captions in Tom's script by eliminating what I felt was superfluous verbiage—knowing in some cases that he was merely stating what I would be drawing in the panel, which the reader could see for himself. I tried not to harm his script in the editing process, but in the end I had no choice but to cut a considerable amount. The number of words Tom wrote simply wouldn't have fit onto the page, no matter how small I lettered. And since all but the first two pages were to be drawn on ditto masters, the lettering would have to be done actual size.

Here was an opportunity for me to show my artistic chops, and as I proudly examined the finished ditto masters, I felt the final result was my best work to date. (The opening two pages, which were drawn for photo-offset, weren't quite as assured, revealing my inexperience with pen and ink, but the result was still satisfactory.)

When I took the issue down to Harrington's to print it, a catastrophe occurred. I had turned up the valve releasing the spirit fluid (which activated the purple ink on the ditto master), thinking this would produce the best result. However, after printing the entire issue front side and back, I examined the stacks of paper to discover that the generous use of fluid had caused the pages to entirely show through. They were an unreadable mess. Since I had already printed two hundred copies of each master, there was no way I could squeeze another two hundred copies from them with good results.

Disaster!

I was bereft. Not only would I have to remaster the *entire issue*, but I would have to pay for several more reams of paper—and I didn't have the money.

Eva Harrington swooped in to the rescue. She generously asserted that the fault wasn't with me but the machine, and she offered to give me enough paper for a second run at no charge. In retrospect, I know for a fact that she saw how upset I was, and she took it upon herself to help however she could.

I did indeed return home and remaster the entire issue. This involved retyping twenty-five pages of text and redrawing numerous illustrations. However, there was simply no way I could redraw "Heisenberg Alley." My only option was to try to get the best possible copies from the existing masters. In the end, the printing on the story—though readable—was much lighter than it should have been.

To make matters worse, I received a letter from Tom Fisher's friend Raymond Miller, who told me that Tom was so upset at my cutting of his script that he couldn't bring himself to write to me. Although I sent him a lengthy letter of apology and explained my reasons for making the edits, Fisher never wrote to me again.

Was I wrong to edit "Heisenberg Alley"? Of course I was, especially when it was a labor of love and I had paid nothing for the right to publish his story. The proper thing—the ethical thing—would have been to write to Tom with my concerns and ask him to make the cuts. Or I could have made the cuts that I deemed appropriate and asked for his concurrence. That would also have afforded him the opportunity to take the script elsewhere if he didn't agree with my treatment of it. By going ahead on my own, I took away his choice in the matter.

I did feel a certain vindication that the story—despite the poor printing—received praise from all quarters. In *Fandom's Agent* #7, editor Chuck Woolley opined:

> "Heisenberg Alley" is the closest thing to a Will Eisner-flavored strip fandom has produced. I won't spoil it by telling you the details, but it is a delightful departure from the super-science madness that infests fan strip efforts. Adding touches of reality and humor, Fisher has turned out a fine story.

Even though I was convinced my edits had been for the best, this didn't justify my lack of consideration for the author. An editor should have a certain amount of basic, unadorned common sense. In this area, I made a decision in the next issue of *Sense of Wonder* that showed me to be deficient in that basic commodity.

In the pages of Wally Wood's *witzend* (yes, it's spelled with a small *w*), Steve Ditko had introduced a controversial new character named Mr. A who was mainly a vehicle for Ditko to espouse views of social morality influenced by Ayn Rand in *The Fountainhead*. The idea was that there was only good and evil, white and black, with no shades of gray between them. To quote Mr. A himself, "When one knows what is black, evil, and what is white, good, there can be no justification for choosing any part of evil. Those who do so choose, are not gray but black and evil … and they will be treated accordingly."

In 1968, I heard that Ditko was doing drawings of Mr. A upon request. Having saved his address from our earlier contact, I wrote to him asking for a cover for *Sense of Wonder*. I soon had a nice piece of penciled and inked original artwork by Ditko for this purpose. (I would have preferred a drawing of Spider-Man, but I was happy with what I got.)

Covers for *Sense of Wonder* #5 by D. Bruce Berry and #6 by Steve Ditko. Ditko was furious when he saw that I'd printed his Mr. A cover on pink, rather than white, paper. Mr. A ™ and © Steve Ditko.

The common practice in the days of ditto fanzines was to have a cover printed by photo-offset to give the magazine a better overall appearance. Generally these covers were printed on colored paper: goldenrod, blue, green. *Sense of Wonder*'s first five issues had used white and all the available colors except for pink. So, when I sent the Mr. A cover to the printer, I requested that it be printed on pink paper.

Wrong.

I received another rebuke from Steve Ditko, more stinging than the first (though without any indication that he remembered the earlier incident), shortly after dropping his complimentary copies in the mail.

To paraphrase, he wrote, "I was shocked and dismayed that you printed a cover featuring Mr. A, whose credo is that there's only black and white with no shades of gray, on colored paper. It goes against the whole basis of the character. It should have been printed in black ink on white paper only. Why is it that I get burned every time I do something for the fan press?"

This time I really felt stupid. Ditko had a valid point that he probably shouldn't have had to explain to me. I suppose it never occurred to me because I didn't associate the color of the paper with anything in the subject matter of the drawing. It was merely to give a slight visual variation from black ink on white. It did occur to me that maybe Steve Ditko wasn't easy to please.

This wasn't the last experience I had as Ditko's publisher. We would cross paths again, once more after a three-year interval.

N

I was beginning to tire of the labor-intensive nature of publishing a ditto fanzine. Not only did I have all the bookkeeping and mailing responsibilities, but I had to print up each issue by hand, assemble it, and staple it. Then I had to address and stamp each copy, again by hand. True, it was only two hundred copies per issue, but the sheer number of issues I had produced in two years had made the mundane aspects more daunting. I was burning out.

On the other hand, my social life seemed to finally be on the right track. Over the summer, Barbara had replaced Mary as the particular object of my affection. I had always enjoyed talking with her, and she encouraged my creative aspirations. Barbara was the only one who had read *The Eyrie*, which she thought was so exciting that I actually wrote a second Richard Stern thriller just for her. In the fall of 1968, I also wrote a brief, comedic novel called *Come with Me*, which imitated elements of Charles Webb's *The Graduate* (I read the book after seeing the movie). Barbara enjoyed that one, too.

My parents rarely objected to me borrowing the Whale—though if they had known some of the antics that I performed with it, they'd have been horrified. (Getting it up over a hundred miles an hour on the two-lane roads on the outskirts of town was one of my dangerous stunts.) Like most teenagers, I had a supreme sense of my own immortality. Some of this was part and parcel of being a high school senior. School itself no longer demanded my full attention, since I had pared my schedule to the minimum number of credits to graduate. Because Barbara was on her way to being our class valedictorian and I was continuing to get straight As, everyone assumed we were models of responsible teenage behavior. This allowed us to derive special glee from an elaborately laid plan to skip school for a jaunt out of town to Spalding Park. We enjoyed playing Bonnie and Clyde for a day, reveling in the sylvan pleasures of the park, and nibbling on cold fried chicken and other picnic-style goodies.

Thus I made my decision. In the editorial of my sixth issue, I announced the demise of the fanzine that had been my pride and joy for the past two years. "Be it known: we're discontinuing *Sense of Wonder*. The fact is, this magazine does not sell enough copies. Recently we had to raise the price to forty cents [from thirty-five cents] due to a poor response to ads and our production costs. We're losing too much [money] per issue." I would publish only one more issue, which saw print in the spring of 1969.

The reason officially given, the loss of money, was only partly true. Burnout was at least as much of a factor. Still, it was true that sales had drifted downward after #2.

The problem? It was probably because *Sense of Wonder* had less and less superhero material as time went on. I was growing up and wanting to experiment with other sorts of stories. Also, I had a hard time finding artists who were good enough to draw comic strips, so most issues featured only one fully illustrated story. The rest was generally made up of two text stories. The Immortal Corpse was the only prose-format character who proved to be accepted and popular in my fanzine. It's also possible that the first wave of fanzine buyers had entered college by the end of the decade and no longer had the time, money, or interest to continue fannish pursuits rather than embracing the college experience.

Sense of Wonder went out of existence in fine form. John Fantucchio, one of comicdom's most talented artists, provided a fabulous (and sexy) cover, and Ronn Foss adapted the Jimmy Rogers song "Child of Clay" into sequential art form. Raymond Miller crafted an excellent comprehensive article on the history of Green Arrow. It felt great to go out on a high note.

My senior year was also approaching its predictable crescendo. I was busy with fittings for my cap and gown, preparing for final exams, and socializing with my new coterie of friends. The time was right to reduce my activity in fandom—but not entirely. As I was bowing out of *Sense of Wonder,* I joined the roster of *Capa-alpha.*

Capa-alpha was an amateur press alliance (APA), which is basically a membership-basis fanzine for which each member prints up his or her own contribution and sends the copies to a central mailer, who collates all the contributions into one big issue and sends a copy to each member. *Capa-alpha,* which had a roster of fifty members at the time, had been established in 1964 by Jerry Bails. It was a less demanding outlet for my creative energy and a way to keep in touch with the fandom grapevine. My Batman-themed cover for #59 (1969) turned out rather well.

I drew the Batman cover for *Capa-alpha* #59 in 1969, about the time I graduated from Lewiston High School.

The main thing that emerged from my *Capa-alpha* experience was the name Hamster Press. Lots of fan publishers came up with lofty names for their publishing enterprises, such as the SFCA, Golden Gate Features, Dynapubs, and so on. When I was typing up the first issue of my APA-zine, I wrote in the indicia that it was published by

Hamster Press. This was something of a satire on those lofty names and also an appropriate choice for a zine only a few pages long. My brother Dave and I had owned two or three hamsters when we were in grade school, and it seemed like an amusing idea.

N

The summer after high-school graduation included the Woodstock music festival, the Apollo moon landing, and the Stonewall riot. They were all fascinating developments on the American scene.

I was startled to read about gay riots in New York City on the front page of the *Lewiston Tribune*. The police had tried to bust the Stonewall Inn, a gay bar in Greenwich Village, one too many times, and they found themselves the targets of an enraged group of disenfranchised young people that rapidly grew into a major melee. I didn't exactly condone violent protests, but I read the story with wonder and a certain satisfaction. If you push people far enough, I thought, this is what happens. I didn't realize that Stonewall would be a watershed event in the gay liberation movement.

As for me, the summer of '69 found me in the frozen-food business. My father used his influence to get me a job at Smith's Frozen Foods, a local plant on the banks of the Clearwater River that processed a large portion of the huge pea harvest from nearby farms. They cooked, froze, and packed zillions of green pellets into boxes that were shipped all over the country. My job was hardly strenuous; as a member of the janitorial team, I was assigned to the area where ladies in hairnets inspected the peas as they flowed along a conveyor belt.

The only catch was that I had to work the graveyard shift. I didn't mind. There was something agreeably eerie about working all night while most of the valley's denizens slumbered. I had stayed up fairly late before, and maybe once or twice I had managed to keep my eyes open all night, but never before or since have I seen so many sunrises in such a short span of time.

While I kept the floors clean, running my squeegee carefully around the tennis-shoe-clad feet of the women who tossed their green debris to the floor, I fantasized what it would be like to be a vampire who could never see the sun. I had been a big fan of Chiller Theater in my preadolescent years in Pittsburgh.

While working the graveyard shift at Smith's Frozen Foods, I got the first glimmer of an idea for a take-off on the Universal Frankenstein films, so beautifully directed by James Whale, in graphic story form. It wouldn't be an adaptation of Mary W. Shelley's imaginative novel; rather, it would look at the basic premise from the creature's point of view. Imagine what it would be like to become conscious in an adult-sized body and find oneself alone in a strange, scary place. What a bizarre, disorienting experience it would be. If set in contemporary times, this perspective would provide the opportunity to show the creature reacting to our modern world, not only as a misfit but as an individual with special powers and abilities. He could be pursued by the doctor who had created him, the police, and others with different motives. Events would swirl around this creature, catching him up in their momentum. The stories would come to him. In some ways, it had faint echoes of *Stranger in a Strange Land*. I decided to call my protagonist the Assembled Man.

12.

BLAME IT ON THE BOSSA NOVA

Fanzines were evolving into something more challenging and complex than they had been at the beginning. By 1968 the "gosh wow" nature of the early amateur publications was being superseded by a spicier, more mature quality. The most superficial symbol of this evolution was the appearance of the unclothed female (and occasionally male) form in the fan press. Comics fans' interests were expanding from superheroes to include the worlds of science fiction (for this was the era of the Edgar Rice Burroughs boom) and heroic fantasy (spearheaded, if that's the word, by the resurgence of interest in Robert E. Howard's pulp tales of Conan the Barbarian).

Even the somewhat stodgy *RBCC* was given a makeover to fit with the times. G. B. Love hired James Van Hise to assist him with layouts and other matters, which—along with the conversion to all photo-offset printing—improved the appearance of the mighty zine significantly. Love also found two extraordinary artists to do most of his covers over the next few years: John Fantucchio and Don Newton. The result was a series of breathtaking covers that enhanced *RBCC* tremendously.

Without a doubt, the fanzine that influenced me most as a writer and artist of comics was Bill Spicer's *Fantasy Illustrated,* which changed its title to *Graphic Story Magazine.* Now the magazine spent fewer pages on amateur comic strips and more on articles and interviews that examined the work of some of the most talented, innovative comics creators of the past, from Charles Biro to Will Eisner. The magazine's letter column, which presented comments on these features from Spicer's far-flung readership, was one of the most intelligent and stimulating in fandom.

For me, it was the "Graphic Story Review" column by Richard Kyle (who, I've already noted, coined the terms "graphic story" and "graphic novel" in 1964) that caused me to raise my sights. I began to realize that the graphic story medium had qualities that are uniquely its own, qualities I wanted to explore more thoroughly than I had done before. It wasn't so much that I wanted the material of my own comics to be of an exalted nature; rather, I wanted to become a more sophisticated user of the medium's storytelling potential. I didn't want to become a journeyman writer/artist who did nothing but repeat the formulas of the past. I had no interest in becoming the leading imitator of Jack Kirby or Al Williamson. I wanted to be the best possible Bill Schelly.

The task was formidable. As Richard Kyle and others around this time pointed out, the comics creator isn't only the director but also the set designer, casting director, costumer, makeup artist, hairdresser, lighting professional, title designer, and much more. The comics creator has to do it all, which requires a wide range of knowledge, a broad perspective, and the right skills. A comics creator makes his or her own universe and is, in short, a god. It's no wonder so few truly excel in the medium.

Throughout the preparations for my freshman year at the University of Idaho, I was developing an outline for *The Assembled Man*. I considered it a totally original concept. It didn't occur to me that doing a take-off on *Frankenstein* was hardly a new idea.

In any case, *The Assembled Man* would be my first major foray into inked art—that is, art created the same way as it was done in the comics industry. That meant it would have to be professionally printed for publication. I didn't know how, but by hook or by crook I would find a way to pay for it.

The initial idea was to produce a fanzine that would showcase the artwork of two high-school buddies, Bob Sanborn and Don Greene, along with my own. Bob and I were set to be roommates in the college dormitory, and we knew Don would be a frequent visitor. All of us were artists with ideas for comics, illustrations, poetry, and short stories. We wanted to do a sort of counterculture publication that we could sell in head shops alongside underground "comix." However, once the school year began, both Bob and Don lost interest in the project, and I was left to fend for myself.

Life as a college freshman, away from home for the first extended period of my life, was an exciting, heady experience. Far from missing my family, I reveled in my newfound freedom. Barbara Barker, my nominal girlfriend, had gotten a full scholarship to attend the University of Puget Sound in Tacoma, Washington, about four hundred miles away. Although we tried to maintain our relationship from a distance, each visiting the other once or twice in the next year, it proved impractical. We decided to see other people but stay in contact as friends. Having my buddy Bob as a roommate guaranteed that I had at least one good friend until I got to know others.

I signed up for a mix of liberal-arts courses and settled into life in the dormitory. I was able to break the ice with some of the other guys in Snow Hall by drawing caricatures of them and taping them to their doors. They got a big kick out of that. It continued my practice of using humorous drawings to make friends. I also did a

This photo, taken at the Carol Drive house, shows me about to return to college after Thanksgiving vacation in 1969, laden with schoolbooks and leftovers from the family feast.

wicked caricature of the middle-aged ladies of the cafeteria staff, which I taped up at the entrance to the dining room for all to see.

In 1969 the University of Idaho boasted about six thousand students and was a respectable institution of higher learning. Even the freshman courses were challenging, if only for the amount of material we were expected to plow through. I was taking Introduction to Life Sciences, English 101, Literature of Western Civilization, Psychology 101, and two art classes. I spent many hours reading texts, doing assignments, and studying for tests. I took my classes seriously.

I also partied seriously. I had smoked a little marijuana during my last year of high school, but pot was hard to find, and smoking was tricky to do when living with the parental units. But in an essentially unsupervised dormitory (part of four dormitories in the brand-new Wallace Complex), sharing connecting rooms with three other guys who were also enjoying their taste of freedom, my marijuana use skyrocketed. That was the only mind-altering substance that I used at first. I was too scared to try LSD for a long time—probably as long as two or three weeks. Then it was "let the good times roll!" Acid was readily available, and a lot of my friends were taking it. In retrospect, I wonder about my lack of caution, but I never had a bad experience; just a lot of unbridled fun, and a certain amount of self-introspection that also comes with it.

Nevertheless, I managed to receive straight As at the end of my first semester. I kept that 4.0 average for three of my four years at the U of I while still doing a lot of the fun things a person does when he or she is finally able to bust loose from parental restrictions. I attribute my good grades to an understanding of how to score well on tests and to my writing ability, which I had honed in my fanzines.

My first art course at the university was figure drawing. We had both clothed and nude models pose for the classes. Nothing drove home the difference between high school and college quite so clearly as the moment when a robed model—usually a woman, not always—would walk to the center of a circle of art students and remove her wrap. All of us were aware of the attributes of the naked human body, yet confronting them in full light in the company of our peers was new. Nor did I expect that I might be acquainted with some of the models. Strangers are one thing, but to have my high-school friend Paula show up for the job one day brought a whole new dimension to the exercise.

The nude figure drawing made an immediate impact on my ability to render the human form. Instead of imitating the way my favorite comics artists drew people, I began to develop my own approach. I have always been blessed with a good eye for drawing—the ability to transfer three-dimensional reality to a two-dimensional page. Before I was in junior high, I was drawing portraits of neighborhood kids for a small fee, and my drawings looked like their subjects. Now I was noticing the contours of the body in real life. I took to it easily, filling up sketch pads and turning in finished drawings that invariably received high marks. This made for much-improved figure draftsman-ship in *The Assembled Man* and the other comics stories I drew later.

Sketches from freshman Life Drawing class at the University of Idaho. We also sketched from nude models.

I made a point of seeing every decent film that came through the two theaters in town, often more than once. *Midnight Cowboy; Last Summer; They Shoot Horses, Don't They?; Z; Bob & Carol & Ted & Alice*—downbeat dramas all, yet with an unprecedented honesty and unvarnished quality that greatly appealed to me. It was a particularly fertile period for the movies. I also liked less intense movies like *Butch Cassidy and the Sundance Kid* and *The Reivers*. I studied them all, especially their storytelling methods and how they framed images.

On a whim, I signed up for Introduction to Acting as an elective. Although I discovered that I was too self-conscious to feel comfortable on a stage, I greatly enjoyed the milieu of the theater. In the spring of 1970, I was cast as the lead in Edward Albee's one-act play *The American Dream.* This was definitely *not* typecasting. The play called for the character to narcissistically flex his biceps. Since I was built like Jimmy Olsen rather than Superman, this moment didn't work too well.

The American Dream had an unexpected benefit: the director, Dale, asked me if I wanted to work as a tour guide at Glacier National Park during the upcoming summer. Dale was returning for another stint at the job himself, and he had been asked to recruit another fellow to fill a vacant slot. Thus I was spared a second summer slopping peas around at Smith's Frozen Foods.

In my spare time, especially while I was in Lewiston on occasional weekends, holidays, and semester breaks, I was furiously working away on *The Assembled Man.* The penciling went well, but I struggled with ink technique. After comic pages are penciled and the balloons and captions are lettered, an inker has to go over the pencils in India ink to make it possible to reproduce the artwork clearly. Inking is a specialty for which technique is paramount. When I tried to use crow quill pens dipped in ink, they tended to splatter and make a mess, and inking by brush required a lot of confidence and hand control. What I needed at this juncture was the chance to observe the working methods of a professional comics inker. If that had been possible, I probably could have broken through that technical barrier.

That sort of training wasn't available to me in Moscow, Idaho. Instead, I chickened out. Rather than working through the challenges of learning to ink by trial and error, I resorted to using a variety of felt-tip markers, which were coming on the market at the time. The Flair pens were my favorites, though they were water-based and nonpermanent. You couldn't correct mistakes with white paint because the result would be a gray mess. One had to paste a paper patch

A portion of a splash panel for *The Assembled Man*, my attempt at a graphic novel. ™ and © Bill Schelly.

over errors. Their virtue was their flexible points, which allowed for more than a sterile, constant line width. You could press hard with them and the line would get fatter, almost like a crow quill pen point with ink. The main thing one *couldn't* achieve with felt-tip pen was the dynamism of real brush strokes. The result tended to look a little stiff. Still, they were easy, clean, and fast to use, and to my eyes the finished product looked *much* better than my awkward inked stuff. (Later I learned that no less a genius than Alex Toth, a comic book artist whose work I revere, was using a variety of pens and markers for his comic art. There's always *someone* who can break the rules and get away with it. Others who tried it were less successful.)

The opening caption of chapter 1 of *The Assembled Man* read as follows:

> Rain slashes down in torrents, pelting a mournful rhythm onto the broken windows and cracked sidewalks of the Hill District. No one from the better sections of town ventures into the slums, especially not when night cloaks its rotting buildings and dark alleys. The Hill District has many tales to tell. At this moment, in fact, in the basement of an abandoned library, an incredible drama unfolds …

Panels of *The Assembled Man* leading up to the title character's creation by Dr. von Krepner. The inking technique wasn't particularly impressive, but my storytelling ability had become considerably more sophisticated. (From *Incognito* #8, 1970).

More *Assembled Man* from *Incognito* #8.

Why did so many of my early stories begin with a rainstorm? It reminds me of poor Snoopy in *Peanuts,* always beginning his ambitious writing projects with the words "It was a dark and stormy night …" In my teenage days as a writer, I left few clichés unused. For example, we have the evil scientist bent on revenge against those who had stripped him of his medical license—the kind of role Boris Karloff played in *House of Frankenstein* and numerous other films. In this case, the scientist's name is Dr. Hans von Krepner, a demented genius who assembles a body from parts of corpses. When questioned by a subordinate, he reasonably responds:

> All I'm doing is assembling parts into a whole man. It isn't much different from all the transplants that go on today. What's more, the parts I'm using are superior. If my experiment is a success, I'll have created a being of phenomenal health and intelligence!

Naturally, his experiment goes wrong. The power lines to the library are old and frayed, and an explosion decimates the premises. The scientist is the only survivor—or is he? When von Krepner searches through the rubble, he realizes his "assembled man" is gone. The creature, it turns out, has come to life and has been taken in by a kindly blind beggar named Audrey who protects and teaches him while the doctor searches the city's slums for his creation. The twenty-two-page, two-chapter origin story ends with a cliffhanger.

The story is a pastiche of Mary W. Shelley, film noir, and sentimental hogwash. Where it succeeded—indeed, where most of my interest and energy was expended—was in the development of specific panel sequences. The buildup to the moment of creation, and the episode where von Krepner discovers Audrey searching through the library rubble, are effectively dramatized in a carefully thought-out series of panels.

Having announced the end of *Sense of Wonder* a year before, I felt it would be embarrassing to bring it back so quickly. I decided to revive it with a different title, mainly as a vehicle for *The Assembled Man.* As my freshman year in college ended, I placed ads for

Incognito #8 in *RBCC* and *The Nostalgia News*. At the same time, I packaged up the artwork and mailed it to the printer, having somehow raised the funds. Then I took off for my summer job at Glacier Park in Montana.

The Glacier Park Boat Company gave me a wonderful summer away from everything, since the lakes we traversed were within the area known as East Glacier. (None of us had cars, so we had to use our thumbs if we wanted to travel to Kalispell or Lethbridge.) The boat captains lived in a rustic cabin with no television or stereo. We had to walk several hundred yards to use the showers in the dormitories for the kids who worked at the big hotel, East Glacier Lodge. Despite the lack of luxury, I found that I liked the job. I excelled at giving tourists on the boats a talk about the sights they were seeing: mountain peaks, glaciers, and animals, including bears—black bears, not grizzlies. The beauty of Glacier Park was awe-inspiring.

Much as I appreciated the park environment, my mind was never far from comic fandom. I wondered if my brother Dave, back in Lewiston, would really be able to keep up my list of comic book purchases in my absence. And I fantasized about the copies of *Incognito* rolling off the presses. It would be great to see *The Assembled Man* in print. Even the beauty of Glacier Park couldn't trump the power of my inner fantasy life.

However, a cloud of worry hovered over me that summer. Student deferments from the draft had been eliminated, and a lottery was to be held that summer to determine if young men my age would be called into military service. With the war at its apogee, the possibility that I would meet my maker face down in a rice paddy was very real. Would I be able to endure the rigors of the military? Or would I take the difficult route of declaring myself a conscientious objector? These thoughts roiled around in my mind, especially at night in bed, making sleep elusive as the lottery approached.

I never had to face that eventuality. My number—105—was high enough to guarantee I wouldn't get called.

Upon returning home, the printed pages for *Incognito* #8 awaited. The artwork, reduced from the larger originals, looked good to me. In the time left before the new school year, I collated them and mailed out my first all-offset fanzine. I took a great deal of satisfaction from this milestone in my amateur publishing career.

Back at the University of Idaho as a sophomore, I geared up for a year that would be more challenging academically. I partied a lot less and spent more time with my textbooks. Still, I found time to write and draw the third chapter of *The Assembled Man*, which was set against a backdrop of riots in the slums, representing a further honing of my storytelling skills. It appeared in *Incognito* #9, which came out at the beginning of 1971.

The second half of that college year found me spending most of my spare time on nonfandom projects. There was increased activity in my drama activities when I landed a small part in an excellent production of *Romeo and Juliet* (I was Friar John, the hapless fellow who is unable to deliver a fateful letter in time). Unfortunately, I somehow lost the letter I was to hand to Friar Lawrence in a crucial scene, and I ended up freezing on stage. How does one ad lib Shakespeare?

Gary Speer, a fellow student who played the prince in the play, was living in a trailer park near the campus. When his neighbor moved out of a small trailer nearby, I happily said goodbye to dorm life and rented the small but cozy abode. Hence, Gary and I, almost roommates, became close friends. Tall, blond, and handsome (although not my type), he was a musician who had been in a band with his brother Paul, who would go on to a high-profile career as a jazz fusion guitarist. I became a roadie for the weekend gigs of his

Gary Speer, high-school photo.

new band, Sunflower (we all hated the name). Before long, Gary and I were organizing a rock festival.

The purpose of the festival, aside from having a good time, was to raise money for the American Civil Liberties Union. Underground comix were being assailed by charges of obscenity. The ACLU seemed like a worthy cause, so Gary and I launched what turned out to be an annual series of all-day rock-and-roll concerts in the campus arboretum. We dubbed it the Blue Mountain Rock Festival, even though the actual Blue Mountains weren't (and still aren't) near Moscow. I designed the posters, which eventually drew several thousand people to the event. We raised over $1,000 for the Spokane branch of the ACLU.

I didn't get back to Fandomland until the summer. I had taken a hard look at the amount of credits I had earned, and I had concluded that it didn't look as if I would accumulate enough to graduate in four years. I would need some extra credits. When I explained this to my parents, they reluctantly allowed me to attend the university's summer session that year.

I signed up for classes in ceramics, painting, and literature. When I wasn't going to classes or studying, I set myself the goal of finishing the last, long chapter of *The Assembled Man* saga. Apparently I had squirreled away enough cash for more photo-offset printing. I decided the artwork would *not* be done with markers—come hell or high water, despite my perennial lack of confidence with inks, I would use pen and ink if it killed me.

The fourth chapter was titled "The King and the Pawn." In it, the story develops to its tragic conclusion, as the Assembled Man sacrifices his life to save the woman who had helped him. As usual, I worked it up in thumbnail sketches and then penciled the pages. I didn't have a photocopier to enlarge my layouts or a light board to transfer them, so I drew each page the old-fashioned way. This chapter represented another step forward for my work in several respects, not just the inking. "The King and the Pawn" was the lead feature in the tenth issue of my fanzine, now returned to its original name, *Sense of Wonder*. Much as I liked the title *Incognito*, it didn't have the magical—almost spiritual—appeal that *Sense of Wonder* had for me.

N

The sign on the student union bulletin board read simply: "Rider or riders needed to share expenses of round-trip cross-country drive to Harrisburg, Pennsylvania." I wondered if this shared ride might be a cheap way to visit Marshall Lanz. The arrival and return dates fell nicely between the end of summer school and the beginning of the fall semester. This could work.

I telephoned Lanz, who was startled at first, but he immediately agreed that it was a good idea. I spoke also with his mother, Kay, who seemed if anything more eager than Marshall that I should visit. The arrangements were easily made because Pittsburgh is on the same freeway as Harrisburg. I would be one of four drivers.

The drive was an adventure in itself. We drove a truck with a canopy nonstop all the way. Two slept in the back, and two drove and navigated. Our course was roughly the same as the train route I had traveled back to Pittsburgh from Oregon as a boy, through Montana, North Dakota, Minnesota, and then south through Chicago and points eastward.

This was toward the end of the hippie era. The promise of Woodstock had sadly given way to the darker portents of Altamont. The drug culture was no longer mind-expanding; it had moved into harder drugs designed to deaden emotion or crank up artificial energy.

My hair was shoulder-length at this point, the longest it ever grew. I had to keep it in a ponytail, or the wind would whip it into a tangled mess. Unfortunately the truck didn't have the luxury of an eight-track player, so we were stuck with the radio. Most of the way, we couldn't find anything other than country-and-western music on the dial; the best we did was to occasionally pick up signals of commercial pop stations from the few larger cities we passed. My memory of the trip is a jumble, what with driving day and night, sleeping odd hours, and hearing "The Sign Song" ("Sign, sign, everywhere a sign ...") dozens of times. Another song that frequently turned up on the radio was Carole King's "I Feel the Earth Move under My Feet." That it did—at about sixty-five miles per hour.

Lanz had not gotten it together yet to attend college. Instead he'd learned to play drums on a kit in the basement of the Lanz home. We were genuinely glad to see each other, after a little initial awkwardness.

Kay Lanz gushed over me, delighted that her "lost adopted son" had come all that way to visit. I soon realized she had an agenda. At the first opportunity, when Lanz was out of the room, she pulled me aside. "Billy, your parents must be so proud of you. You're a college student with a good career ahead of you. But my Marshall is so lacking in direction. I'm afraid he's going to turn into a bum. He won't go to college. All he wants to do is play that horrible rock and roll and hang out with his bad friends. Please do me a favor. You can be a good influence on him. See if you can convince him to drop those awful friends."

I was skeptical. It sounded like things had been kind of rocky between Kay and her son, but what could I do? I didn't know the situation. Lanz wouldn't listen to me, and I had no idea what direction he should take. I was barely out of my teens and had no idea where I was heading. How could I help anyone else? To mollify Kay, I told her I would talk to Lanz about his friends. When I halfheartedly did so, he replied succinctly that she was crazy and his friends were fine. College didn't seem to be in his immediate future, although I later found out he did pursue higher education.

Both of us had plans for an upcoming fanzine. Our ostensible goal for getting together, besides being able to visit in person, was to work on material for these publications together, like the old days. I wrote and penciled an EC satire titled "Tales from the Script," which Lanz inked. It was great fun to work on this with him, since he always had tremendous enthusiasm for parody. Meanwhile, he set about

Lanz in the early 1970s.

doing a nice job inking a second Brimstone story that I'd brought with me, already fully penciled and lettered. It would appear in my upcoming *Sense of Wonder* #10. The EC parody would appear in *Flotsam* #3, the last fanzine Lanz ever published. (Collectors: Don't bother looking for *Flotsam* #1 or #2; it was merely a name change from *The Irving Forbush Gazette*.)

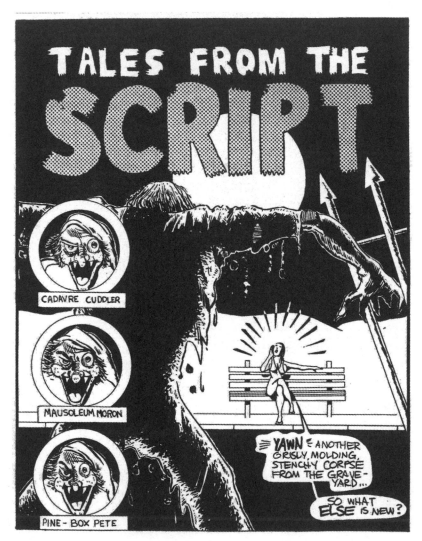

Lanz and I collaborated on this EC satire during my visit. (From *Flotsam* #3).

One day I had an experience at that house that I'll never forget. Lanz had gone out on some sort of errand, and I used the opportunity to take a shower. Knowing that Kay might barge in at any time, I locked the bathroom door. Later, when I was done, I couldn't get it unlocked. The door was stuck. I tried every kind of pressure and jiggle on that damn lock. Nothing worked.

I knew Kay was somewhere in the house, so I pounded on the door. And pounded, and pounded. No response. Then I realized that the music from downstairs was coming from her electric organ. Because Lanz hated her organ, she only played it when he was gone. She was blissfully playing a samba while I was trapped in that tiny bathroom.

While I wouldn't call it a full-blown phobia, I do suffer from mild claustrophobia, and this confinement began to get to me. What were my options? I could simply wait for her to come looking for me, but that might take an hour or longer.

The situation reminded me of the traps that would often confront a comic book character like Batman. What, I asked myself, would the Caped Crusader do in this situation?

I considered the window. It was a small one. Opening it, I peered outside. I was on the second floor, and it was a long way down to the lawn below. And me without my Bat-rope.

Wait. There were rocks piled up against the side of the house, covered with ivy. Maybe if I could get out the window, they would break my fall enough so I wouldn't get hurt.

I finally screwed up my courage, and as Kay launched into a perky rendition of the song "Blame It on the Bossa Nova" (a big hit in 1963), I somehow climbed out that little window feet first. Taking a deep breath, I slowly eased my way down until I was hanging full-length by my fingertips from the brick sill, while wondering how I could have gotten myself in this fix.

I steeled myself and let go.

Whoooosh.

I dropped heavily onto that ivy-covered rock wall, and bounded back from it, landing hard on the lawn on my back. For a moment I couldn't breathe, and I panicked … until I realized I'd only had the wind knocked out of me. Soon the air was rushing back into my lungs. In a few moments I stood up, shaken but all right.

I tried to act nonchalant, while glancing around to see if anyone had noticed the odd spectacle. When I walked (still somewhat unsteadily) into the house, Kay turned from her organ, her eyes as big as saucers. "Who—are—you?" she gasped. With my long hair, she didn't recognize me. Kay's first thought was that I was a random hippie who had walked into her home uninvited. When I told her my story, she was aghast and effusively apologetic.

I was just glad to get out of that goddamn bathroom.

13

A SUCCESSOR FOR *ALTER EGO?*

Despite printing problems that marred parts of *The Assembled Man,* I felt a great deal of satisfaction in having completed the sixty-page saga. I wasn't yet an expert inker, but I had increased my proficiency in that difficult craft.

The reader response was encouraging. While my artwork received mixed reviews, the story was singled out for praise. Larry Herndon, editor of *Star-Studded Comics,* wrote:

> I feel *The Assembled Man* is the best thing you've ever done. The story was beautiful—a genuine human interest story that was truly moving. I would have been proud to have written that myself. It was handled just right. It was one of the finest examples of human interest illo-fiction that fandom has produced, and you should indeed feel proud of what you have done with the story.

I had maintained contact with premiere fandom artist Ronn Foss since the days when he had contributed to my earlier fanzines. He wrote some nice things about *The Assembled Man,* and he ended his letter with some almost fatherly advice:

> You say you're twenty years old. To this old man of thirty-six, the days when I was that age don't seem long ago, and yet if I had known what life would bring I would have enjoyed those times more. Maybe you can benefit from my experience.

Don't be in a big hurry to take life too seriously. Though surely your university studies require steady effort, try to relax ... enjoy yourself ... and don't let your youth escape unappreci-ated. I know from experience that adulthood will soon pile on its burdens and responsibilities. Youth is precious. You may never again feel as carefree as you do now. *Live!*

Peace,

Ronn

If I gave Ronn any reason to offer such advice, it could only have been a sentence or two in a letter where I bemoaned the effort involved in maintaining my straight-A average. But Ronn was a sensitive, highly intuitive individual who probably read between the lines. I *was* feel-ing the pressure of school, despite my various diversions; after all, I hadn't even had the summer off from classes. Later I found out that Foss was looking for his own escape from the pressures of urban living. He soon moved with his wife, Coreen, to the Ozarks to live a more relaxed, rural lifestyle.

Ronn's advice touched me and caused me to stop and examine my life and my priorities. I began to let up on the pressure to get all As. Would it really matter that much if I got an occasional B? A tightness lifted from me, and I seemed to breathe easier.

Changes in fandom were inevitable. Many of fandom's original founders (Jerry Bails, Biljo White, Paul Gambaccini) had scaled back their participation as the 1970s arrived. The Academy of Comic Book Fans and Collectors was officially dead (having more or less achieved its goals, such as establishing a system for grading the condition of individual comic books). A new breed of slick photo-offset fanzines filled with art by professionals were begin-ning to dominate the scene. Fans tended to spend their money on these flashy publications, and as a result, outlets for aspiring amateurs to show what they could do received less support. Bob Overstreet was now publishing his *Comic Book Price Guide,* which changed forever the way comics were bought and sold. In addition to its pricing information, it was the first attempt at a comprehensive index of every comic book published. Buyers complained that it caused prices to go up, but sellers appreciated knowing how much to ask for their wares. When greedy dealers discovered little old ladies with an attic full of old comic books, those ladies might now be armed with Overstreet's guide and would no longer give such treasures away for a song.

After Roy Thomas got a job at Marvel in 1965, it took almost five years before another issue of *Alter Ego* was published. He was too busy with his duties as Stan Lee's right-hand man to publish the magazine on a regular basis. Yet *AE* had been fandom's flagship fanzine, presenting a nicely balanced mix of informative articles on Golden Age comics, clever cartoons and parodies, interesting letters, and an occasional original comics story. The artwork was provided by fandom's foremost talents, and the overall package was always literate, attractive, and tastefully assembled.

Fandom *needed* gen-zines (general-interest fanzines) like *Alter Ego.* Much of the history of comics lay unexplored, since the vast majority of fanzines, mostly produced by younger fans, largely focused on the post-1956 Silver Age of comics. Would-be successors might never have the prestige or pedigree of that seminal superhero fanzine, but they could still offer features of similar quality.

One of the first to try to fill the gap was Robert Schoenfeld, a prominent member of St. Louis fandom. Bob had made many contacts when he took over the reins of Jerry Bails's *The Comic Reader* (under the alternate title *On the Drawing Board*) and was able to put together three excellent issues of a gen-zine called *Gosh Wow!,* which presented work by hot new artists Vaughn Bodé and George Metzger, among others. Another was Martin Greim, whose *Comic Crusader* improved by leaps and bounds in the early 1970s until it, too, approached *AE* in quality.

Once again, I was ready for a change. Having spent the last couple of years producing and publishing *The Assembled Man,* I was ready for something different—and something that would *sell.* Photo-offset printing couldn't be financed on paid circulations of one or two hundred copies. Next to ad-zines like *RBCC* and a new upstart called *The Buyer's Guide to Comic Fandom,* fanmags providing informative articles sold the most copies.

The new *Sense of Wonder* would tilt more toward well-written articles and less toward amateur comic strips, with accompanying artwork by top-name fans and pros. The change was announced in the final pages of #10. In an editorial titled "Transition," I wrote, "Our emphasis, which has always been on original comic strips, will shift to include a series of articles on aspects of the graphic story." By this time, I was a confirmed acolyte of Richard Kyle, who espoused the serious potential of the graphic story medium, and I wanted to do my part to spread the word.

The major article in *Sense of Wonder* #11 would be nothing less than an attempt to discuss the entirety of Will Eisner's illustrious career as a comics creator. It would be not merely a look at *The Spirit* but also at Eisner's early, lesser-known work, as well as the characters he created or cocreated in partnership with Busy Arnold for Quality Comics and the material he produced for the U.S. military in the 1950s. Eisner was my idol and, along with Ditko, my primary artistic influence, and I wanted to celebrate his contributions as fully as possible.

Since I had obtained my Spirit sections from Raymond Miller, it was only natural that I would ask him to write the article. Raymond responded that he was already working on such a piece, which I was welcome to publish. This was a great stroke of luck on my part. Then he told me that he was writing it in conjunction with his friend Tom Fisher.

Ulp!

This was the same Tom Fisher who had written "Heisenberg Alley" and had been infuriated by my editing job. Would he be willing to take another chance on me? I promised Raymond that I would do no more than correct spelling and grammar in the article, if necessary. Armed with that assurance, Miller obtained Fisher's okay. I would have my article. They even agreed to use the title I suggested: "Eisner: A Man and His Work."

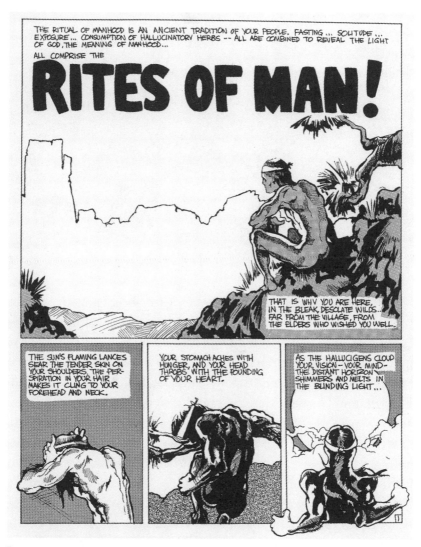

I wrote a script titled "Rites of Man!" and convinced Bob Sanborn to do the artwork, which he agreed to do as long as I did the layouts. He'd never done a comic strip before (nor has he since). From *Sense of Wonder* #11.

Yours truly holding a copy of *Sense of Wonder* #11, hot off the presses.

While this substantial piece was being finished, I pulled together the rest of the issue. The other major text piece would be a discussion column in which fandom's leading lights responded to the question, "What direction would you like to see the graphic story take?" I elicited commentary by Guy H. Lillian, Jan S. Strnad, Fred Patten, Gordon Matthews, and others. The issue would also contain a couple of short stories that I already had on hand. The first was "Captain America Bunny" by Alan Hanley, a funny-animal version of the classic Marvel hero. Second was "Rites of Man!," a short moralistic piece inspired by Harvey Kurtzman's *Frontline Combat* war comic of the early 1950s. It was a collaboration between Bob Sanborn and me which showed off Bob's excellent artwork. A review of the new Nostalgia Press book *Horror*

Comics of the 1950s, an editorial, and some other miscellaneous items would complete the issue.

I found myself with energy for more fannish activity. Despite carrying a full credit load, I decided to rejoin the ranks of *Capa-alpha.* My new mini-zine was dubbed *The Speakeasy,* named after a campus hangout. In its pages I originated a comics feature that was the best I ever did in fandom. It was inspired by the works of two great comics artists: Jack Kirby and Alex Toth.

Kirby had stunned the comics industry by leaving Marvel Comics in 1970, and now he was setting fandom on its ear with his Fourth World saga (as it came to be known) in *New Gods, Forever People, Jimmy Olsen,* and *Mister Miracle,* published by DC Comics. I couldn't get enough of Kirby's explosive power, cosmic majesty, and unflagging inventiveness.

Toth, who had established his reputation with DC in the late 1940s, was a maverick who tended to steer clear of superhero stories. He had carved out a reputation for unparalleled storytelling and design skills in romance, mystery, television adaptations, and crime comics over the past twenty years. In 1970 his art on the new *Hot Wheels* book from DC caught my attention because of its simple yet effective character designs and its brilliant page and panel layouts. Toth's action shots were forceful, direct, and highly effective. I still think "The Case of the Curious Classic" in *Hot Wheels* #5 (which he both wrote and drew) is a masterpiece of the medium.

I conceived of a hero team of three superpowered brothers who are commanded by an overbearing mother. Thus was born the O'Brian Gang, introduced in a full-page portrait of the group in *The Speakeasy.* When I sent a copy of the *Capa-alpha* zine to my correspondent, Chuck Robinson II, he immediately requested the feature for his ditto fanzine *Comique.* I returned to ditto gratefully, knowing I could produce the strip much more easily that way. The first installment appeared in *Comique* #7 later that year.

From *Comique* #9: in "The O'Brian Gang Freak Out!!!," the villainous Soulslayer put LSD in the water system of the O'Brian mansion, leading to a wild series of events.

I had a blast with the O'Brian Gang. After all that elaborate and painstaking inked work on *The Assembled Man*, drawing the O'Brians on ditto masters was a sheer delight. My character designs had something of the simplicity of Toth's *Hot Wheels* cast, which I found suited my natural drawing style. A new energy seemed to infuse both my story and my art, which I attribute to the influence of the new Kirby comics. Also, a slapstick, sarcastic quality that surfaced in the familial banter made the story especially fun. Everything seemed to fall into place, and I was suddenly producing work at a higher level. Maybe Ronn Foss's advice to relax and enjoy led partly to the free-wheeling quality of the O'Brian Gang.

The initial O'Brian Gang story was merely an introduction to Ma O'Brian and her three sons, Kevin (the not-too-bright big bruiser), P. R. (the long-haired hippie), and Timothy (the bespectacled kid-genius). We meet their nemesis, Soulslayer, and his beautiful assistant, Mavis. All

At the Blue Mountain Rock Festival on the University of Idaho campus. Photo: Anita Hoyle.

this is a teaser for the long second part, an elaborate thirteen-pager titled "The O'Brian Gang Freak-Out!!!" In it, Soulslayer penetrates the security systems of the O'Brian mansion and laces their water supply with LSD. They then must fight for their lives against Soulslayer's minions, even while they are fully in the grip of the powerful hallucinogenic drug.

In addition to school and fanzine activity, Gary Speer and I mounted the second Blue Mountain Rock Festival on the university campus in the spring of 1972. This time we had a raft of volunteers to help, so I was able to relax on the appointed day and enjoy the festivities.

In *Sense of Wonder* #11, I scored a real publishing coup: I was able to feature one of the earliest and best of the Mr. A stories that Steve Ditko was doing at the time.

It happened like this: I had phoned Larry Herndon in Texas to see what he thought of some art samples I had submitted. Was I good enough now for an assignment in the pages of *Star-Studded Comics*? That had long been an ambition of mine.

"Yes, the sample was fine," Larry said. "You're definitely good enough now."

"That's great."

"The only thing is, we're backed up with inventory. We have an awful lot of stuff on file that we want to use before we accept anything else."

"Oh."

"Also, we're thinking of discontinuing *Star-Studded*."

"Then maybe I should—*what did you say?*"

"We're probably only going to publish one more issue," he explained.

I could hardly believe my ears. *SSC* had been around before I'd even gotten involved in fandom. "Why would you stop publishing it?"

Herndon seemed hesitant to explain. "Let's say we've been doing it for a long time, and now we want to do other things."

Panel from the Mr. A story "The Defenders" by Steve Ditko. My final "close encounter" with Ditko went without a hitch—finally! Mr. A ™ and © Steve Ditko.

"Damn. Just when I get good enough to contribute."

Then Larry turned the tables. "Are you going to continue publishing *Sense of Wonder* photo-offset?"

"Yeah, I'm putting together the eleventh issue right now."

He paused, then asked, "How would you like to print a new Mr. A story by Steve Ditko?"

"Would I? Of course. But how?"

"Steve offered it to us, but we don't have an issue coming out soon. He wants it to see print as soon as possible since he did it back in 1969. He asked if we knew anyone else who was publishing a good fanzine where it would fit."

After reeling with surprise for a moment, my heart racing, I reiterated my enthusiasm about putting it in *Sense of Wonder*. Yes, I'd published a couple of full-pagers by the cocreator of Spider-Man, but this was a complete story—a real coup for any fan editor. "Do you have the original art?"

"No, and he won't send it, either. He says he's had a problem with some fanzine editors keeping his originals, so he said to tell him when and where to send the original art when you're submitting the remainder of the issue to the printer, and he'll send it to them directly."

That's why I have Larry Herndon to thank for giving me the opportunity to debut the six-page Mr. A story titled "The Defenders"—that, and Ditko's apparently forgiving nature, since surely he remembered the pink Mr. A cover on *Sense of Wonder* #6 that had upset him.

As a result of having Ditko's name prominently placed in my advertisements, as well as the names of other well-regarded artists—Frank Frazetta, Dave Cockrum, Don Newton, Rocke Mastroserio, and Ronn Foss (all of whom contributed single illustrations)—I received a flood of orders. *Sense of Wonder* #11 was my first publication to sell more than a couple of hundred copies. I printed five hundred, and I sold out within two or three months.

I was quickly learning that connections made all the difference. The old axiom "It's not what you do, but who you know" was proving true for me, although I had only made my contacts as a result of a great deal of hard work. Herndon wouldn't have recommended *Sense of Wonder* as a place for Mr. A if I hadn't gained some sort of credibility in my seven years in fandom. My plan to follow in the footsteps of *Alter Ego* was off to an auspicious start.

14.
THE LIFE YOU SAVE MAY BE YOUR OWN

Many and varied were the letters that flowed into my mailbox at my college apartment that spring. Orders had been directed to my parents' house in Lewiston, since I had a habit of changing residences frequently during my college years. However, my personal correspondence required more expeditious handling, especially since I wanted to produce another issue of *Sense of Wonder* during the summer, and I was busy lining up contributions.

The return addresses on those letters bore the names of fans who were considerably better-known than my usual correspondents, making my eyes bug out when I saw them: John T. Ryan, who was Australia's best-known comic art enthusiast; Don Newton, whose covers on *RBCC* were a precursor to his brilliant art on *Batman* and other comics in later years; Richard Kyle, Roy G. Krenkel, Rich Buckler, and many others.

Then there were the days when I received drawings done especially for me from Will Eisner and C. C. Beck. Those moments were almost dreamlike in their wonderment.

The most eyebrow-raising letter bore the return address of one Frederic Wertham, MD. The German-born psychiatrist, the most reviled figure in the history of comics, had written a notorious indictment of the medium called *Seduction of the Innocent* in 1954. A well-meaning liberal, Dr. Wertham blamed comic books for the phenomenon of juvenile delinquency in the postwar era. He inveighed against the crime and horror comics that were so popular in the early 1950s, going so far as to testify in 1954 as an expert witness before the Kefauver congressional committee on media violence. Not content to stop there, he painted nearly *all* comics, including *Superman* and *Donald Duck*, with the same brush. It was Wertham, with his oh-so-impressive credentials, who gave legitimacy to the pressure groups that brought an end to the great EC comics line of the era, as well as any other comics that couldn't pass by the blue pencil of the sharp-eyed screeners employed by the newly founded Comics Code Authority.

Why was the infamous Frederic Wertham writing to *me*?

Inside the envelope was nothing more sinister than a friendly letter and a check for *Sense of Wonder*. He reminded me that he had ordered a subscription to *SofW* in 1969 when I was on the brink of discontinuing it. (I had forgotten our earlier contact.) He was pleased, he told me, that I had started up publication again.

Wertham's clinical mind had turned toward the subject of comic fandom. He was now reading and analyzing comics fanzines.

As the old EC comics used to say, "*Choke*! Good lord!"

Was Wertham now going to raise alarms about comicdom? To what end? We were a small enough subculture. What kind of public uproar could really be incited, especially when the worst that could be said was that some fanzines portrayed the unveiled female form in all its glory?

When I wrote asking what form his study of fandom would take, his response calmed my concerns.

> I find the whole phenomenon of fanzines to be very interesting indeed. Here are hundreds or perhaps thousands of teenagers and young adults who are working mightily to produce magazines simply as a form of their own creative expression. This seems like a positive, healthy activity that merits study. I'm not sure at present exactly what form my final study will take. I'm working on a paper that will likely be published by a university press.

The doctor enclosed a copy of the paperback edition of *A Sign for Cain,* his most recent book, for my comments.

Wertham was true to his word. His book, *The World of Fanzines,* was published by Southern Illinois University Press in 1973. Much to the surprise of fandom, it offered an entirely positive view of fanzines. Echoing some of the wording of his letter to me, he wrote, "In my analysis, the editing of fanzines is a constructive and healthy exercise of creative drives. Fanzines are a healthy part of society."

Imagine my surprise when he alluded in the book to *Sense of Wonder* in one instance. With regard to the issue of the erratic publishing schedules of fanzines, he wrote, "One can't always know for certain whether a fanzine has stopped for good, either," he wrote. "For example, in 1969 I ordered a subscription to *Sense of Wonder* from its editor Bill Schelly in Idaho. He wrote that he had discontinued its publication. But two years later he started publication again and sent me a copy. I've had a number of similar experiences."

The World of Fanzines—for many years the only book written about the comics and science fiction fanzines—marked the beginning of something of a reassessment of Dr. Wertham's character, if not his actions. In it he emerges not as a self-righteous witch hunter but as a kindly, white-haired clinician who wants nothing more than to see the good in everyone. However, that didn't mean he'd revised his views of comic books themselves. In an interview in 1974, he was quoted as saying, "That comic books are used in remedial reading [is] completely wrong. There have been important scientific studies made. They're *not* good for reading. Yes, comic books have become legitimate and I don't think it's a good sign for the cultural state of the nation."

After *Sense of Wonder* #11 was published, the number of letters and orders I received for the next issue was astounding. The new format met with resounding approval. I was especially proud that "Rites of Man!" received kudos from most respondents. Everyone enjoyed the article on Will Eisner's career. Of course, there were both pro and con opinions of Steve Ditko's controversial Mr. A story, but that was to be expected. This time I didn't hear from Ditko, so I presume he was satisfied with his treatment at my hands—at last.

The most significant response to "Eisner: A Man and His Work" was an offer from John T. Ryan to write a follow-up piece to fill in various gaps left in the article by Raymond Miller and Tom Fisher. His "Eisner & Company" became the main feature of the next issue. In addition, John offered me material on the superb Australian comics artist Stanley Pitt, including an article on his version of Tarzan, called Yarmak. Essentially, John Ryan handed me half of *Sense of Wonder* #12 on a silver platter.

I also heard from Will Eisner. Along with the sketch of the Spirit that he did for me, he readily gave me permission to reprint whatever brief examples of his work I needed for the second part of the overview of his career. It wasn't long afterward that he had a meeting with James Warren that resulted in a new series of magazines reprinting the Spirit stories, as well as an entire book written about his work. This eventually led Eisner to return to the graphic story medium to create non-Spirit stories, with his seminal book *A Contract with God* (1978, Baronet Books), which initiated a whole new phase in his stellar career.

The remainder of *Sense of Wonder* #12 came together quite easily. I was able to adorn the letters page and editorial with spot illustrations by noted fantasy artist Roy G. Krenkel, Richard Buckler, and Bill Black. The final icing on the cake was a beautiful front cover of Yarmak by Don Newton. (This was Don's second attempt; the first had been destroyed when his basement flooded.)

The Spirit.™ and © Will Eisner Studios Inc.

Sense of Wonder #12 (1972) represents the zenith of my fanzine publishing efforts. The front cover features the "Australian Tarzan," Yarmak the Fearless One, as rendered by Don Newton. Newton achieved considerable success as a professional comic book artist, most notably on *Batman* in the early 1980s, before his untimely death. Yarmak ™ and © respective copyright holder.

Having placed advertisements in *RBCC* and *The Buyer's Guide to Comic Fandom* early to raise money for the printing, I was inundated with orders. An unexpected surprise was the number of overseas customers who wanted copies. At least fifty copies would be going to England, Italy, Australia, Japan, and points in between.

I was charging seventy-five cents a copy. The bill for printing and shipping one thousand copies was about $500. As soon as I passed the break-even point, I sent the pasted-up pages off to the printer.

The day the printed fanzines arrived, about a month later, I experienced an incredible high. I opened a carton and pulled out a copy. Though the cover was black and white, it was printed on glossy stock. It shimmered with a silvery glow as I tilted it this way and that. Paging through the issue, it all appeared exactly as I'd hoped.

I had done it!

I had finally—after years of printing problems and other frustrations—produced a magazine I was proud of in every respect.

I had done my *Alter Ego*.

Including the bulk orders I received from Bud Plant and G. B. Love, I had sold eight hundred copies of the thousand-copy print run by the time I got the boxes back from the printer. In a few more weeks, all copies were gone.

Selling one thousand copies was a threshold I had yearned to attain, for in comic fandom it was a benchmark that only the top fanzines achieved.

The response from the fan press was glowing.

In *Graphic Story World*, Richard Kyle wrote, "*Sense of Wonder* 12 is a must for every serious comics fan."

In *RBCC*, James Van Hise enthused, "This is a very well done publication and deserves much more recognition than it receives."

In the venerable *The Comic Reader*, Richard Shanklin said, "*Sense of Wonder* … offers interesting information on untrodden subjects. The information on Stanley Pitt's Gully Foyle is fascinating and enlightening. The back cover by [Joseph] Wehrle deserves to be framed."

My only regret was that I hadn't been able to include even a brief comics story or any major art of my own in the issue. I planned to rectify that in the next one with a special project.

When the pea harvest was over and I had a few weeks to fill before the start of my senior year in college, I embarked on what was to be my best comic strip yet. The O'Brian Gang had been a fun diversion, but I asked myself: "Why are you fiddling around with publishing a lot of other people's work, or working on ditto strips, when you want to break into pro comics?" Prominent fan artists like Mike Kaluta, Alan Weiss, and Bernie Wrightson were getting their work published in DC comics, so it seemed that the closed shop of the 1960s was opening its doors.

I needed to concentrate my effort on improving my sequential art abilities and producing work specifically to build up a portfolio. I had lots of figure-drawing sketches from class and a number of other single illustrations that would fit, but I could see that *The Assembled Man* pages weren't good enough. I needed evidence that I could produce professional-quality comics material. At the same time, I wanted to do something that I could publish in my next issue or in one of the other top fanzines of the day.

This time, I wouldn't make the mistake of trying to do something so long that it would take forever. I would draw a story that was no more than ten or eleven pages. It didn't have to be the usual superhero stuff. Many of the top fanzines were printing comics stories of other types. DC was trying out new artists on their noncostumed hero books like *House of Secrets* and *House of Mystery,* where the ability to draw normal people was required.

I decided to do an adaptation of a short story I had read in a literature class and admired greatly: "The Life You Save May Be Your Own," by acclaimed southern writer Flannery O'Connor. (Her best-known work is probably the novel *Wise Blood,* published in 1952 and made into a movie by John Huston.) I didn't have the rights from the O'Connor estate to do this adaptation, but I blithely went ahead, assuming they would approve my effort when it was done (and if not, it could still be in my portfolio).

"The Life You Save May Be Your Own" is a short story about a one-armed drifter named Tom T. Shiftlet who comes to live with an old lady and her developmentally disabled daughter on a remote southern farm. He becomes a handyman for them for a time, and the old lady hopes he will stay on and help take care of her daughter upon the old lady's demise. The end is suitably sad and moody, with

Shiftlet trying to fulfill that wish but being unable to do so. I found it mysterious and affecting. The story conjured images in my imagination. I felt called to this project and set to work.

My pencil seemed somehow blessed as I laid out the story, broke it down into panels, and began filling in the details. There was a sureness, a confidence, and even an inspired quality to the work that I hadn't achieved before. I was on fire with enthusiasm as I carefully crafted each panel. I finished it shortly before I left Lewiston to begin my senior year, and I carefully tucked it into my portfolio. I would find time to ink it once I registered for my classes and got myself settled.

My new home was one of Moscow's landmarks, a remodeled mansion/apartment house that had been built in 1884. It was located next door to contemporary-style apartments where my brother Steve was living. (By now Steve was out of the army and attending school at the University of Idaho on the G.I. Bill.) The house I moved into had been subdivided into six units, two per floor. I took one on the third floor, which smelled of fresh paint. It had many windows that let in a great deal of sunlight and was quite spacious—a sort of large studio apartment. Over Labor Day weekend, I moved my belongings (including my trusty drawing table and some of my comics) into my new home.

Less than a week later, shortly after registration, I showed off my new place to a buddy, then left with him for a swim in the campus pool. Afterwards, I dropped in on some friends on the walk home. We were sitting in their living room when someone came in and said, "Hey, there's a fire downtown. Come have a look."

My friends went outside. I remember thinking, *I'm not going to move my butt off this couch to gawk at some stupid smoke.*

When they didn't come back inside right away, my resolve crumbled and I got up to take a look myself. It was getting dark. *Yes,* I thought when I joined my friends in a clump outside, *there's definitely a fire downtown.* There were big, black clouds of smoke rising from the north end of town, alarmingly close by.

The Daily Idahonian

BUILDING FOR TOMORROW   IN THE PALOUSE EMPIRE

VOL. 79 NO. 244 · MOSCOW, IDAHO   —Wednesday, September 6, 1972—

Fire Damages Moscow Landmark

SCENE OF FIRE — The Almon Asbury Lieuallen mansion, pictured above in an old photo, was extensively damaged last night by fire. At left below, Betty Hansen disconsolately surveys the havoc in her apartment. The blaze started in the William Schelly apartment, below right. (Philip Feinstein photos)

One of Moscow's landmarks, a remodeled mansion-apartment house at First and Almon, was badly damaged by fire last night.

The blaze, first noticed by a passer-by, was confined to the top, or third floor of this historic building, once the home of Almon Asbury Lieuallen. Lieuallen, the maternal grandfather of Mrs. Robert (Lillian) Otness, of 522 S. Monroe, built the home in 1884. It was remodeled into six apartments in 1917 by Lieuallen's daughter, Mrs. Jay Woodworth, and her husband. It was the town's first modern apartment house, with running water and electric ranges, according to the late Mrs. Woodworth's memoirs.

At the time it was built, the 12-room mansion was the only home in that part of town, standing in the midst of a wheat field. The third story was floored, but not partitioned, and the Lieuallen children and their playmates used the area as a skating rink, said Mrs. Otness.

Last night's fire was fought by 45 Moscow volunteer firemen, using seven pieces of equipment. Apparently the blaze started in a corner of the south apartment rented to William Schelly. As yet, no cause for the blaze has been determined and firemen are still investigating.

Mrs. George Nelson, the present owner, said this morning that she "hasn't given a thought to restoration. . . I don't know if the building is worth it." Insurance adjusters were scheduled to examine the structure this afternoon.

Inhabitants of the apartments, in addition to Schelly, were Betty Hansen, a University of Idaho student and recent delegate to the Democratic National Convention; Mr. and Mrs. Jonathan Turner, Mike Lind, Dwight Sawin, and Mr. and Mrs. James Sampson.

Mrs. Turner, alerted by the passer-by, turned in the fire alarm at 9:30 p.m. Other residents ran upstairs with fire extinguishers, but were unable to douse the blaze. Schelly's apartment was gutted and Miss Hansen's rooms, which she had occupied for only one week, were badly damaged by heat, smoke, and water. The lower four apartments also received smoke and water damage, although the occupants were able to remove most of their personal belongings.

Firemen remained at the scene until about 2 a.m. to make sure that the fire was out.

I frowned. "That's not far from where I live." My friends turned and raised their eyebrows.

"In fact," I continued, something inside me awakening to a dire possibility, "that's coming from *really close* to my place." We were about half a mile away, and it was impossible to see which building was on fire, but the glow from the flames was growing more noticeable since the sun had set and darkness was rapidly falling.

I walked back inside and dialed the Moscow fire department. "Hello, um, can you tell me where that fire is located? What building?"

"Why do you want to know?" the disembodied voice asked.

"Because I live right around there."

"Hold on, I'll check." A few seconds passed, and then he came on and said, "It's at 101 Almon Street."

My heart jumped in my chest. "That's where I live! I have an apartment in that house!"

"What's your name, sir?"

I answered his question and then hung up, in a daze. My friends had straggled in and couldn't help but notice my stunned expression.

"That fire's at my place. I've gotta go."

I took off running, muttering "holy shit, holy shit" to myself the whole way. By the time I got there, in a few minutes, darkness had fallen.

I came around the corner, and there it was: the house where I lived was now burning at full throttle through much of its upper floors. There were numerous fire trucks around, and several water hoses were trained on the building. Neighbors were milling around to watch. I made my way through them, stepping over hoses.

A voice yelled out to me. "Bill! It's you! Thank God!!"

It was my brother Steve. He came up with a bit of a crazed look in his eyes. "We didn't know … we thought you might have been *in there!*"

I shook my head. For a few moments, I didn't know what to say. I stared at the blazing building. The fire had not yet reached the lower floors, but it had clearly decimated the two top-floor apartments, especially mine.

It was only later that I realized that the fire had destroyed not only my clothes and other mundane possessions; it had burned a good portion of my comic book and fanzine collection. And it had immolated just about *all* the artwork I had done in college: my oil paintings, my sketchbooks, my finished drawings.

Worst of all, it had destroyed my portfolio. All the original art to *The Assembled Man,* all the inked pieces I had done for various fanzines—everything was lost, including my completed pencils for "The Life You Save May Be Your Own."

It's difficult to describe the emotional aftermath of that terrible fire. My feelings ran the gamut from disbelief to anger to a kind of giddy happiness that I hadn't lost my life in the blaze.

There was also guilt, for it was clear that the fire had originated in my apartment. This was stated in the newspaper article that appeared the next day in *The Daily Idahonian,* and the pattern of the fire supported the contention. Was I responsible for the fire? Had I left the stove on or a candle burning before I went out? I didn't think so, but the building's wiring had been recently updated, so that probably wasn't the cause.

One image haunted me: flames lapping at my precious artwork and belongings while I was immersed in the waters of the campus pool, blissfully unaware.

The next day I went up to inspect what was left of the apartment. "Maybe there's something I can salvage," I told my brother.

"You won't find anything," Steve said. "Whatever wasn't burned is soaked. There was water damage all through that side of the building."

I had to check it out for myself. "Is it safe to go up there?"

"Yes, but be careful."

It was more than a little strange, climbing the steps of the damaged building. When I got to the third floor, I saw that my apartment's door was gone. I peered inside. The floor was intact, as were the inside walls. Where the outer walls and ceiling had been was now sky.

I gingerly stepped inside. Some of the furniture was at least recognizable. I could find nothing salvageable amid the rubble. It was shocking in a whole new way to see everything familiar to me turned into black, charred debris. My trusty Smith Corona portable still sat on its table, but now it was melted into a blob of metal and plastic. Part of my drawing table had survived, but everything made of paper or canvas had been vaporized by the heat or turned into a soggy mess by the dousing. I found the occasional anomaly, such as some cooking utensils sitting on a surviving portion of the kitchen counter, now coated with black soot undisturbed by the high-powered hoses.

Fortunately, most of my comic book collection escaped the fire because I kept it stored at my parents' house. But what could compensate for the artwork that had been lost? It represented years of work—my whole life up to that point.

What now?

The emotional response—the frustration, the anger, the nausea—came in aftershocks over the ensuing weeks and months. At times it seemed as if I could barely go on; at other times, in my despair, I almost saw the fire as a blessing.

I thought, *Maybe this makes things simpler. Maybe I should forget about my dream to become a comic book artist.* With no portfolio and little time to build up a new one from scratch, it seemed fate had made the decision for me. Thus, I embarked on my senior year in college, glad to be alive—but more lost than ever.

15.

SECRET IDENTITY NO MORE

Growing up as a gay youth, a member of a sexual minority, will probably always be difficult, even though there's much greater acceptance today, and there are support systems to help. Still, bullying continues, as do hate crimes, and the rate of suicide attempts by lesbian, gay, and bisexual youth is four times higher than that of straight youth. (Suicide is the second-leading cause of death among young people ages ten to twenty-four.)

Back in 1964, when I was beginning to recognize my gay feelings, there was no societal acceptance of homosexuality. There was only condemnation. When I looked for information in the public library, I found out that homosexuality was classified as a mental disorder by the American Psychiatric Association. There was no concept of a healthy gay person. This was hard for me to fathom, because I didn't feel ill. I didn't want to hurt anyone or force anyone to have sex with me.

I tried to stop having those feelings, and I probably used my involvement in comic fandom as a way of pushing such thoughts out of my brain as best I could. Instead of pining away or becoming depressed, I wrote articles, drew comic strips, and wrote letters. I read comic books, as many as I could afford, while still putting in enough effort to get good grades in school. I kept busy.

Despite the obstacles, human nature is such that I wanted to find someone I could tell about these feelings. Coming out, the process of revealing one's minority sexual identity, is said to have three stages. First comes knowing your identity and admitting it to yourself; second is telling others, such as family and friends; and third is living openly as a gay person. For me, the first phase, sometimes described as an internal coming-out, was happening within me throughout my teenage years. It was a secret, and it was a struggle, and it was lonely.

In college, while my friends were dating, I spent time going to every movie that came to town and continuing to work on various fanzine projects. Comic fandom kept me company. And those projects, fun as they were, involved real work: hours spent at the drawing board, drawing comics and laying out pages; hours spent at the typewriter. Given how intertwined fandom had become with my life, I suppose it's no surprise that fandom was the avenue I chose when I was finally ready to come out—just a bit.

In the summer of 1972, when I was pasting up the pages for *Sense of Wonder* #12, I continued to write to a couple of diehard correspondents. The topics we discussed included our opinions of new comic books and developments in the comics industry, but the door was open to any sort of topic. Perhaps emboldened by the rise of the gay rights movement after the Stonewall riot of 1969, I took the plunge, cautiously averring that "I might be bisexual or gay." I figured those two correspondents, having known me a long time, would be open-minded and supportive. That's all I was hoping for. My heart raced as I posted those letters.

One of them never wrote me again. That fan chose that moment to end our correspondence, and I could only conclude that my confession was the reason. However, a letter from correspondent Mario Vitale showed up at 2211 Carol Drive in short order. It turned out that he was more than supportive; imagine my shock when I read his words, "I'm also gay." Eureka! I had my first gay friend! I had peeked out the closet door, and it had turned out so much better than I expected. He even had a boyfriend of sorts. No words exist to describe the euphoria that filled me as I read and reread that letter. Naturally, this gave our correspondence a major shot in the arm. Many letters flew between Lewiston and Providence in the coming months.

N

Empowerment fantasies are the heart and soul of the appeal super-heroes have for readers of any sexual orientation. The desire to escape the humdrum world around us motivates all of us to enter into a world where people have powers and abilities "far beyond those of mortal men" and where things can transpire that don't happen in everyday life. Also driving us is the human race's universal need for stories. There are, however, ways in which the appeal of superheroes is different for a homosexual male than for a heterosexual male.

My straight buddy Jeff Gelb likes comics featuring what collec-tors call "good girl art," that is, comics that feature the female form prominently and use sexual titillation to at least partly generate sales. For gay comics fans, virtually all superhero comics feature "good guy art." Obviously straight guys notice the prominence of the male phy-sique in comics; they just don't experience it as anything sexual. For gay comic book readers, superhero comics had always presented that extra *frisson* of the male body drawn as if covered but delineated in ways to reveal the hero's every rippling muscle.

Beyond the semierotic male imagery, it's not much of a stretch to point out how the perennial superhero trope of the secret identity could be meaningful in a different way for the gay reader. Should he tell his friends his secret? What if, in the case of Peter Parker's frail Aunt May, it would be too much of a shock? His enemies might use that knowledge to destroy him or his loved ones.

Then there's the wearing of a colorful costume. I used to fantasize about how cool it would be to wear such a getup, which was beyond the pale in the real world for anyone but a ballet dancer or a circus performer. This wasn't true of me, but I can imagine other gay readers being attracted to the wearing of a superhero costume almost as a form of drag. Wasn't that what "camp" was more or less about? One can imagine the young, hot members of the Legion of Super-Heroes voguing at a meeting in the Legion Clubhouse, each one playfully displaying his or her outfit before the others.

I do wonder what straight readers made of Jimmy Olsen's adven-tures in female impersonation in such stories as "Miss Jimmy Olsen!" (*Superman's Pal Jimmy Olsen* #44, 1960), where Jimmy disguises himself as a woman to get close to a gangster and find out where he's hiding stolen gems. I can only imagine what a boy experiencing what is now called "gender dysphoria" felt while reading "Claire Kent, Alias Super-Sister!" (*Superboy* #78, 1960), a story where Superboy dreams an alien has changed him into a girl. That tale is overdue for reprinting.

My next step in coming out—a bolder step, because it involved coming face to face with others—occurred some weeks after my apartment fire. I'd found a room in a house full of students on Almon Street, a few blocks from campus, and I'd pulled together the items necessary for school: new clothes, an electric typewriter, some bed linens, and a few replacement textbooks. A small check from an insurance company for my lost property helped. I continued my senior year with no major interruption.

While reading *The Argonaut,* the student newspaper, I found an interesting notice among a schedule of upcoming events at Washington State University, eight miles across the state line in Pullman, Washington. WSU had more than twice as many students as the U of I and a more diverse group of student organizations. My eyes widened as I read about an upcoming meeting of something called the Gay

Overtly gay themes weren't explored in comic books when I was growing up, but there were stories that flirted with issues of cross-dressing and gender dysphoria, such as "Miss Jimmy Olsen!" from *Superman's Pal Jimmy Olsen* #44 (1960) and "Claire Kent, Alias Super-Sister!" from *Superboy* #78 (1960). Jimmy Olsen, Superboy ™ and © DC Comics.

Student Alliance. In the wake of Stonewall, such organizations had been formed on many university campuses as a way for gay and lesbian students to come together, self-identify, and support each other.

It was a cold, dark December night when I parked a borrowed car on the WSU campus and approached the address given for the GSA meeting. Coming out in a letter was one thing. Preparing to come out to real people, even if they were gay, was different, and that was what it would mean to enter that meeting room: coming out for real. But I was ready, and—on wobbly legs, with heart pounding—I walked into the room and took a seat in a circle of chairs with perhaps a dozen people.

I don't remember the details of the meeting, only some of the people. It probably began with introductions, going around the circle. I'm pretty sure we were told that it wasn't necessary for us to say if we were gay or bisexual, but could if we wanted. It didn't matter. You were there for a meeting of the Gay Student Alliance. The meeting itself was brief, quickly segueing into announcements of upcoming social events. I got an invitation to one of those "some of us are getting together at so-and-so's apartment next Saturday, would you like to come?" gatherings. When I walked away, it was with the knowledge that my "secret identity" was no longer quite as secret. I became an active member of the group. Its Christmas celebration a couple of weeks later was also, in a way, my coming-out party.

Further exploration of gay possibilities was briefly interrupted by the Christmas visit with my family. Still, as I opened gifts with my family and participated in the ritual holiday feast, somehow I felt like a changed person. Only later did I realize upon reflection that I had walked through a door that opened up a new world. Maybe it was sort of like Earth 2 in the DC comics. In this case, it might be Earth Λ, because the Greek letter lambda was adopted as a symbol of the gay rights movement.

$\mathcal{N}$

In the new year, it was time for my mandatory student-teaching assignment. Remember, my folks had required me to get a teaching degree to fall back on. I was informed before the Christmas break of 1973 that I would spend the first half of my last semester in college at Sacajawea Junior High School in Lewiston. For those nine weeks, I would live at Carol Drive with my parents.

Student teaching was a nightmare. I hated it. I was only twenty-one years old, and yet I was expected to be an authority figure for classes of thirty students? I hated having to prepare lesson plans, and I was intensely uncomfortable being a focus of attention at the front of the room. I barely got through it, and when I returned to Moscow to complete the term, I knew one thing: I would never, ever teach secondary school. As I look back, I have to wonder why I disliked it so much. Was I still suffering some sort of post-fire emotional trauma? Or was it simply that I had never intended to teach? Perhaps part of the problem was that I was tired of college. Graduation would soon be upon me. I was ready to get on with my life.

What about my long-held dream of working in the comics industry? Was that really out of my reach?

An announcement grabbed my attention in the comic book *Shazam* #4 (July 1973), the issue on sale in April. In a column titled "Behind the Scenes at the DC Comic World," a new program was announced: "The Junior Bullpen Project." The text read, in part:

> DC is starting a program under which promising talents can enter the business as apprentices. We will be offering twelve such jobs to young people this summer. All twelve will work in our new offices ... and meanwhile will have their skills polished by some of the most accomplished people in the business. These will be paying jobs: the first rung on the ladder of comic success. You will be guaranteed a basic wage while you learn. Six writing trainees and six artistic trainees will be chosen.

> The details: The jobs are only open to people who would be able to live in the New York Metropolitan Area. Many of the lucky people will be chosen at the annual Comic Art

Convention here in New York City, when DC will examine portfolios and scripts. The convention will be held from July 4th to 8th.

The column, which ran in many DC comics that same month, went on to indicate that the people who would be evaluating the art portfolios were looking for any and all renditions of the human form, whether they be sketches or finished comics pages. Drawings could be in pencil or inked.

J. Michael Kaluta illustrated this advertisement for the 1973 New York Comic Art Convention, done in the 1930s style similar to that of the new *Shadow* comic book he was drawing for DC.

How could the Junior Bullpen Project, as it was called, not fail to grip my imagination? I was suddenly inspired again. I would do it. I would create a brand-new portfolio. I would go to that convention, and I would enter, and by God I would be one of the six artists chosen.

The question of my future would be settled. I would have my dream after all. Happily, my parents didn't object. I think they realized that it was a way to get this dream out of my system, and besides, I had enough money—possibly because my grandparents had given me a check for college graduation a little early—for the hotel (single rooms cost $17 a night). My father could work his magic with the Northern Pacific and wangle me a round-trip coach seat for a fraction of full price.

I wrote to Mario Vitale and urged him to go to the convention so we could meet. Unfortunately, he couldn't because he had to work to make money for college, and he couldn't afford to take time off or spend any of that precious lucre on a trip to New York City. We did, however, hatch a plan for me to visit him after the con. Before riding the rails home, I would take a bus jaunt to Providence and visit him for a few days.

College graduation came off without a hitch. It was anticlimactic to me, but not to my parents, who carefully clipped out the article in the *Lewiston Tribune* that named me, among others, as a member of the Phi Kappa Phi honorary fraternity for graduating with a high grade-point average (3.79), and noted that I'd been selected for an Outstanding Senior award. I was more relieved than anything else. My mind was elsewhere. I had a portfolio to prepare.

16.

THE PULSING HEART OF FANDOM

With every *click-clack* of its iron wheels on metal tracks and every high-pitched shriek from its whistle, the powerful diesel train brought me closer to my destination: New York City.

Odd, I thought, how much trains were intertwined with my love of comics. There was the westward trip when, at eight years old, I had discovered the adventures of the Man of Steel. On a similar cross-country train trip in 1963, I'd taken along a stash of my own comics, the better to enjoy even more time on the trip with comic book characters who had become old friends. Now I was hurtling eastward on another train to attend my first major comics convention and break into the comics field as an artist.

I wasn't unrealistic about my chances to be selected for DC's Junior Bullpen Project. I had just spent a month preparing several sample pages of comic book art, and the work had not come easily. I still had much to learn about human anatomy, and my inking was uncertain. I had done a Batman page, a Superman page, a full-page illustration of Star Rangers (from *Sense of Wonder*), and a couple of pages of pencil drawings without inks. The Batman page had turned out the best.

Over the years I had been lucky enough to be able to study pages of professional art, and I knew how good they could look. Professional pages are assured, with no wasted effort and no unnecessary noodling. Professional comics art avoided techniques that didn't reproduce well on newsprint, like cross-hatching. The inking was a study in confidence.

One of the better pages from my New York portfolio. I didn't claim it was of professional quality, but did feel it showed that I had potential. According to DC's announcement, they were looking for apprentices. Batman, Robin ™ and © DC Comics.

Though my sample pages were good by fanzine standards, I knew they weren't professional caliber. I reasoned that the judges for the DC initiative, which was designed for "apprentices," according to the announcement, wouldn't expect candidates to present a totally slick product. How would that make sense? They would be looking for *potential.* I had plenty of that. I also had the optimism and naiveté of a twenty-one-year-old.

On this railroad journey, I was not afforded the luxury of a private compartment, but it didn't matter. At that age, one can endure personal discomfort with relative equanimity. During the long hours of passing through wheat fields and other vistas, I alternately read a book (*At the Mountains of Madness* by H. P. Lovecraft), conversed with another passenger, or dozed. When the train slowed upon entering an urban core, I occupied myself by watching the passing tableaux through the giant windows.

Minneapolis-St. Paul, Chicago, and Pittsburgh are all cities with visual appeal if viewed when flying in from above or from another advantageous prospect. Trains, however, are a mode of transportation intended less for passengers than for bulk freight, so they generally move through the less attractive industrial parts of a city. Rather than basking in views of the cities' polished edifices, I had ample opportunity to study each one's underbelly. The sight wasn't often pretty, but it was interesting in a different way.

The industrial areas of town—warehouses, loading docks, train yards—are places of unadorned reality. Especially in the older eastern cities, they are simply the arenas of basic economic function. As we slowly rolled through, I watched the working-class people toiling away at their jobs, and I wondered: how is it that I am on this train, college educated, and with a world of opportunity before me, while they are (so I imagined) stuck in a bleak, dead-end existence?

The luck of the draw, I knew, accounts for much that we end up with in life. Individual focus and hard work count for a lot too, but a goal can either be within reach or so far beyond it that only the most exceptional individual can leap across that chasm. I wondered whether the luck of the draw would favor me in my current endeavor.

I had done my part to the best of my ability. Would fate lead me into work in the comics industry? As the train barreled through Pennsylvania, my anticipation grew. The answer to that momentous question was coming closer.

Not that I wouldn't have had butterflies in my stomach at the mere prospect of attending America's largest comics convention. I would soon meet people whom I had previously only known on the printed page or through correspondence.

The guests of honor of the 1973 New York Comic Art Convention included Bob Kane (cocreator of Batman) and C. C. Beck (principal artist on the classic Captain Marvel comic books of the 1940s and 1950s). The convention ads proclaimed that William M. Gaines (publisher of *Mad* magazine), Jim Steranko (innovative writer-artist of *Nick Fury, Agent of S.H.I.E.L.D.*), Vaughn Bodé, Russ Heath, Burne Hogarth, Jeff Jones, James Warren, and many other industry legends and top talents would be there. I knew from other sources that many of the most active fans and dealers would be in attendance. I was especially eager to meet Alan Hanley, Bud Plant, Tom Fagan, Mark Gruenwald, Bill Thailing, and of course Phil Seuling, the man who had organized the con.

I got off the train at Pennsylvania Station. Stepping out onto the sidewalk, I was hustled into a yellow cab by an aggressive fellow who then slid behind the wheel. I gawked out the cab window as the driver threaded our way to the centrally located Commodore Hotel in Manhattan. The energy of New York seemed to press in on me.

The Commodore was a comfortable, older hotel that was apparently chosen because it wasn't too expensive for comics fans—once they got their convention rate, that is. I ventured inside, lugging a large suitcase and my portfolio. Glancing around the lobby, I expected to see people wearing superhero t-shirts, maybe someone dressed in costume, or possibly Stan Lee. After all, the convention had officially started the night before, though I was advised that little would be going on other than registration and an early look into the dealers' room, where all the collectable items were on sale. However, now that the con was really underway, there still weren't any visible signs of comics fans as I headed toward the registration desk.

The room wasn't much. I didn't care. I pulled up a window and leaned out, imagining I was Joe Buck in *Midnight Cowboy*. I could almost hear Harry Nilsson singing "Everybody's Talking" in the background.

I had made it!

The door opened. A guy about my age, with longish brown hair like my own, entered. It was Clay, my roommate, a fan whom I'd met through the mail. We quickly became acquainted in person. Although Clay had attended major cons before, this was his first sojourn to New York City. He wasn't there for the DC portfolio review; like most fans, he had come to meet the professional artists and writers, attend the panel discussions, and look for old comics at reasonable prices.

"Let's have a look at your stuff," Clay said.

I pulled some pages from my portfolio and laid them on the bed. He nodded approvingly at what he saw. "You're good."

"Good enough?"

He shrugged and smiled. "Yeah, depending on the competition."

On this note, we headed downstairs. The portfolio review wasn't until tomorrow morning. However, the convention had opened its doors at 10 a.m., and time was a-wasting.

I was pleased to discover that the volunteers handling registration were polite and efficient. We paid the entrance fee ($2.50 a day) and were handed a thick, professionally produced program, as well as a mimeographed list of the daily events. Soon Clay and I were entering the Commodore's Grand Ballroom, which served as the main location for the dealer tables.

My roommate quickly disappeared into the crowd, but I lingered a moment near the entrance, taking it all in. For a comics fan who endures tolerance at best from his friends and family, nothing is so affirming as entering a huge room full of true-blue, dyed-in-the-wool lovers of comic books. I surveyed the scene and thought, *These are my people.*

Everywhere I looked were displays of four-color wonders, from as recently as the previous month to as long ago as the 1930s. Some of the booths were backed by walls displaying row after row of awesome treasures. Also for sale were science fiction movie posters, prints of sword-and-sorcery scenes painted by Frank Frazetta, a huge assortment of promotional pins and buttons from cereal boxes of the 1940s, superhero games and record albums, Star Trek items, pulp magazines, tapes of old radio shows—an almost endless selection of fantasy-related goods.

I began to see some familiar faces. William M. Gaines was unmistakable with his shoulder-length gray hair, wide girth, and black-framed glasses. I also recognized a tall, handsome man with graying hair making his way through the crowd: famed Green Lantern artist Gil Kane.

The 1973 New York Comic Art Convention grand ballroom. Photo by Howard Siegel.

Here I was, after all my years of writing letters and publishing fanzines yet knowing only a handful of comics fans in person, finally stepping into the pulsing heart of fandom. With a pang of regret that I had only a couple of hundred dollars to spend, I plunged into the ballroom like I was diving into a familiar swimming pool.

Moving through that room was like traveling through an amusement park ride—one never knew who or what one would find at the next booth, coming around the next corner, or making his way through the next crowd of fans. In this way I got to meet Jim Steranko, who was miffed when I asked him to sign not the cover but the inside splash page of a copy of *Nick Fury, Agent of S.H.I.E.L.D. #2.*

I couldn't have been prouder when I discovered copies of *Sense of Wonder* #12 staring back at me from one of a group of tables overseen by Bud Plant, who greeted me with warmth. Yes, I fit right in.

Bud Plant.

At one point, I passed by a large fellow with slicked-back hair and a beer belly. "Hey, how are ya?" he asked cheerfully. It was none other than Phil Seuling himself. "Are ya having a good time?" he asked. I nodded enthusiastically and was about to introduce myself when he was hailed by someone else and turned to speak. I never did get to talk personally with Phil. Every time I ran into him at the con he was rushing madly about, dealing with one emergency or another.

The professional guests of the convention were anything but aloof. I encountered James Warren, publisher of a group of popular black-and-white magazines including *Famous Monsters of Filmland, Creepy,* and *Eerie,* who stopped to chat. When I mentioned that I was an artist looking for work in comics, he gave me his card.

"Call my editor at this number. His name is Bill DuBay. We're looking for some help."

Left: Ken Barr's design for the official convention logo. Below: Mark Gruenwald was one of many fans whom I met at this convention. A few years later he would become a successful writer and editor for Marvel Comics. Photo by David Lofvers.

"I know Bill DuBay."

"You do?"

"Well, not personally. He contributed to my fanzine a few years ago."

Warren nodded. "Give him a call. Maybe you're what we need. We need help in the production department."

I didn't know exactly what a production department was, but I thanked him and immediately made my way out of the hall and to a pay phone in the lobby, where I set up that appointment through DuBay's secretary.

One slight difficulty was finding people I knew. The name tags at the con were too small to read from a distance, and I had little idea what Mark Gruenwald or Tony Isabella looked like. Eventually I resorted to asking Bud Plant to point out some folks to me. Then I approached them and introduced myself.

The impact of Bob Overstreet's *Comic Book Price Guide* was obvious. (By this time, a second, expanded edition had appeared.) As I compared prices for old comics at various dealers' tables, I found a remarkable consistency among prices for items in similar condition. There were few real bargains to be found, and recent back issues were routinely priced at seventy-five cents to a dollar, in an era when new comics cost twenty cents.

After a couple of hours of the convention, my stomach told me it was time for a break. I made my way out onto the sidewalk and looked for a place to grab a bite. Again I felt overwhelmed by the immensity and the energy of New York. I wasn't some Idaho hick, either; I'd been in the urban center of Pittsburgh many times. Still, that didn't prepare me for the impact of downtown Manhattan. For one thing, I hadn't a clue how the streets were arranged or how to find my way around.

Conveniently, a pizza-by-the-slice place was located a block or so from the hotel; nothing fancy, which was exactly what I wanted. While eating a piece of genuine New York pizza, I sat in the window on a stool and watching the teeming masses pass by. I knew full well that working in DC's Junior Bullpen meant I would have to move to

New York. For the first time I thought to myself: *What am I going to do if they actually pick me?*

That evening I palled around with some of the young fans who were dipping their toes into the pool of professional work in comics: Tony Isabella, Carl Gafford, Anthony Tollin. My mind was elsewhere.

Friday morning, I was rested, breakfasted, and in line for the DC portfolio review as soon as anyone would say where the line should form. It wasn't long before at least a hundred people were in line. While waiting, some of us showed each other our work. Mine garnered its fair share of compliments, and I took solace from the inferior work that some of my competitors displayed.

Someone official announced that the location of the review had been changed at the last minute. We should line up in the mezzanine lobby, one floor up. The ensuing chaos was like a scene out of a Keystone Cops movie. In a herd, we trampled up the stairs, racing each other to be in the front of the line like a bunch of grade-school kids. When the new line had formed, I found myself with only two people in front of me. We waited impatiently at least half an hour longer before the DC people arrived.

A door flew open. A stocky, middle-aged man with white hair entered. Noticing the size of the line, he gave a quick laugh, then took his place on a chair. Several people in the line whispered, "That's Vince Colletta."

Colletta was a long-time inker and was acting as an art director for DC comics at this time. We had found out at the convention that he was the person who would be reviewing our portfolios.

Moments after Colletta appeared, a thin gentleman with a bald head and glasses arrived. This was Julius Schwartz. At the time it seemed logical that he was there, since he might be looking for talent he could put to work in his editorial stable of comics.

Each person in turn took a chair next to Colletta and was permitted to display various items from his or her portfolio. Being third in line, I didn't have long to wait.

Official program book for the 1973 New York Comic Art Convention, with cover art featuring Broom-Hilda by Russell Myers. Broom-Hilda ™ and © Tribune Media Services.

Bob Kane was a guest of honor at the convention, and he contributed this drawing to the program book. Batman ™ and © DC Comics.

I nervously shook hands with Colletta.

"Hi," I said. "I'm Bill Schelly."

"What have you got to show me, Bill?"

"I have a few comic book pages here that I worked up." I pulled them out of my portfolio. The first one was a page that I had done in pencil only (no inks).

Colletta said, "We don't do artwork that size anymore."

"I know that, but I didn't think it mattered for this."

"Well, you want your work to look as professional as possible."

"Okay, I can see that."

"You shouldn't darken in the areas for the blacks in pencil," he continued. "It takes too much time."

I knew that too, but I had thought the pencils would look better if I did so.

Schwartz leaned over, and commented, "The action doesn't flow real good."

"Yeah," Colletta concurred.

Searching for a compliment, I asked what he thought of the best panel on the page. "It's okay," Vince said. "But we're not looking for impressive pictures. We're looking for good storytelling."

I went directly to my big guns and pulled my Batman page to the front.

"Hm," Colletta said, nodding. "Your anatomy is weak."

"What's that?" Julie said, leaning over and pointing to a portion of the page.

"This?" It seemed he was referring to some white paint I'd used to differentiate between two black areas.

"Yeah," he said. "What's that, black on black? We don't do that."

My heart was sinking. When Colletta said, "What else you got?" I showed him some figure drawings I'd done in school. They were among my best, and they were the only ones that escaped the fire because I'd left them in Lewiston.

"Not bad. We're not looking for this kind of stuff, though. I don't mean to discourage you. You've got talent, but that's not enough. I'm no great talent, but the main thing is, I get the work done on time, and it's professional. Am I right, Julie?"

"Yeah," Julie said.

"Keep on working on it, kid," Colletta said, dismissing me.

That was it. In five minutes, perhaps less, the hopes and dreams of a lifetime were dashed. In a daze, I put my artwork back into my portfolio. It had all happened so fast. I almost staggered out of the area. How could this have gone so terribly wrong?

I found I was shaking, and had to sit down on a bench in the outer mezzanine.

Hardly a positive word had been uttered about my samples. Yet I knew that, despite weaknesses, my work showed a basic grasp of comic art techniques.

There was only one answer: DC Comics—or at least Vince Colletta—wasn't looking for young artists with obvious potential. They were looking for someone who was already producing work of professional quality, someone who would be presumably available at bargain rates.

Then, too, it seemed that both Colletta and Schwartz focused mainly on the most superficial elements of my presentation: the size of the page or how I indicated the areas of solid black. It felt like they were testing applicants to see if they knew the secret handshake.

Upon reflection, I decided it was probably a bad strategy to be so close to the head of the line. It would have been far wiser to let Colletta see the large amount of wretched work that he would undoubtedly encounter so that when I appeared, my work's obvious merits would stand out in stark relief. Plus, he wasn't likely to pick someone at the front of the line. What if there were a dozen prodigies behind me? Being in the front was a disadvantage in more ways than one.

I wasn't angry because I thought my work was perfect. I couldn't argue with Colletta's comments about weak delineation of anatomy. I knew I had to be able to accept constructive criticism. I was upset because I knew I was qualified to fill an apprentice position, which was what they said they were looking for in their announcement. I had been given short shrift, and it hurt.

Swallowing my disappointment, I told myself that I at least had a meeting with Warren Publishing about a possible job. Maybe that would be the silver lining in my cloud.

Warren Publishing was located in a typical older office building in New York. When I was ushered into DuBay's space, he was seated behind a desk and wearing a distracted expression. By way of introduction, I mentioned that he had contributed to a fanzine of mine several years before. He seemed to barely remember being a part of fandom, as if it had been in the distant past.

"We're looking for someone to paste up advertisements and such for our magazines. What have you got to show me that you've done?"

I pulled out a copy of *Sense of Wonder* #12 and handed it to him.

DuBay paged through it till he noticed something. "What happened here?"

"What?" I asked, leaning forward.

"Here. See where the typed lines are skewed?"

"Um, I think I was having trouble with the typewriter."

He shook his head and tossed the fanzine back to me. "Sorry. Everything in our magazines has to look completely professional."

I cleared my throat. "Don't you think the fact that I did this magazine at home in my bedroom says something about my abilities?"

His eyebrows shot up. "I suppose so. You probably wouldn't want to do the kind of work we have, anyway. We can't pay much, maybe $100 a week."

"Well, you're right. That's not much."

DuBay stood up and reached to shake my hand. "So, thanks for coming by." The interview took scarcely longer than the brush-off I'd been given by DC.

17.

THE FAN SITTING TWO ROWS BACK

My ebullient mood had been stomped on. I felt like Bambi to their Godzilla. Only gradually and in small increments was I able to get out of my funk enough to enjoy the rest of the convention.

By chance I ran into Alan Hanley, one of fandom's most talented cartoonists, who had contributed to *Sense of Wonder.* He was sitting at a table in the registration area, working on a sketch. I was surprised and pleased to learn that Charlton Comics had shown some interest in his work. He was at the con trying to drum up assignments from some of the other publishers, but he was looking rather dour—not what I expected from the writer-artist of the jovial Captain America Bunny.

Clay introduced me to a number of his acquaintances at the event, including the lovely Heidi Saha, who (although a mere teenager) was already dressing as Vampirella, with James Warren's blessing. Heidi was one of the first "spokesmodels" to attend a comics convention at the behest of a publisher to draw attention to his products.

At one point I found myself in the elevator alone with Vaughn Bodé, who was at the con to do a slide show about his Cheech Wizard character. I was about to say hello, and perhaps comment on the comely shade of fingernail polish he was wearing, when the elevator stopped and Gil Kane entered. Kane—who had been the main cover artist of Marvel Comics for the past couple of years and had penciled Spider-Man's adventures for a time—was one of the most highly respected professionals in the business. I screwed up my courage and introduced myself to him, and I said I was looking for work. Since I was (for some reason) carrying my portfolio, he asked if he might take a look at my samples after we got off the elevator.

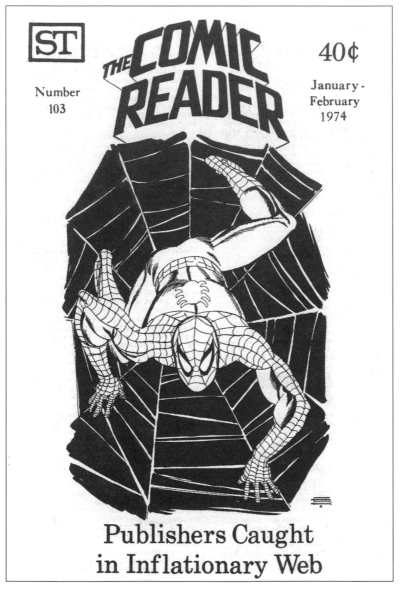

Gil Kane's cover of the news fanzine *The Comic Reader* #103. ™ and © Marvel Characters Inc.

Kane didn't say much when he quickly examined a couple of my pieces; he merely nodded and said, "If you're interested in working with me, I could probably use you."

"You can?"

He glanced at his watch. "I don't have more time to look through your portfolio right now, m'boy. My studio is in Connecticut. Can you bring it up there? That's where you'd have to work."

"Well, er ... yes, I guess so."

"You're from out of town?"

"I'm from the Pacific Northwest."

"Oh. Well, here's my card. If you want to come up, give me a call. We'll set something up." With a quick handshake, Kane strode away, leaving me wondering what to do about his semi-offer. Regardless, it raised my spirits somewhat.

The last event I remember attending at the convention was devoted to DC's revival of the original Captain Marvel from the Golden Age of comics. DC had recently launched the new series under the title *Shazam!* There were probably a number of people on the panel, such as editor Julius Schwartz or writer Denny O'Neill, but the only one I remember was C. C. Beck.

Left: In *Shazam!* #1 (1973), the original Captain Marvel returned to DC Comics, with art by his cooriginator, C. C. Beck. Right: Beck did this personalized sketch for me a year before the 1973 con, where he was a guest of honor. Captain Marvel ™ and © DC Comics.

Charles Clarence Beck was a legend in comics by 1973. He had been the main artistic force to define the look of Captain Marvel in the 1940s, when that character actually outsold Superman for some time. Beck had left comics after Captain Marvel (and his entire brood of related characters) was relegated to publishing limbo in 1953, and he'd been working in the commercial art field for the past twenty years. He had only returned to comics because of the DC revival. To their credit, they engaged him to do the art for *Shazam!*.

The rumor mill had it that Beck was feuding with Julie Schwartz over the quality of the scripts. He had apparently been chastised for making changes to some of them and by now was drawing them exactly as written. The results were just plain bad. The DC writers hadn't caught the spirit of the Big Red Cheese.

During a question-and-answer session, someone asked Beck, "What do you think of the scripts you're getting for Captain Marvel?"

There was a hush in the room.

Beck hesitated, looking owlishly around the room through his thick glasses, then answered, "Let me turn it around. What do you *fans* think of the scripts?"

The applause was half-hearted at best.

"That's very interesting," Beck said, a wry smile creasing his face. Nothing more needed to be said. It wasn't long before the man's dissatisfaction rose to the point where he stopped drawing Captain Marvel. It wasn't, we found out, because he was tired of the character—not at all—but he wouldn't be a party to a travesty.

Once the panel discussion was over and most of the audience had filtered out of the room, I sat in my seat reflecting on the fact that even the great C. C. Beck had been miserable working in contemporary professional comics. It was beginning to dawn on me that the companies that had produced the comics I'd loved as a boy, and that always seemed like such congenial venues in their ads and letter columns, might not be exactly idyllic places to make a living.

At that moment, a fan who was sitting two rows behind me during the panel came forward and introduced himself as Howard Siegel, a name I instantly recognized. Howard's long-time "Comic

Collector's Comments" column in *RBCC* had been one of the best parts of that publication for years. Howard was a knowledgeable fellow when it came to the comics industry. He took the seat next to me, and we began sharing our assessments of the convention. I was familiar with his column, and Siegel was aware of *Sense of Wonder* and my writing and art. Soon I poured out my tale of woe.

Siegel heard me out. When I was done, he said, "Count yourself lucky, Bill."

"Huh?"

"I mean, do you think Beck sounded happy about working in comics these days? It's no picnic."

I said, "That may be, but I've always wanted to draw them. It's been my lifelong dream."

"Then stick to fandom. It's a better place, believe me."

"What do you mean?"

"Look," Siegel said. "I've met a lot of comic book artists, and few of them like what they're doing. It's repetitious. You draw the same things over and over and over again. There's no time to do a really good job because you've got to get it done by a deadline. There are no benefits, the pay is low, you have to buy your own supplies, and you get no respect from the publishers. Why should they care whether you're happy or not? There's always another kid itching to break in who will happily fill your place if you make waves."

I said, "Don't tell me Jack Kirby doesn't make decent money." After all, Kirby had cocreated most of the Marvel Universe.

"He does, for comics. But Kirby's at the top of the game, and what he gets is still nothing great. It's a tough racket, and most guys ache to get out of it by the time they're

G. B. Love, publisher of *RBCC*, with Howard Siegel, "the fan sitting two rows back." Photo courtesy of Howard Siegel.

in their forties. Their eyes aren't as good. Their hand control gets shaky. They go into commercial art if they can. Talk to anyone who leaves comics for commercial art. None of them regret it."

Siegel continued, "Bill, I've seen your work. You're a reasonably talented guy. So why get mixed up with comics at all? Get a job in commercial art or some related field. If you want to do comics, do them on the side and publish them in fanzines. Take it from me, you'll be a lot better off."

"But I've always wanted to be a professional."

"There's no disgrace in being a dedicated amateur. H. P. Lovecraft exalted the idealistic amateur who didn't have to make commercial compromises. Most of his writing was for fanzines."

I persisted. "Gil Kane saw my stuff and offered me work if I could go up to his studio in Connecticut."

"Forget it. That's bullshit."

"What do you mean? It sounded like a bona fide offer."

"I'm not saying it wasn't. He might very well put you to work. But is that what you want to do? Learn to draw so your work can pass for Gil's? I'm not putting him down, but I don't see why you would want to waste your time ghosting for him."

"I might learn a lot."

"Where are you from? Idaho, right?"

"I grew up in Pittsburgh, but I live in Idaho now."

"My advice is, if you're looking for work, go to Seattle or another city around your part of the country and get into commercial art. Keep comics as something you do for fun on the side. You'll be much happier, and it will be something you can enjoy for the rest of your life."

※

When the convention was over, I boarded a bus for Providence, Rhode Island. I still had one more exciting adventure ahead of me: a visit with my correspondent Mario Vitale. But the scenery on the trip was just a blur. I was lost in my reflections on the events of the prior three days.

Howard Siegel's words echoed in my brain. What he said wasn't what I wanted to hear, but much of it rang true. Everything I had experienced in New York City confirmed it. Even if he had overstated the case—for there were surely people working in comics who thrived on it—I now understood that the comics industry had a pronounced downside. I didn't want to become bitter, negative, or cynical about comics. I began to realize that it would be possible to lose my sense of wonder by making comics my profession.

A job in DC's Junior Bullpen wouldn't have paid much, probably the same as the $100 a week for that Warren job. I was at the bottom of the ladder, and no one—including Gil Kane—was going to pay me more than a pittance. Even if I could have found a shared living arrangement with other young hopefuls, I would have been living on a shoestring budget three thousand miles from my family. It took a trip to the Big Apple for me to figure all this out. Now it was clear that I had to find a new direction to look for employment. Teaching, I already knew, wasn't for me. Well, there was time to figure it out. Perhaps I would move to Seattle and look for work in an art-related field, such as the commercial art arena suggested by Siegel. Or I could look for something that seemed more attractive, given my abilities; maybe a job in publishing.

My mood lightened. I reflected on how much comic fandom had done for me. It had given me practical lessons in writing and editing, it had allowed me to explore my creative talents, and it had provided a showcase for my work that reached across the country and around the world. I had learned much about the process of collaborating on creative works with others, and I had developed a set of personal ethics in the process. Many aspects of running a small business had come into play in my fanzine publishing efforts, including leading others in a shared endeavor.

On a deeper level, my involvement in comics had helped meet a need inside me, a need to find somewhere to belong, to be a part of something larger. It had given me a purpose and the means to actualize who I was. Along the way, my life had been touched by quite a few people who'd made a marked difference in my life: Dick

Trageser, who had typed up my first stories and contributed to most of my fanzines; Don Thompson, who challenged me to always strive to improve myself; Ronn Foss, who taught me that nothing is worth working for if one isn't enjoying process of getting there; and Howard Siegel, who helped me understand the benefit of keeping comics as a hobby rather than a job. And there had been many more whom fandom had brought into my life for adventures big and small: Marshall Lanz, Jim Shooter, Raymond Miller, and Don Newton, among so many others.

Now comic fandom was giving me one more gift: a get-together with my first gay friend. As the bus trundled through the streets of Providence on its way to the terminal, I felt my heart beating faster. The second phase of my post-graduation vacation was about to begin.

PART 2

18.

BREAKING UP IS HARD TO DO

My visit with Mario Vitale was a success from the moment I stepped off the bus, suitcase in hand. His friend Jeannie Rossiter met me at the station because Mario was working his shift as a busser at Barney's, a local restaurant. He and I were naturally excited as we planned to meet in person after corresponding for several years, but neither of us had any idea how exciting it would become when we found ourselves in the grip of sudden mutual attraction.

Mario was seventeen and had just graduated from high school. The photograph he'd sent in advance didn't do him justice. He was a handsome, slender young man of Italian descent, with dark, curly hair and olive skin. I was twenty-one and, at a height of six feet, two or three inches taller than he was. Face to face at his apartment door, we both instantly realized there were sparks between us.

While his parents were on the other side of the wall, we sat on his bed and got to know each other better. I showed him some of the goodies I'd bought at the convention. When he particularly admired an issue of the fanzine *Heritage* devoted to artistic interpretations of Flash Gordon, I gave it to him as a gift. I told him about my experiences at the con, and he told me about his plans to attend Amherst College in western Massachusetts. Soon we were doing more than talking. We were falling in love.

The days I spent with Mario were beautiful and intense. We didn't want them to end, so I phoned my dad and arranged to have my train tickets changed so I could stay several more days. A lot can happen in nine days. There were languorous hours together in the bedroom at the Rossiters' house, where I stayed for the latter part of the visit. Apart from the lovemaking, we went to movies *(The Paper Chase, Forty Carats),* walked along a nearby reservoir, listened to and discussed popular music, and created a small fanzine together. One momentous night, we took peyote and spent hours staring into each other's eyes—a true mystical experience. We had so many things in common and forged such a profound emotional connection that it felt like we were one.

Inevitably, the visit came to an end. The rest of my world receded and all that mattered, besotted as I was, was being with Mario. I promised to come back to him. Although it was sad to watch him waving forlornly from the sidewalk as my bus pulled away, I was happy. I would get a job to earn some money and return to be with him as soon as possible.

Back in Lewiston, I wrote Mario impassioned letters and received the same from him in return. Meanwhile I looked for a job, any sort of job. I don't remember how much I told my parents about my plans, except that it didn't look like drawing comic books was in my future. They smiled knowingly, barely concealing their "we told you so" attitude. They agreed that it was too late to find a teaching position for the upcoming school year, and they were satisfied when I got a job as a night watchman and janitor at a large appliance store.

As I gradually came back down to earth in the weeks and months after the convention, I realized that, as much as I loved Mario, I couldn't go back to live with him in Amherst, a town with a population of twenty-seven thousand. What would I do there while he was attending classes? I knew my employment prospects would be slim because I'd be competing with lots of college students who were also looking for work. Also, once I began seriously considering moving across the country, I found it to be a daunting prospect. (I'd already faced the fact that moving east to work at DC Comics would have been very difficult.) Hopes and dreams had to give way to the practical and possible.

I exchanged numerous letters with Mario, then ensconced in a dormitory on the Amherst campus. When my job in Lewiston ended after Christmas, our exchange continued to and from my new address in Moscow, where I moved at the beginning of 1974 to take a job at a state-run liquor store. Mario's letters became more plaintive. He was lonely in a town without much of a gay scene, and he missed me. I missed him too. My heart ached over the situation.

About nine months after our visit, I told him I wasn't coming back. I felt awful about it. I broke Mario's heart and my own at the same time. He began calling on the phone. On the advice of a friend who said, "Make a clean break, it's better that way," I asked him to stop calling. I didn't blame him for the bitter things he said about me in his last letter. He was justifiably upset. My first great love was over, and I felt like a heel.

N

Once I decided not to move to Amherst, I needed a new plan. I couldn't stay in Moscow, my old college town. I was now a graduate with a bachelor's degree, ready to embark on some sort of career. I thought back to Howard Siegel's advice at the New York con. The closest large city was Seattle. There would be publishing there, I told myself, as well as commercial art firms and many other opportunities. And Seattle was much less intimidating than New York City.

My move to Seattle in September 1974 was both eased and encouraged by a chance encounter. I'd reconnected with the Gay Student Alliance crowd in Pullman. At one of their social functions, I met a fellow named John who was visiting from Seattle. He and I hit it off, and I asked him about life in the city. He told me that the Seattle gay and lesbian community had had its first Gay Pride celebration the prior June, and the city had several gay bars I ought to check out. He also said he'd be happy to show me around. John talked about Seattle in a way that made me feel like it was a place where it was safe to be openly gay. "If you want to move there," John said, "you can rent a room in my house for as long as it takes you to find a job and get your own place."

The twin prospects of career opportunities and gay liberation made his invitation irresistible. He gave me driving instructions to his house in the northern suburb of Bothell. I announced my decision to my parents, and I was soon ready to go. I packed almost all my earthly possessions into the back of my green 1973 Vega hatchback, a recent purchase made possible by combining my savings with the remainder of the generous graduation check my grandparents had given me.

I couldn't take all my comics and fanzines to the city with me. They would have to be transported later, after I got settled. But I couldn't contemplate the move without bringing at least some of my four-color treasures. Among the essentials I brought was the copy of *Giant Superman Annual* #1 that Dad had purchased for me in the train station in 1960. I waved goodbye to my folks and was on my way west.

⚡

I received a suitably enthusiastic welcome from John and his roommates when I pulled into the driveway of his manufactured home in the grandly named Cascade Vista Estates. This was the height of the disco era, so they insisted that before I did any job hunting, I needed to sow some wild oats—which meant availing myself of the gay bars and all they had to offer. Bothell, I learned, was about a forty-minute drive to downtown Seattle, where those bars were located.

Nervous? The first time I entered such an establishment, I was petrified. What would it be like to walk into a room full of people who all knew or assumed I was gay? Would everyone's head turn as I entered—*Whoosh!*—to check me out? Would I have to walk a gauntlet of catcalls and groping hands? As it happened, no one paid much attention when we entered the Golden Horseshoe and found a table. I soon discovered that a gay bar wasn't that different from any other bar: loud music, beer (no hard liquor), a small dance floor, a smoky atmosphere, and lots of people having a good time with their friends—and the friends they wanted to make.

The only true disco in Seattle in 1974 was Shelly's Leg, located near Pioneer Square in the downtown city core.

The Horseshoe played disco music, but Seattle only had one true gay disco (no one ever called them discotheques). It was called Shelley's Leg because it had been paid for by an insurance settlement received by the owner, Shelley Bauman, after she was injured during a Seattle parade in 1970. The place had all the usual features of such establishments: a waiting line to get in, a dance floor with a large disco ball and swirling lights, and a disc jockey spinning the latest dance music played ear-splittingly loud, always with an insistent, thumping beat. The place had been open for a year when I arrived, and it was the undisputed center of the young gay scene in Seattle. I wasn't a fan of disco music, so it wasn't to my taste, but I got swept up in the frenzied scene anyway.

Still, job hunting took top priority. I figured I could probably do production work pasting up pages for a magazine or small newspaper, but it wasn't long before I learned that Seattle wasn't a publishing hub. The two big newspapers (the *Seattle Times* and the *Seattle Post-Intelligencer*) didn't need me, and the days of lively, small, alternative newspapers (*Seattle Weekly, The Rocket,* and *The Stranger*) were years in the future. As for commercial art, I soon found out that it required specific skills I didn't have. If you wanted to work in publishing at that time, you pretty much had to live in close proximity to New York City. Therefore, to survive "while looking for other opportunities," I swallowed my pride and took the first clerical job on offer. That was for Pacific Marine Schwabacher, a hardware wholesaler located near Pioneer Square, barely a stone's throw from Shelley's Leg.

Back in Lewiston for Christmas, I noticed that my dad looked a little peaked. Not long after the New Year, I received a chilling call from my mom.

"Your father has liver cancer," she said. "He's very sick."

"Should I come home right away?"

"Let's wait and see."

The news didn't improve. About six weeks later, I got another call that was even more chilling: "You'd better come home right away. Your father might not be around much longer. You should see him."

My last visit with my dad was profoundly disturbing. He had lost a lot of weight and could hardly focus on the conversation. When I held his hand, it seemed enormous, all bones and knuckles. The next time I returned, it was for his funeral. My father, Carl Schelly, passed away on March 23, 1975, two weeks before his sixty-third

My father, Carl Schelly, is caught puttering with his stamp collection, not long before he became ill in early 1975. Photo by Steve Schelly.

birthday. After a lifetime of working for the railroad, he didn't live long enough to enjoy the retirement he had earned.

Of the seven hills Seattle was built on, Capitol Hill is closest to the downtown core. In the mid-1970s, it was Seattle's equivalent to San Francisco's Castro district, a notably bohemian area with a large gay population. That's where I found my first foothold in the city, a one-bedroom corner apartment on Harrison Street. The rent was $130 a month. After Dad died, Mom was forced to sell their home, so I furnished my new abode with items I brought from the Lewiston house. I also brought my fanzine and comic book collections and my record albums. Now I had a home in the city, conveniently located a mere fifteen minutes from work.

Despite my job disappointment, it was thrilling to be living in such a vibrant city, set amid green hills and sparkling waterways. The weather in Seattle is moderate, and rain is less of a factor than reputation would have it. Yes, the winter was dark, rainy, and long, but my first spring in the Emerald City was breathtaking.

I soon heard about Rod Dyke's Golden Age Collectables, the city's first comic book specialty shop, which was located in downtown's touristy Pike Place Market. The shop had roots in the market as Ron Layton's Books and Records Cellar, founded in 1961, which was known as a place to buy "used comic books ... at rock-bottom prices." Rod bought the store in 1971 and has run it ever since (as of this writing, it's still in business). When I first saw the place in late 1974 or early 1975, it was a small space crammed with old and rare comics, general back issues, monster magazines, Big Little Books, pulp magazines, fanzines, and other related comic book and pop-culture merchandise. The only thing Rod didn't have was the new mainstream comics. DC and Marvel comics weren't yet widely sold through comic book specialty stores; if you wanted those, you had to find them on newsstands or in drug stores.

And if you didn't? Something had happened to me since I'd graduated from college: I stopped buying new comics. Nothing on the spinner racks looked good. Many of my favorite artists from the 1960s had moved on or were doing work that didn't interest me as much. I'd pick up a comic book from time to time, conclude that the content looked uninspired or shoddy, and put it back on the rack. Had I paid closer attention, I might have bought the excellent *Giant-Size X-Men* #1 (1975), with the introduction of the new X-Men by writer Len Wein and artist Dave Cockrum. Or I might have thrilled to *Master of Kung Fu*, superbly scripted by Doug Moench and beautifully drawn by Paul Gulacy. I stopped by Golden Age Collectables occasionally, especially if I was visiting the Pike Place Market for some other reason. I'm pretty sure that's where I bought the *Apex Treasury of Underground Comics* (1975), mainly for the stories by Robert Crumb, who was my favorite of the underground writer-artists. It wasn't long before my visits to the store tapered off.

With roots in Seattle's Pike Place Market going back to 1961, Golden Age Collectables is one of the oldest comic book stores in existence. Shown here is the small venue where it was located when I first entered its doors, with a photo of owner Rod Dyke taken in the early 1970s. Shortly thereafter, Rod lost weight and became the slim version of himself that most people now know. Courtesy of Roderick Dyke.

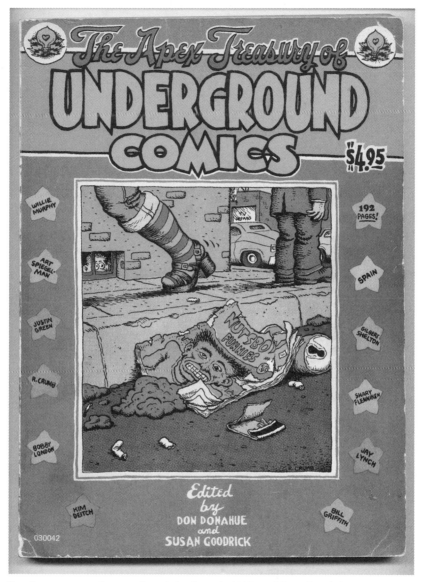

I read numerous underground comix in the early 1970s, and I purchased the *Apex Treasury of Underground Comics* in 1975 to get some of the best in one book.

Perhaps even more surprising, comic fandom lost its luster for me. Fanzines had become pricey because of the proliferation of high-end publications with work by professionals and semiprofessionals. They cost at least $1 and were often $2 or more. For a guy on a limited income, they were too costly; and besides, they didn't really interest me. The charm of the early fanzines had been superseded, in my view, by soulless publications more interested in making money than in celebrating the form and the hobby.

Why didn't I participate in the friendlier aspects of 1960s fandom that survived into the 1970s, such as comics APA *Capa-alpha*? I reasoned that if I couldn't find new comics that interested me, it was time to give comics a rest. I didn't understand until later that what really caused my drift away from the hobby was the death of my dream of becoming a professional comics artist, combined with my guilt and depression over the way my relationship with Mario Vitale—who had initially come into my life as a reader of *Sense of Wonder*—had ended. Those two traumatic experiences were the underlying reasons why I turned away from the art form, the hobby, and community of people who had meant so much to me and had given me a place to establish my identity and potency.

Now I spent my disposable income, such as it was, on things like movies, records, clothes, and pitchers of beer. I did what most young, single guys do: party and try to get laid as much as possible. Maybe my life looked a little different from the heterosexual version, but it was much the same. My immersion in the gay bars, including Shelley's Leg and the Golden Horseshoe, continued through 1975 and much of 1976.

One night at Shelley's Leg, I had a surprising encounter. I had paid the cover charge and was walking in when someone leaning against a wall nearby spoke to me.

"Bill?"

I turned my head. The music was, as usual, incredibly loud, so I wasn't sure I'd heard right. There was a guy there dressed in women's clothes, wearing a red wig. Was he talking to me?

"Bill … don't you recognize me? It's me—Gary."

My jaw could have hit the floor. It was my buddy from college, the rock singer, actor, and fellow trailer-park denizen, Gary Speer—dressed as a woman.

Despite my surprise, I was naturally happy to see him. I stammered some sort of greeting, having to practically yell to be heard.

"So," he yelled back. "Are you gay?"

"Yeah," I nodded, smiling. "You?"

"Well, no, not gay," he said. The din defeated us. "We should talk sometime."

Gary gave me his address, and a couple of days later I visited him at his apartment, not far from where I lived. As in the bar, he was again dressed as a woman, although his hair didn't look as good this time. "Oh, that was a borrowed wig," he said. "I'm saving up for a good one."

I don't remember much from our conversation, except that he explained that he wasn't gay, and he wasn't a drag queen, either. He haltingly told me, "I want to … be a woman." It was the first time I met a person experiencing gender dysphoria. When I left, I came away with the feeling that Gary had a rough road ahead of him. I hoped he—she?—would be okay, but for reasons I can't recall—I think Gary planned to move back to Idaho—we didn't see each other again. I wish I had been able to help in some way.

Apart from the bars and dance clubs, the city offered plenty of things that had been unavailable in Idaho, such as major rock concerts. In 1975 alone, I saw the Faces with Rod Stewart, Queen, Pink Floyd, Kiss, and Eric Clapton. Most impressive of all was Bruce Springsteen's first concert in Seattle. The venue was the Paramount Theater, which seated about two thousand people, and the concert took place on October 26, 1975. I'd only heard Springsteen's "Born to Run" single before entering those doors; upon exiting, I immediately found a record store that was still open and bought the album of the same title. I felt like I had just experienced a rebirth of rock and roll. Disco could be fun, but it was thin as paper and phony as a three-dollar bill. Springsteen's rock and roll was the perfect antidote to disco: heartfelt, genuine, and inspiring. In a way, Bruce revived my interest in my own art. In my post-concert enthusiasm, I drew a large portrait of "the Boss" and proudly displayed it on my living-room wall for many years to come.

Portrait of Bruce Springsteen, drawn after seeing him in concert on October 26, 1975.

As the 1970s marched along, I was unable to find better jobs. A career in art never materialized. I shifted restlessly from one clerical position to another, but I found myself trapped in low-paying jobs doing the kind of work that led nowhere. I could afford to rent an apartment and take care of my basic expenses, but I had little extra. When a sudden large expense came up, like a car repair, I was forced to dip into my savings. I was alarmed to watch those savings slowly but inexorably shrink to almost nothing. So-called "real life" was grinding me down. By 1978, I was living in a rooming house and using a shared bathroom. It was a nice, old house on a corner, and my room was large, with a big bow window, but it had no cooking facilities. My car was burning oil, and its cheap vinyl seats were coming apart at the seams. So was I, it seemed.

I found myself making few romantic connections that lasted more than a few dates. That was partly due to the nature of gay subculture, where young men in their twenties were less interested in finding Mr. Right than in finding Mr. Right Now. It was about the thrill of the hunt and immediate gratification. The names and faces became a bit of a blur.

Just as I was frustrated by my jobs and unfulfilled by my love life, I had difficulty finding ways to express my creativity. About all I'd done since moving to the city was a drawing here or there for my own amusement. I was still the same person who had written stories at eight, discovered his art ability at ten, published a fanzine at thirteen, and written a novel at fifteen. In college I had done a lot of drawing and oil painting. No matter what else was going on in my life, I had always been involved in a creative endeavor of some kind. Creativity was a fundamental part of my personality and identity, as well as an outlet that was good for my mental health.

In 1978, I decided to try to write a novel, visions of a bestseller dancing in my head. My protagonist was a newswoman who discovers some sort of mysterious government facility near her resort cabin in the Adirondacks. This untitled thriller began auspiciously enough, but it meandered to a stop after several chapters. The problem was that I never was able to figure out what was going on inside that mysterious government facility. The facility was nothing more than a plot device, and when I had to work out the more specific plot details for the middle and end of the book, I found myself confused and discouraged. My problem was that in fiction, anything is possible—and "anything" is a little too nonspecific for me. I stopped after about thirty thousand words, thoroughly demoralized.

Taken in a photo booth in downtown Seattle, after a chance meeting with Barbara Barker. We've been in sporadic contact ever since.

At least there was good news on the job front: my constant search for a better job turned up a decent opportunity. The Boeing Company, the biggest employer in the Seattle area, was gearing up to design some new airplanes, and they needed more draftsmen. I had some background in mechanical drawing, and I was willing to take an eight-week crash course sponsored by the company. If Mom was able to loan me a little money to get through the training period, I could easily pay it back because my starting annual salary was almost twice what I'd made in the past year working as an office temp for Kelly Services. I passed the eight-week course handily and reported for job orientation at the Boeing Airplane plant in Everett, Washington, in October 1978.

After four years in Seattle, it seemed like my fortunes were looking up. I could even say I was working at an art-oriented job, although I was well aware that doing layout drawings to assist the engineers in designing the Boeing 767 was hardly imaginative work. That part of the dilemma remained. I knew I couldn't be happy unless I found a real creative outlet, a way to channel the need for expression that was so central to my personal fulfillment. The planes would fly. But would I?

19.

GIVING VOICE TO SILENT FILMS

In 1925, the Woman's Century Club, a feminist organization founded in Seattle in 1891, built a grand brick structure to house its meetings, social events, and offices, from which it managed various philanthropic activities. Located at the north end of Broadway, the main street that runs through the Capitol Hill business district, the clubhouse was sold in 1968 and was converted into a movie theater named the Harvard Exit.

When I became aware of it, the Harvard Exit—named after a street running along one side of the building, where one exited after a movie—was running an ongoing repertory program of classic movies. These were the days before home video, when there was no way for the average filmgoer to see great films of the past, apart from woefully inadequate late-night television showings on a total of five stations. Now, Seattleites could see big-screen presentations of such classics as *Grand Hotel, Casablanca, Top Hat, All about Eve, It Happened One Night,* and *The Philadelphia Story,* as well as slates of the movies of the Marx Brothers, W. C. Fields, Alfred Hitchcock, and many others. The movies were constantly changing, only showing two or three times each at most. After the show, one could cross the street to Cinema Books, a specialty store catering to the Exit's clientele.

Although Cinema Books was owned by Stephanie Ogle, the store was sometimes manned by an energetic young gymnastics instructor named Jim Holt. Jim, I quickly discovered, was a silent film fanatic (enthusiast is too mild a word) who couldn't stop talking about the greatness of director D. W. Griffith, the Gish sisters, Buster Keaton, and Charlie Chaplin. I'd seen a couple of Chaplin films, the Lon Chaney *Phantom of the Opera,* and a handful of other silents, and I had a modicum of appreciation for the form. Hence, I was receptive when Jim showed me a new, oversized book titled *The Silent Clowns* by film and theater critic Walter Kerr. The book had originally been published in hardcover by Alfred A. Knopf in 1975, and it was now, in 1979, being released in a more affordable paperback edition.

I was sharing an apartment near the Harvard Exit with a friend named Diana Borasio. She was as much into movies as I was, and she grabbed my copy of *The Silent Clowns* whenever I put it down. We were both captivated by Kerr's knowing, perceptive prose and by the book's cornucopia of large, beautiful photographs featuring the "big four" silent clowns: Charlie Chaplin, Buster Keaton, Harold Lloyd, and Harry Langdon. This, of course, made us yearn to see the comedians in action. Our wish was granted when, a few weeks later, a flier appeared touting the Exit's upcoming movie repertory program called "The Silent Clowns." Although not officially linked to the book, the program would present twenty-one days of films starring Kerr's big-four comedians with live organ accompaniment by silent movie specialist Lee Erwin. The program, which had already played in New York, Washington, DC, and Los Angeles, would arrive in Seattle in September. By the time it started, Diana was already deep into her second or third book about Buster Keaton, and I was reading Jim Holt's copy of Kevin Brownlow's *The Parade's Gone By,* one of the best books written about the silent film era.

Unsurprisingly, we went gaga over such great movies as *The Kid* and *City Lights* (Chaplin), *The Navigator* and *Sherlock Jr.* (Keaton), *Speedy* and *The Freshman* (Lloyd), and *The Strong Man* and *Long Pants* (Langdon). Diana fell completely under Buster's spell, and so did I to a great extent, but it was Harry Langdon who particularly fascinated me. On the last day of "The Silent Clowns," the Exit showed Langdon's feature *The Strong Man,* the movie Brownlow described as "one of the most perfect comedies ever made." I was thoroughly charmed by Langdon's elfin screen persona and his subtle pantomime skills, which had once been favorably compared to Chaplin's.

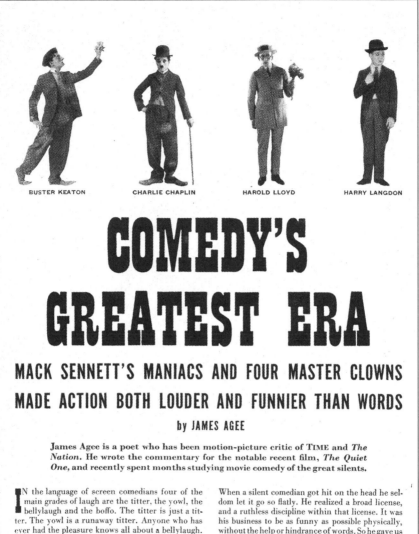

BUSTER KEATON   CHARLIE CHAPLIN   HAROLD LLOYD   HARRY LANGDON

COMEDY'S GREATEST ERA

MACK SENNETT'S MANIACS AND FOUR MASTER CLOWNS MADE ACTION BOTH LOUDER AND FUNNIER THAN WORDS

by JAMES AGEE

James Agee is a poet who has been motion-picture critic of TIME and *The Nation*. He wrote the commentary for the notable recent film, *The Quiet One*, and recently spent months studying movie comedy of the great silents.

IN the language of screen comedians four of the main grades of laugh are the titter, the yowl, the bellylaugh and the boffo. The titter is just a titter. The yowl is a runaway titter. Anyone who has ever had the pleasure knows all about a bellylaugh. The boffo is the laugh that kills. An ideally good gag, perfectly constructed and played, would bring the victim up this ladder of laughs by cruelly controlled degrees to the top rung, and would then proceed to wobble, shake, wave and brandish the ladder until he groaned for mercy. Then, after the shortest possible time out for recuperation, he would feel

When a silent comedian got hit on the head he seldom let it go so flatly. He realized a broad license, and a ruthless discipline within that license. It was his business to be as funny as possible physically, without the help or hindrance of words. So he gave us a figure of speech, or rather of vision, for loss of consciousness. In other words he gave us a poem, a kind of poem, moreover, that everybody understands. The least he might do was to straighten up stiff as a plank and fall over backward with such skill that his whole length seemed to slap the floor at the same instant. Or he might make a cadenza of it—look

Writer and critic James Agee's seminal essay "Comedy's Greatest Era" in *Life* magazine (September 5, 1949) included Harry Langdon in his pantheon of the most important silent film comedians, along with Buster Keaton, Charlie Chaplin, and Harold Lloyd.

I also didn't fail to note that the movie was directed by Frank Capra, his first such screen credit. In his autobiography *The Name above the Title* (Macmillan, 1971), Capra wrote, "In a day when comics out-exaggerated each other, Langdon played scenes delicately, almost in slow motion. You could practically see the wheels of his immature mind turning as it registered tiny pleasures and discomforts. With [Langdon's] limited range … his art approached genius. As a director, I had two sticky problems. One, to keep him on the narrow beam of his range; the other, talking him out of scenes that were not in character … without bruising his fast-inflating ego." Shortly after *The Strong Man* was released in 1926, Capra left him, and Harry Langdon's career collapsed. Capra called him "the most tragic figure I ever knew in Hollywood."

I was captivated reading about the heights that Harry Langdon's comedic talent had attained and his precipitous fall from grace. I wanted to know more, and I was frustrated when I discovered that little had been written about him. Film historian Leonard Maltin's *The Great Movie Comedians* (Crown, 1978) neatly summarized all I'd found about Langdon, but that was it. There was no book on him, which seemed strange. After all, if the influential critics James Agee and Walter Kerr ranked Langdon with Chaplin, Keaton, and Lloyd, and if there were many books about the other three, didn't Langdon merit at least one—a single source that told his life story and dealt with his career in depth?

"All these books on Buster Keaton," I said to Diana one day, referring to several that she had collected, "and not one on Langdon? It's crazy."

She agreed. Aware that I'd been casting about for a writing project, she suggested, "Why don't you write one?"

"That," I said, "is a great idea."

"But how will you research it?" she asked.

How indeed? I got to work.

N

Publicity photo of Harry Langdon in *The Strong Man* (1926), and a poster for his subsequent film, *Long Pants* (1927). Silent film historian Kevin Brownlow described *The Strong Man* as "one of the most perfect comedies ever made."

More than anything, the glue that held my life together through 1979, 1980, and 1981 was the Harry Langdon project. Finally, I had a creative endeavor with which I could completely engage. The first order of business was scouring the local libraries. I found the main branch of the Seattle Public Library not only had a small cache of eight-millimeter Langdon two-reelers (twenty-minute comedies), but they even loaned out projectors so you could watch the films. I spent time in two excellent libraries on the University of Washington campus, which had a substantial number of helpful books. Every little squib was important to me; every tiny fact was one more piece of the puzzle. Contemporary magazines like *Film Comment* and *Films in Review* had run interesting pieces on Langdon, as did vintage magazines from the 1920s and 1930s, such as *Photoplay*. Gradually, I was able to see a fuller picture and construct an outline.

Next, I began writing letters to anyone who I thought could help. Langdon had died in 1944, but I discovered that his widow, Mabel, was still alive. Leonard Maltin was kind enough to give me her address in North Hollywood, California. I wrote to her, asking for help. No letter that I wrote to research the Langdon book was more important than that one. When I received an envelope with her return address on it, my fingers shook as I opened it. On November 8, 1979, she wrote:

> Dear Mr. Schelly:
>
> In reference to your intention to write the biography of Harry Langdon, please be advised that I own the rights to his biography. I am interested in knowing your qualifications to write this type of book, and also what have you written and had published that I might read?

Was she looking for a writer to work with her on such a book? I telephoned her. Mabel Langdon was polite, even friendly, but she made it clear that she was working on her own book on her late husband's career, so she wouldn't be helping me. Since I had no desire to ghostwrite her book, I didn't say much about my qualifications, such as they were. As we were wrapping up the conversation, she said I might enjoy getting in touch with a Langdon fan in Seattle named Michael Copner, and she gave me his address. Mrs. Langdon also followed up by sending me a copy of a program that had been published in 1966 on the occasion of a Langdon film retrospective at the Gallery of Modern Art in New York. The program included an interview with her and mentioned that her biography of Harry was "imminent."

"Maybe I'd better forget it," I told Diana. "If her book is coming out, what publisher would want mine?" Diana observed that if a book was described as "imminent" in 1966 but hadn't been published by 1979, it had probably stalled. I decided to forge ahead, even without the assistance of the Langdon estate, although this meant my book couldn't be definitive. It would have to be more of a study of Langdon's work than a book about his life. A compromised book, I told myself, was better than none.

What about Mabel's other point? What made me think I was qualified to write such a book? Beyond some juvenile novels, I'd never written any long-form or book-length works. However, as a result of classes I took as an English minor in college, I knew how to write essays that regularly received top marks. I had forged a bond with one professor in particular, James Malek, who thought highly of my writing ability and encouraged me to strive for excellence. In my mind, a nonfiction book was just a long essay with multiple sections, i.e., chapters. Yes, it would be a lot of work, but I never doubted my ability to write an intelligent, well-organized, thoughtful book. This self-confidence, coupled with my enthusiasm for my subject, would see me through. I had to start somewhere.

I've never wanted to write articles. For me, it's always been about writing books. That dream emerged when I was nine years old, when I imagined having my own book stand in the neighborhood, full of books that I would write. For some reason I felt that a writer of books was someone worthy of great respect, the kind of respect that I hoped to be accorded.

I followed Mabel's recommendation to get in touch with Langdon fan Michael Copner in Seattle. As luck would have it, he lived a few short blocks from our apartment. Mike turned out to be a friendly young man about my age who bore a certain resemblance to Marshall Lanz. He was tall, had dark hair, and evinced an air of self-confidence. More to the point, Mike owned sixteen-millimeter prints of some of Langdon's sound films, which were hard to find. He also owned a projector to show them and was quite willing to do so. In addition, Copner had a collection of still photos from Harry's films. He admitted that he'd considered writing his own Langdon book but was willing to help with mine.

Assistance from other quarters was less forthcoming. Frank Capra wrote, "I have written all the pertinent facts I know about Harry Langdon in my autobiography. Anything I could add to what I have already written about him would be hearsay or rumor which I have no wish to pass on to posterity." Under the signature, there was the notation: "Dictated by Frank Capra, signed in his absence." It

seemed he was guarding against me selling the letter for its genuine
Capra signature. Others who didn't have much to offer in the way of
help, like Walter Kerr, wrote letters of encouragement. So began the
process that would continue over the next two years.

N

My "wonderful opportunity" at the Boeing Company ended in mid-
1980. The forty-minute commute each way to Everett had grown
tiresome, but moving closer to the plant would put a damper on my
social life, just when I was building up a circle of friends. At the same
time, Boeing began expecting—almost requiring—us to work overtime on an ongoing basis. Adding ten-hour days (or longer) to a total
of eighty minutes on the road each day was too much. On top of that,
the creative component of the job vanished after the layout phase of
designing the 767 was complete. The work had devolved into doing
highly technical drawings of rivets and metal plates. Besides, Boeing
was notorious for its boom-and-bust cycles, with a "last in, first out"
policy. It wasn't like I was giving up great job security.

Before I left, I had a job lined up in the accounting department of
a company called Wilbur-Ellis, a fertilizer and chemicals wholesaler.
True, it put me one step above the clerical pool, but it paid about the
same as Boeing, and had its offices in a building on Lake Union, near
the city core. My commute went from forty minutes each way to about
ten, and there was no overtime. I had worked there as a temporary typist
before going to Boeing, and I knew I liked the people. What I didn't
know was what a dramatic effect one particular person there, a youthful
coworker named Stephanie Seymour, would have on the rest of my life.

That came later. Meanwhile, work on the Langdon book shifted
into higher gear. I received movie stills from the Museum of Modern
Art in New York and the American Film Institute in Los Angeles. A private collector named Wayne Powers contributed numerous
crucial images for the book. The project was coming together. The
excitement I felt reminded me of the old fanzine days, when I was
starting work on a new issue of *Sense of Wonder*.

Program for a Seattle performance by Marcel Marceau, who contributed a quote to the Harry Langdon biography I was writing in 1980 and 1981. ™ and © respective copyright holders.

An advertisement for a local performance by acclaimed pantomime artist Marcel Marceau caught my eye. Diana and I went to see him perform and were thoroughly impressed by his creativity and talent as an entertainer. The biographical profile in the program indicated that he considered Charlie Chaplin and Harry Langdon his two earliest influences. Since the program also listed the address of his management agency, I sent him a letter asking for a quote for the book. He graciously responded, in a letter dated June 19, 1980, which read (in part):

> Harry Langdon is, in my opinion, the last great Pierrot who played in silent movies. If you compare him to Charlot, you will notice that Chaplin has revealed both sides of human nature: Joy and Tragedy which always will make of him an [sic] universal Artist. In Harry Langdon, we see only one side of human fragility: a terrible loneliness and melancholy of a poor soul lost in a dark and wild world.

When Marceau refers to a "Pierrot," he is referring to a stock character of European pantomime and commedia dell'arte, the sad clown. I was delighted and thrilled to have this eloquent quote for the book. Eventually, I was able to meet the great mime backstage when he returned to Seattle, and I thanked him for his help in person.

I began to piece together the first draft. One of my key theses was that far from his career ending with the coming of sound, Langdon went on to a long and productive career in talking pictures, albeit low-budget ones. He hadn't died in poverty and obscurity, as some would have it. Langdon's fall from grace may have been tragic, but he went on to have a good life and worked in sound films until his untimely death due to a cerebral hemorrhage.

↯

I finished the second draft of the Harry Langdon book in the summer of 1981 and sent it off to various publishers. Among numerous rejections, I received an offer from a company called Scarecrow Press. They published short-run books on specialized subjects, sold mostly to libraries in North America.

I immediately accepted the offer, although my joy was tempered by the fact that Scarecrow's books had no dust jacket or any kind of cover art, and the interiors were typed (via typewriter) rather than typeset. However, there could be interior photographs, and it would be a hardback book. Scarecrow wanted to publish it as part of their new Filmmaker Series, which would be edited by noted film historian Anthony Slide.

Among his comments on my manuscript, Slide asked if I'd been in touch with film impresario Raymond Rohauer, who had helped put together "The Silent Clowns" film retrospective and was the agent for the films of both Keaton and Langdon. I hadn't bothered to contact Rohauer since Mabel Langdon had made it clear that he was involved with her book. However, I duly dispatched a letter asking for his help. It wasn't long before I heard from his attorney. The three-page letter from Stephen P. Rohde stated in part:

> Please be advised that Mr. Rohauer and Mrs. Langdon exercise exclusive ownership and control over all of the materials and information to which you refer concerning Harry Langdon.

We must respectfully advise you that by reason of state and federal law, your plans appear to infringe upon our clients' protected rights concerning the name, photograph and likeness of Harry Langdon, as well as his films and public performances. Any wrongful publication in contravention of our client's rights will be met with legal action seeking appropriate injunctive relief as well as compensatory and punitive damages together with attorney's fees and court costs.

Please notify Scarecrow Press promptly of the contents of this notice. In the event you elect to ignore this notice …

And so on. You can imagine my reaction. All seemed lost. Depression! I had found a publisher for my book, and now someone was trying their best to crush my dream.

Diana advised, "Call Anthony Slide."

I did and was quickly reassured. After I read various passages of the letter to him, he said, "Send me the letter. But I can tell you, they have no legal right to stop you from writing a biography of Harry Langdon. He was a public figure, and you are perfectly within your rights. It sounds like they're just trying to intimidate you."

Slide was right. I had a local attorney respond with a letter stating just that, and while Rohauer and Rohde answered with further threats, there was ultimately nothing they could do to stop me. I had called their bluff, but it had cost me money for the attorney and at least one sleepless night in Seattle. I later found out that Rohauer was widely disliked in the vintage film

Harry Langdon from Scarecrow Press, 1982—three years in the making.

community for his business practices, which included intimidation, false charges, neglect of films in his so-called archives, claiming to own things that he didn't, and so on. Most people were afraid to speak out against him until after his death in 1987.

On January 29, 1982, I sent in the completed manuscript to Scarecrow. Over the past couple of years, I had unleashed every bit of my creativity on the book. Now what remained was the activity necessary to finalize it, such as reviewing proofs. Then it would go to press.

On a day in October much like any other, the receptionist at Wilbur-Ellis turned to me and said, "There's a box here for you." My box of author's copies had arrived! I took it down to my car, opened it, and sat there, holding my first book in my trembling hands.

20.

SUPER UPS, SUPER DOWNS, SUPER COMICS

I'd made several close friends in my eight years in Seattle. Diana Bora-sio was one; another was Ed Brooks, a young rock-and-roll fan whom I met in line for Bruce Springsteen tickets in 1980. Ed would parlay his love of rock music into a career as studio engineer and producer working with many of the best-known musicians in the Pacific Northwest in the coming years. Today, he owns his own studio and continues to be a vital force in the Seattle music scene. There were others, but strange as it might seem, none of them were gay. Sure, I went on dates and even saw the occasional person on a regular basis for a while, but they didn't stick around to become friends. I wanted to know people like me whom I didn't meet through the bars, which I had all but stopped patronizing.

Somewhere I read that volunteer work was a good way to meet people, and it occurred to me that there was one place that was entirely populated by gay men and women: the Seattle Counseling Service, a nonprofit entity that provided various services to the gay community. I figured I would at least have the opportunity to make some friends among the volunteers there. Sometime in July 1982, I contacted SCS and went in for an interview in their Capitol Hill offices. Before long, I was in a training program to become a telephone counselor.

SCS had a hotline that was both a referral service and a place where lesbian, gay, bisexual, and other sexually nonconforming people could call and talk about anything. It also functioned as a crisis line. Calls from people feeling suicidal were not uncommon. After a few weeks of training, I signed up for the Wednesday night phone shift, which lasted from 6:00 to 10:00 p.m. There were always two people on duty, sometimes three.

Shortly after I started with SCS, we began getting questions about a "gay cancer" that was beginning to make newspaper headlines. Although recent research has shown that HIV was being spread as early as 1970 in New York City, the Centers for Disease Control in Atlanta didn't recognize the distinct syndrome we now know as AIDS until 1981. By May of 1982, reported cases numbered at least 335 (most of them gay), of whom 136 had died. The disease was briefly called GRID (gay-related immune deficiency), but it soon became clear that anyone, gay or straight, could be infected. The name was changed to AIDS (acquired immune deficiency syndrome) in September 1982, as I was sliding into my chair at the SCS switchboard for the first time. The first case of AIDS in Washington wouldn't be reported until November, yet the phone lines were buzzing with questions. Little was known at that point, but it was thought that the virus—if it was a virus—spread through blood and semen, so we were recommending at a minimum that people should use condoms without fail.

To be frank about it, I was having occasional intimate contact with people who were essentially strangers. Given that I was living on Capitol Hill, such one-night stands would almost certainly have exposed me to the HIV virus. The fact is that if I hadn't gotten the word about AIDS as early as I did, I would probably have been an early victim of the disease. It's chilling to think how close I came to being one of the 3,500 people in Seattle who would die from AIDS. As soon as I heard about it, I immediately changed my behavior to avoid any chance of contracting the virus. Good fortune—and recognizing the seriousness of the illness as soon as I heard about it—saved me from the awful fate that befell too many, including some whom I knew and even dated.

I did make two long-term gay friends as a result of volunteering at SCS. One evening, a substitute volunteer named Dale Nash served on a shift with me. He perked up when I told him about my

Langdon book. "My boyfriend and I are both into movies," he said. "We ought to get together." I found out that Dale and his partner, John Teegarden, were more than casual fans of cinema. John had majored in film history and criticism at the University of Southern California, and the two of them had quite a collection of vintage movie stills, lobby cards, and posters. They were living in an apartment on Queen Anne Hill, close enough to Capitol Hill that we could easily get together for dinner and a movie. They also gave parties where I met other gay people, local newspaper and television film critics, and people who worked for the Seattle International Film Festival and local movie chains. Thanks to John and Dale, my social network was greatly expanded, but the best part about meeting them was their friendship. John was a particularly insightful and knowledgeable writer about film for the magazine *Audience* and other places, and we've had many great conversations (and some spirited arguments) about movies.

The fall of 1982 was also when I met Howard Cruse, the openly gay cartoonist who edited *Gay Comix* for Kitchen Sink Press. Stan Henry, a local writer who had befriended me, invited Howard to town for a visit. I met him at a small party given in his honor and was favorably impressed by his obvious intelligence and soft-spoken

Gay Comix #1 (1980), cover by Rand Holmes. ™ and © respective copyright holders. By the time I met the comic's editor, Howard Cruse, I was living at the Union Manor.

manner. Howard signed my copy of *Gay Comix* #1 (1980) and announced that the third issue would soon see print. I brought along a copy of *Sense of Wonder* #12, my self-publishing pride and joy, and Howard was suitably complimentary. Later, he sent me a small piece of original art, which I still have. He was the only comics professional I'd met in almost a decade.

Now that I was a published author, I began thinking about what I would write next. Another film book? A novel? It would take some figuring, but I was certain of one thing: I was on my way as a writer of books.

As such, I needed quiet in order to write, so I moved from my place with Diana to an apartment of my own in an enormous brick building not far away, called the Union Manor. My place took on the look of an office when I set up an enormous work table made from a door and set my IBM Selectric typewriter (the latest technology) and my drawing board on top.

In the coming months, I worked on several book ideas that all began promisingly enough, but they eventually stalled for various reasons. Most were film books, such as a general history of comedy in the movies. The idea was to capitalize on my credential as a published writer about cinema. Initial outlines were easy to generate, but then the question became: "How will this book be any different from other books—especially those by well-qualified people, such as Leonard Maltin—that are about the same thing? What will I bring to the table that's new or different?"

I considered doing a book on a movie director and his films. I would have loved to write about Alfred Hitchcock, but there were already plenty of books about him. I settled on Francis Coppola, who hadn't yet received the full biography treatment. There was one problem: I couldn't get access to him. With no contacts in the film business, about all I could do was call his production company, American Zoetrope in San Francisco, and ask to set up an interview. After a few attempts proved fruitless—probably because my credentials weren't all that impressive—I gave up.

This was when I learned that merely stringing together material from other books, magazines, newspaper articles, press books, and other sources wasn't enough. Perhaps a worthwhile book could be written from such information, but potential publishers wanted to know what sort of access I had to my subject. Had I interviewed him? Had he opened up his files to me? My answer had to be no. Even the folks at humble Scarecrow Press weren't interested.

I was also facing a different problem I'd encountered before, while trying to research the Langdon book in Seattle. If I wasn't able to visit film archives in Southern California or New York City, and if I couldn't view special collections in certain libraries across the country, then I simply wasn't in a position to be a credible film historian. A true historian works from primary sources to find little-known or undiscovered information. A better plan might have been to find out what special collections were held in the Seattle Public Library or the local university libraries and then consider what I could do with that information. However, that idea didn't occur to me.

Okay, I thought, if nonfiction doesn't look promising, what about fiction? True, my attempt at a best seller had ended in frustration, but I had an ace in the hole: my coming-of-age novel titled *Come with Me,* which I'd written when I was sixteen. I thought it could work well as a young-adult book. S. E. Hinton's novel for teenagers *The Outsiders* (1967) had spurred an upsurge in such novels in the 1970s and early 1980s, and it had just been made into a movie. So I spent several months rewriting my story about a teenage boy with an unbearable home life who convinces his girlfriend to run away with him. They have various comedic, romantic, and harrowing adventures on the road before returning home, chastened and wiser.

I thought the revision turned out quite well, and I found an agent who was willing to read it. Still unsure, he gave it to his twelve-year-old daughter, and she liked it, so he accepted me as a client and did his best to place the novel. When he couldn't find a publisher for it, I found a second agent who also tried to find a publisher.

Unfortunately, after working to revise it over several months, the new and improved *Come with Me* went nowhere.

Discouraged by its rejection, I slid into a period of depression. It seemed like whichever way I turned, I was stymied. Yet my need for creative expression was as strong as ever.

I had written *Harry Langdon* and revised *Come with Me* over the course of four years working at Wilbur-Ellis. Adding to my frustration was the realization that my job had reached a dead end. There was no possibility of a promotion (or more money), and in fact a computer system was being put in place that would eliminate some or all of what I was doing. I felt like the ground was sinking under me. I remember staring out a window in the office, wondering what to do, as work piled up in my inbox. My life had hit bottom.

⚡

In late 1984, I decided to step back and take a good, long look at my situation. I'd been working more or less nonstop for the previous 11 years, and I needed a break. I didn't feel badly about turning in my notice at my dead-end Wilbur-Ellis job. The somewhat better money I'd been making there and at Boeing had allowed me to start an IRA and build up a nice amount in savings. And I would need those savings, because I planned to be unemployed for a while.

Maybe that looked like a stupid move from the outside, but after all, I didn't have any dependents. The only person whom it would affect negatively was my mom, who would of course be disappointed. She was living in an apartment in Lewiston, and she naturally wanted all of her sons to be successful. She couldn't accept any reason for leaving a paying job without another one lined up. I had enough faith in myself to know I would be okay.

For the next eight months, I did all kinds of things. I rested. I got back to the gym and started working out again. I started a journal and began seeing a counselor to help me sort out my thoughts. And I got back in touch with a man who had been a kind of mentor to me: Dick Trageser.

1985 photo of Dee and Dick Trageser, with Pittsburgh in the background.

Dick was the fellow who worked in the Northern Pacific office for my dad in Pittsburgh, who typed up my stories when I was eight years old, and who wrote Immortal Corpse tales for *Sense of Wonder*. He was now married, and he was glad to hear from me when I phoned. I was taken aback when he asked me "How's your dad?" I'd felt sure he would have heard about my father's passing, but it turned out Dick had left the railroad sometime after we moved. He was saddened to hear the news. "I really liked and respected him," he said.

I told him I was thinking about visiting Pittsburgh to see some of my old haunts. He immediately offered to put me up at his place, a house he'd bought when he got married. "There's something you should know before you accept," he said. "We have fourteen cats."

I'm not allergic to cats, but I'm also not particularly a cat lover. Fourteen cats sounded like a bit much, but I figured I could put up with anything for a few days. When I got there, I found it was more than I bargained for, especially when they stalked in and around our feet meowing as we tried to eat dinner. But we were away from the house much of the time, and I could shut the door to my bedroom at night.

It was great to see Dick again, older than before but still with the same twinkle in his eye. He and his wife Dee (short for Dorothy) were more than willing to drive me around to see my old houses on Lantern Hill Drive and Lovingston Drive, as well as some other old stomping grounds. We went to Kennywood, the amusement park I'd gone to with my family so many times, and rode the roller coasters. Most important of all was the time Dick and I spent together, reminiscing about the past and filling in each other about our lives in recent years. I asked if he had any advice for me in my situation. He didn't have any magic solution, but he told me that, having watched me grow up, he was confident that I would work things out. I had a good time with him, and I came away feeling a little better about things.

In the mid-1960s, Dick exposed me to Golden Age comics by loaning me his copy of Jules Feiffer's *The Great Comic Book Heroes.* Now, twenty years later, as a going-away gift he gave me a book that also had a comic art connection: *The Lives and Times of Archy and Mehitabel* (1940) by Don Marquis. Archy, a cockroach, and Mehitabel, an alley cat, appeared in humorous verses and short stories in the writer's column in the *New York Evening Sun.* The poems and prose in the book were accompanied by cartoons by George Herriman, creator of the classic comic strip *Krazy Kat,* which ran from 1913 to 1944 and is considered one of the greatest strips of all time. I'd heard of *Krazy Kat,* but this gift from Trageser provided my first exposure to a substantial amount of Herriman's cartooning. For the first time in a while, I was reminded of how much I responded to cartoons and comic art.

When I got back to Seattle, I continued seeing the mental health professional who I hoped would help me sort things out. After discussing my options and possible courses of action over a period of weeks, he finally stopped me midsession and said, "I know you're depressed over these things, but I'm getting the impression that it isn't entirely what we call situational depression. I'm thinking that an antidepressant medication might help." He explained generally how such medications worked, and I began to think perhaps he was right. On top of dealing with my specific problems, I was having to struggle to stay in a positive frame of mind. I was finding it harder to get interested in doing anything, even normal social activities.

"An antidepressant won't fix your life," he told me, "but it could help make you more able to take action to change things." I figured it was worth trying. He couldn't write prescriptions, but he referred me to a doctor who could and who would advise me about which medication might work best for me. Thus, in the spring of 1985, I started taking the antidepressant imipramine (marketed as Tofranil), one of the first such drugs to hit the market in the 1960s. Before long, I felt my general mood gradually lift.

Although it looked like I went from job to job rather aimlessly, I had a reason for each change: to try to find something better. My mistake was that when I left Boeing, I went back to what was essentially another clerical job. If I wanted something better, I couldn't repeat that mistake again. Thus, when the time came for me to look for a new job, it was with an eye toward something with growth potential.

Almost immediately, I spotted an ad in the newspaper classifieds for a management trainee. From past experience, I'd learned that this usually meant some sort of sales position or an assistant-manager job in a fast-food restaurant, or it was a come-on that employment agencies used to get you in the door. In this case, the position wasn't listed by an employment agency; the employer's name was Surety Insurance Services. What was "surety insurance"? Was this another sales job in mufti? I dialed the number and spoke to the office manager, who assured me it wasn't a sales job. After asking me a few questions, she invited me to come in for an interview, and I was soon sitting on a leather couch in the office of the firm's owner, Tom Kohoutek. He was fiftyish and well-dressed, although he seemed a little on the rough-hewn side.

We went over my résumé. Then he told me about his business. "There are basically two kinds of surety bonds that we provide," he explained. "One is a license bond, which every contractor is required to have in order to become a legal, registered contractor in the state of Washington. Those are more or less routine. The second, the main part of our business, is writing construction bonds. Those are surety bonds that contractors must have before they can do specific projects for any government entity, be it the federal government, state government—any job funded by taxpayers. Our job is to underwrite those contractors. If, in our judgment, they qualify for the job, then we're authorized by a surety company to give the employer a bond which says if that contractor defaults, the surety will fix the problem. To get the bond, the contractor pays a premium based on the dollar amount of the contract." Surety Insurance Services represented several corporate surety companies who made money from assuming those risks. He told me he was looking for someone to train in underwriting construction companies that applied for such bonds.

I didn't quite follow what he was saying, but I thought underwriting might be interesting. The interview went well. Kohoutek did most of the talking initially; then there was a little back-and-forth. He asked me why I didn't become a teacher and about my jobs since I'd been in Seattle. Finally he said, "Bill, you strike me as an intelligent person who hasn't been able to find a way to reach his potential. I don't think anybody has given you a chance to show what you can do. I want to give you that chance." That sounded good to me. The salary he offered to start was low. "But," he assured me, "if you work out for us, you'll get a substantial raise." When I pressed him on that, he said that within a year I'd likely be making about the same as I had at Wilbur-Ellis. As I gained experience as an underwriter, my earnings would grow from there. I accepted the job and began the probation period. Would I like the work, and would the people there like me? I did and they did.

The office was in the Jones Building in downtown Seattle, a structure much like the Park Building in Pittsburgh where the Northern Pacific offices were located. The offices had high ceilings, wood-cased windows, and metal desks. There were seven employees in the agency, counting Tom Kohoutek and me. I began by reading surety bond manuals and learning how to prepare license bonds.

Zanadu Comics was on the same block as my new job. When I walked in the door and said hello to owner Perry Plush, the first comic book I noticed was *Crisis on Infinite Earths* #7. Superman, Supergirl ™ and © DC Comics.

It must have been the second or third day on the job when I noticed there was a comic book specialty store called Zanadu Comics on the same block. I had visited Golden Age Collectables in the past, but the fact that this store was located so close to where I was now working felt like a sign of some kind. It was as if comic books were calling to me, urging me to return to the fold.

Perry Plush, the owner of Zanadu, shared the space with a used bookstore called the Paperback Exchange. Zanadu been subleasing space in the used bookstore since July 1977. When I walked in the door, the first thing I saw was a display featuring the cover of DC's *Crisis on Infinite Earths* #7. That was the issue with the shocking, now iconic "death of Supergirl" cover, which shows Superman holding the wounded body of Kara in his arms. What a reintroduction to comic books! It reminded me of the DC comic that was most important to me in sixth grade: *Batman* #156 (1963), titled "Robin Dies at Dawn!" The cover showed a bereft Batman holding Robin's dead body in his arms in a similar position. I had to have it. Since Perry also had the previous six issues of *Crisis on Infinite Earths* in stock, I bought them all. He was also selling reprints of *Swamp Thing* on high-quality paper, and there were comics featuring Spider-Man wearing an all-black costume. I thought: maybe comic books have made a comeback. I walked out with eight or nine of them, thoroughly intrigued. When I got home and checked them out, I found that I enjoyed them even more than I anticipated. It was fun reading comics again, and these were better than what I had seen on the stands in the 1970s. I decided to buy more, and soon I was hooked again. I even experienced some of the sense of wonder that had drawn me to comics originally. It helped that I had a convenient place to find them.

On my second or third visit to Zanadu, I noticed Tom Kohoutek's son Mark browsing in the store. I had seen him around the office, dropping by to see his father. He seemed startled to discover that his father's new employee was a comic book fan. We shook hands and introduced ourselves. Mark was in his late twenties and heavy-set with dark, longish hair. We acknowledged that we liked comic books, and I told him I was only now getting interested again. That was about all we said at that meeting. (Later I told him about my former participation in fandom.)

It wasn't long before Mark said something to me about wanting to open his own comic book store. I responded that it sounded like a cool idea to me, but starting a business was a big deal and you needed a lot of money to do that. "Oh, that wouldn't be a problem," he said. "My dad has tons of money. Funding it would be small potatoes to him. Would you be interested in coming in on something like that?" I responded affirmatively. I don't remember exactly what I was thinking, except that the idea of running a store full of comic books sounded appealing, and if his father would finance it, maybe it could really happen. Still, it sounded kind of far-fetched.

Shortly thereafter, Tom Kohoutek summoned me to his office. When I entered, I found Mark sitting on the leather couch, where I joined him. Tom said, "Mark tells me you might be interested in becoming a partner in a comic book retail store." When I cautiously replied in the affirmative, I didn't know that I had begun the roller-coaster ride that would become known as Super Comics and Collectables.

Putting the first comics to arrive on our brand-new shelves. By this time, it was apparent that I was losing my hair.

In the ensuing discussions, Tom made it clear that while he would put money into the store, I also had to put money into it if I wanted to be an owner and not merely an employee. "Share the risk, share the reward" was his philosophy. Since the financial upside would only go to the owners, it was a no-brainer. It ended up with me agreeing to put in an initial investment of $2,000 to get the doors open and the store running. Tom would put in the same amount in Mark's name. He explained that we should be able to pay the bills from the profits generated by sales and that we would get the comics and other merchandise on credit.

The preparations involved in opening Super Comics and Collectables are now a blur in my memory. We did everything at breakneck speed. I wanted to slow things down and spend time studying the feasibility of such an enterprise, but research on the costs and potential profitability of comic book stores wasn't available. Tom's point of view was simple: "Either it will work, or it won't work. If Zanadu Comics stays in business, it must be profitable. So sell the same things Perry does, and it will work." I was worn down and also excited by the prospect of being a comic book retailer. I figured that Tom was right. If it worked, it could become a full-time job for Mark and me. How cool would that be? We forged ahead, doing all the practical things required to get a retail business started: setting up a corporation, scouting for locations, and meeting with a distributor (Second Genesis in Portland). We opened a bank account, ordered merchandise, got the retail space ready, and bought comics for back-stock from a local dealer.

Why does it seem somehow prophetic that our opening day was April 1, 1986? As Puck says in *A Midsummer Night's Dream* of the human beings who have wandered into his forest, "Lord, what fools these mortals be!"

Mark and Tom Kohoutek at the "night before opening" party.

Super Comics and Collectables storefront. We opened in April 1986.

We rented a storefront in the University District (5226 University Way), the main drag where the students who attended the University of Washington shopped. While Mark worked with a hammer and saw to build a wooden display rack along one wall of the store, I painted a temporary sign for the window and designed some ad flyers. A large magazine rack and glass display case on loan from distributor Second Genesis arrived. The cash register was free from Marvel Comics (part of a special program to help get new stores on a full professional footing). A desk was installed to give me a place where I could do the daily bookkeeping functions and prepare the nightly deposit. In due time, the first shipment of comics and merchandise arrived, and everything else was made ready. On the night before opening day, we had a little party on the premises for family and friends.

At the beginning, being a partner in a comics store was fun. There was a lot to do, but we had high hopes. It was exciting to hear the cash register ring up another sale or to see new faces appear, happy that there was now a place to buy comics in the University District.

We signed up lots of people for our subscription service. The weekly shipments of new comics each week were always fun to unpack. Most of this work fell to Mark, while I was doing my daily duties at Surety Insurance. The big event in comics at this time was *The Dark Knight Returns* by Frank Miller, Klaus Janson, and Lynn Varley. Copies of the second "prestige edition" flew off the shelf so fast that we had to reorder them the same day. Other popular titles that I recall from those days were *Teenage Mutant Ninja Turtles*, *Watchmen*, *Man of Steel*, and *Usagi Yojimbo*.

Generally, after the shop was closed, Mark and I would drive to the bank, put the deposit into the night drop, and go to my place to fix dinner. Although we were very different people, we got along well and soon became friends, although it was more of a coworker friendship than otherwise.

Soon it became apparent that revenues weren't covering expenses, and those expenses didn't even include paying Mark a salary. Tom agreed to take care of Mark's financial needs for the time being, but the store would have to make enough to pay both Mark and me soon, and of course Tom, too, at some point. What we needed was advice from someone who knew how to successfully run such a business. None of us had a clue how to fix the problem. We couldn't very well ask Perry Plush, as he was now our competitor. Instead, we stumbled along, taking whatever measures we thought might help (sales, special promotions, coupons, etc.). There's no doubt that we sold a lot of comic books. The store had a regular clientele. We had some good days, which gave us hope. Even then, something often went wrong. For instance, on one day when we had a deposit of about $500 (a good day for us), Mark and I had a celebratory dinner after making the night drop. A few days later, when one of our checks bounced, we found out that the bank had no record of receiving that $500 deposit. Since I had been in the car and watched Mark make the deposit, I was convinced the bank had messed up, but they weren't budging. The money simply wasn't there.

Later, when Tom and I were alone, he asked me, "Are you sure that deposit got made?" I assured him it did. He persisted: "Are you sure Mark didn't fake like he was depositing the money and keep it?" I was outraged that Mark's own father would suggest that his son was a thief. Tom reminded me that he had been a bank manager before he started Surety Insurance, and banks just don't lose $500 deposits. It was a baffling situation, but the bottom line is that we were out $500, which we desperately needed. Both Tom and I put another $500 into the business.

By September, as we approached six months in business, I had lost heart. The store wasn't any closer to profitability than it had been all along. I was getting tired of the grind of having to work one job and then spend time on store business. Also, Mark's behavior gradually began to deteriorate. I would call the store during business hours and no one would answer. Or I would find out that against our strict no-smoking policy, Mark had been smoking in the store again. Then I discovered that unsold comics had been piling up in the storage room for months, comics we would never sell. I had thought we were doing a good job of calculating the number of copies to order, but my partner was hiding the fact that we were regularly overordering.

The Dark Knight Returns #1 and *Watchmen* #1, two of the biggest comic book hits of 1986, when Super Comics was in business. Characters ™ and © DC Comics.

I caught Mark in other little lies here and there. One night my mind went back to that mysteriously missing bank deposit, and in light of subsequent developments, I realized what had most likely happened (which Tom had suggested): Mark had made up a dummy envelope that looked just like the deposit. While I watched, he put the fake deposit into the night drop and kept the $500. That *had* to be what had happened. It was staring me in the face, but I wouldn't believe it because I thought Mark would never do that to me. I didn't confront him, because I had no proof and I knew he would deny it—and once you accuse your partner of theft, where do you go from there? However, when the company needed another cash injection, I put my foot down.

I told Tom, "That's it. I'm not putting any more money into the store. It's not working and we have no solutions, so the only thing to do is shut the doors and just end it." I don't remember how much I told Tom about Mark's various shenanigans. (Later, a former customer alluded to "someone" snorting cocaine off the glass display case in the store, although I never got specifics.) One might think the situation would have had repercussions in my day job, but by this point I was no longer working for Surety Insurance. I had quit to work for Construction Bonding and Management Services, a similar surety agency owned and run by Tom's brother-in-law, Nicholas Fix. A younger man, Nick was just getting his business off the ground, and he needed a good "number two man." I continued learning about surety bond underwriting, leaving the realm of clerical work behind. I hoped it would be my ticket to financial stability, and eventually, security. But it wouldn't happen overnight.

Tom and Mark decided to keep the store open, so I had my name removed from the incorporation papers filed with the state and washed my hands of it. I also called Richard Finn at Second Genesis and told him I was leaving. In the end, Tom agreed that Super Comics was a lost cause. It continued only a few months after I dropped out. I chalked up my losses to experience. I didn't like losing $2,500, but I was philosophical about it. The misadventure had had an upside: it got me back into regularly reading and collecting comic books.

Still, there were quite a few areas in my life that were up in the air. Here I was turning thirty-five years old, living on a small income, with no appreciable assets, no romantic involvements, and no creative outlet. I wanted more out of life. It was time to take the bull by the horns, but how?

21.

PUTTING DOWN ROOTS

It might seem strange that I enjoyed learning the surety bond business and the ins and outs of underwriting bonds for construction firms. It wasn't creative work in the sense that it wasn't like writing or drawing or publishing, but each construction firm is unique, so each case was different and presented different hurdles. An underwriter needs to be able to detect hidden problems; to succeed, he or she must be a problem solver. After all, we didn't make any money unless we issued the bonds and were paid the premiums. This made the job both interesting and challenging.

The only drawback was the amount I was getting paid. One couldn't master the arcana of the surety business in six months or even a year, but after doing it for a couple of years, I felt I had a reasonable handle on it. Still, by 1988, my income had increased only slightly, and I was beginning to get frustrated. Patience, I was told, patience.

Making a lot of money has never been my goal, but I was beginning to think I was lagging behind. I saw my friends doing better financially, buying new cars, taking vacations overseas, and becoming homeowners. Even my friend Jim Holt, who wasn't making much himself, had recently bought a house in the city's Roosevelt District. We met for pizza and beer, and I bemoaned my fate.

"I want to buy a house, too, but I'll probably never be able to," I said. "Real estate prices in the city have increased a lot in the past couple of years. By the time I can afford to buy a house, they'll probably go up even more. I may never be able to catch up to match those rising prices."

Jim responded, "It didn't take that much for me to get into my house. For a first-time home buyer, you just need enough for closing costs and mortgage insurance."

"How much would that be?"

"For a starter home, probably about $3,000."

"Well, I don't have it." At this point, my personal savings had eroded to almost nothing.

"I thought you said you have an IRA."

"Yeah, but I can't spend that. It's for my retirement."

"Retirement? What better investment could you make toward your retirement than buying a house? That's how the average person can afford to retire, because at some point the house will be paid off, and your expenses will drop. Instead of paying rent, you'll be creating an important personal asset. It's great to save for retirement; I'm just saying that IRA money could get you into a house. If you want it that bad, there's a way you can do it. Even with the tax consequences of taking the money out now, I'll bet you can cover it. When your income goes up, you can replenish the IRA."

What Jim said made a lot of sense. He put me in touch with his real estate agent, Michelle. Soon I was looking at houses in my price range in neighborhoods in the north end of Seattle where I wanted to live.

Anybody who has shopped for houses knows it can be a grueling process. You shouldn't make that kind of a decision in a hurry. My first day with the agent was discouraging. I was seeing bungalows that needed complete overhauls, houses where the foundation was noticeably sloped, and homes adjacent to public schools. The same happened during the second go-round. Then another big eureka moment occurred in my life. We pulled up to a neat little white house on a corner lot. I immediately liked the look of it. Inside, it had hardwood floors, a fireplace, a full-sized unfinished basement, and a detached garage. The flyer called this one "Grandma's House." It only had 780 square feet, but there were two decent-sized bedrooms, and the basement could eventually be finished. About the only negative factor, other than the house being on the small side, was that it needed a new coat of exterior paint and the yard needed work. But it was an attractive, classy little house. I told Michelle I liked it, and she said, "Okay, let's make a note of that. I have several more houses to show you."

A bit later that same day, after seeing a few unsatisfactory places, she said, "I think you really liked that white house on the corner. Do you want to go back and take another look at it?" I did, and I decided then and there to make an offer. It was so much better than everything else I'd seen, and it suited my needs, so I knew in my gut that it was the one.

It took a bit of wangling back and forth with the mortgage company because my income wasn't quite enough to qualify for the loan, but finally it was done. On July 31, 1988, I officially took possession.

Jim was happy for me. "You won't believe how good you'll feel, owning your own home," he said. He was right. Oh how right he was. It was a fantastic feeling, knowing that the money I was spending for my housing was going toward something I would own someday. I was also nervous as hell about it, because the monthly payments took more than a third of my take-home pay. It would be tough at first, but I had pride in ownership. The exterior needed painting, which I would do myself. That was a huge job; luckily, some friends pitched in and helped. But no one helped me more than Jim Holt, who opened my eyes to the opportunity right before my eyes.

A great deal of my income went toward the house and my car payments, but I still managed to buy a few new comic books (I kept buying and reading them after the store failed), and I saw an occasional movie. Friends came by and were at least mildly impressed. They nicknamed it "Stately Schelly Manor." It just needed a Bat-Cave to make it complete—and the unfinished basement had potential.

ⴝ

I'd had an occasional date over the prior several years, but eventually I would think back to the experience of falling in love with Mario Vitale, and I had to admit that nothing I'd had with anyone else had approached that magic. Was I just fooling myself? Had that been just an idyllic fantasy that had ended because it hadn't been real in the first place?

I decided to try a more pragmatic approach. I would take out a personal ad in a newspaper that seemed likely to be read by someone I might like. The *Seattle Weekly* classifieds were rife with such ads, including some by people seeking same-sex partners. For me, a better choice seemed to be the *Seattle Gay News,* which by this time had been around for over a decade. I figured it was more likely to be read by guys who were out and proud, which was what I wanted. At the time, I wasn't out at work, but I was out to everyone else in my life. So I placed an ad.

While I was waiting for responses, I got together with Stephanie Seymour, who had been a friend since we both started work at Wilbur-Ellis on the same day back in 1980. Now I discovered that she had a "significant other"—an expression becoming popular at the time—named Maureen (nicknamed Renie) Jones, and they were living only half a mile north of me. They talked about wanting children and the different ways lesbian couples went about it. One way was the anonymous donor route, using the services of a sperm bank. Another was finding a man who would agree to father their children, perhaps a gay man. That way could be complicated, but it had the virtue of allowing the children to know their father.

This made sense to me, and it struck a chord. In my search to understand who I was, I had often asked my parents and my mother's parents about family history. Did I inherit any artistic genes? Being able to know about one's forebears is important. At some point, Stephanie, Renie, and I started discussing the possibility of me being that man for them. I knew they were good people. I also knew I would never be in a traditional marriage with a woman and have children of my own. The possibility of becoming a father bounced around in my head in the months to come.

I received a response to my advertisement in the *Seattle Gay News* from a man named Larry Summers, who had moved to Seattle from Kansas City, Missouri, a couple of years before. Larry was thirty-seven, like me. We met, began dating, and liked each other. He was a respiratory therapist by trade, which meant, of course, that he smoked. (So did I.) Larry had come to Seattle to be with another man, but when that hadn't worked out, he decided to see if he could find someone else. He was nice-looking and warm, and it wasn't long before we were discussing whether he ought to move in with me. His lease was expiring, so he had to move somewhere. We had only known each other a few months, but not long after the arrival of 1989, Larry moved into Stately Schelly Manor, and we were suddenly a couple.

Even with Larry's help, the house payments were steep, and I felt my salary at work should be growing faster than it was. I was underwriting all the license bonds we were doing as well as many of the construction bonds. Most of the bonds for specific projects were done with guarantees from the Surety Bond Guarantee Program, a federal program run by the U.S. Small Business Administration, which was established to give an incentive to bond companies to provide surety bonds to small construction firms. I prepared the applications to the SBA for each bond guarantee and took them to the SBA's local office.

I'd been in the surety bond business for three and a half years, three of them with Construction Bonding and Management Services, on the day when I asked Nick for a raise. He responded with about the worst thing he could have said. "Well, you know," he said, "I have to consider whether I could hire a clerk to do your job." It was not only insulting, but it made no sense, since nearly all of what I was doing presupposed knowing how to underwrite the bonds. I told him that was ridiculous, but I didn't blow up. I seethed.

Larry Summers, my significant other in the early 1990s.

By this time, I had a working relationship with Tom Ewbank, head of the SBA Bond Guarantee Program in Seattle, and I was talking with him on the phone shortly after that talk with Nick. Out of frustration, I (inappropriately) vented about my job frustrations, ending with: "If there's ever an opening for an underwriter at the SBA, let me know."

"Actually," Tom said, "the junior underwriter here is leaving, so I'll be interviewing for replacements in the next few weeks. Why don't you apply?" The job with the SBA would initially pay about the same as I had been making, but it had two substantial salary jumps built in for one and two years hence. By my second anniversary, assuming everything went well, I would be making something like 30 percent more than at the start. After that, there were step increases one would receive in the subsequent years, in addition to cost-of-living increases. I saw it for what it was: a big fat opportunity, and immediately decided to go for it.

The application for federal employment was the most in-depth, involved job application I'd ever encountered. It required several essays to display my knowledge of different aspects of the surety industry, and here my writing ability worked to my advantage. The job also required a college degree, any kind of degree, and now my degree was finally useful, too. By the time I finished the application, I was brimming with confidence. My interview with Tom and another interview with his supervisor went well. In late July, I got the call. The job was mine.

N

Shortly before I got the verdict from the SBA, I had one of the greatest cinema experiences of my life. Not because the movie itself was up there with *Citizen Kane* or *The Godfather* or *Schindler's List,* but because it was a major motion picture about my favorite comic book character: Batman.

JUNE 23

The advance screening of Tim Burton's *Batman* (1989), starring Michael Keaton and Jack Nicholson, gave me one of the biggest cinematic thrills of my life. Bat symbol, Batman ™ and © DC Comics.

Excitement for Seattle's advance screening of Tim Burton's *Batman* had reached a fever pitch by the time the event finally took place. The fans who poured into the Oak Tree Cinema that night seemed to be mostly hardcore comics fans. The media had been beating the drum for this movie, which had been highly controversial due to its casting of comedic actor Michael Keaton as Batman, and for its sensational casting of Jack Nicholson as the Joker. Burton's previous movie, *Beetlejuice* (also starring Keaton), had been a substantial success. It showcased Burton's way with quirky, dark material, which seemed to bode well for the comic book adaptation. The campy *Batman* TV show of the 1960s had cast the Dynamic Duo as figures of fun. Many doubted that the public would accept a serious story with a man in a bat costume. How in the world would Burton and Keaton pull this off?

After a wait that seemed interminable, the lights came down and the noisy crowd hushed. From the opening, brooding strains of Danny Elfman's soundtrack, and the revelation of the giant bat logo, I felt chills down my spine and a thrill second to no other I'd felt in a theater in my adult life. When the title "Batman" appeared on the screen, the crowd erupted in applause and cheers. I was completely spellbound as Anton Furst's amazing conception of Gotham City was revealed, and Batman made his first appearance on a rooftop. When the unfortunate thug gasped, "Who—are—you?" and Keaton rasped, "I'm Batman!" I, and the entire audience, knew this was going to be good.

Eleven years earlier, *Superman* starring Christopher Reeve had been a big hit, yet it took the meteoric box office success of Tim Burton's *Batman* to start the modern cinematic trend in comic book movies that continues to the present day. *Batman*'s success was all the more exciting because the film was an unprecedented artistic triumph that respected—nay, celebrated—its comic book roots.

⚡

Shortly after Larry and I became a couple, I decided to father a child with Stephanie and Renie. Stephanie had gone back to college to become a computer programmer, so they decided Renie would be the first to become pregnant. They wanted to know if I was serious about being the father. Again, they emphasized that they didn't want to go the artificial-insemination route, a common choice for lesbian couples. They wanted their children to know their father. This said a lot to me about the kind of parents they would be.

Early photo of Jaimeson and dad. He was born March 14, 1990.

I discussed it with Larry, and while he wasn't sure it was a good idea, he left it up to me because I was the one who had known them, and he and I hadn't been together long. In a written agreement between Renie and me, it was established that I would give up my parental rights and would have no financial obligation to the child. They would be the parents. As the father, I could be as much a part of the child's life as I wanted to be. This sort of arrangement was highly unusual at this time. It was based on trust, since a written agreement could conceivably be broken or superseded by state laws regarding parental responsibility, but I had given the matter more thought, and I wanted to go ahead. I wanted the son or daughter that I couldn't have any other way.

With the help of an accommodating shot glass, followed by a quick drive from my house to theirs, we began the process. Renie became pregnant on our first try, and eight months and one week later she gave birth at Virginia Mason Hospital in Seattle. Due to issues with Renie's blood pressure, labor was induced three weeks early. I was in the delivery room and witnessed the birth, the most profound experience of life to be had on planet Earth. Despite weighing a little under six pounds when he came into the world, Jaimeson Carl Jones was a healthy baby boy. No problems arose from his premature birth. Renie chose the name "Jaimeson" simply because she liked it. She also chose his middle name, "Carl," to honor his parentage. Carl is my middle name and was my father's first name, the patriarchal name of the Schelly family going way back.

For his first two weeks of life, I saw Jaimeson almost every day. When he was three months old, I took him to my place for the first time, and it was just him and me. We got along fine. Of course, if a baby's crying, it can only mean one of four things: he needs a bottle, a burp, a diaper change, or sleep. Larry seemed a little uncomfortable with his boyfriend having a son, but he pitched in as best he could. I must admit, two men with a baby in a stroller attracted some funny looks on the day we took him to Northgate Mall. It wouldn't seem so odd today. I don't know if I'd call us pioneers, but I guess we were, of a sort. Eventually, we settled on having him over once a week. He would grow up calling this occasion "daddy day." This gave Renie and Stephanie a bit of a break, and it gave me a chance to bond with my son.

Perhaps not too surprisingly, considering how quickly he had moved in with me after we met, my relationship with Larry came to an end a little more than a year after Jaimeson's birth. It had nothing to do with me being a father, or (as far as I know) with the fact that I had agreed to father a second child (this time with Stephanie). It was simply the fact that he and I didn't have enough in common. I wanted to stay friends, but that seldom works. Larry decided Seattle had been a bust for him, and he moved back to Kansas City. Within months I was hearing about his new friend Andy, who became his partner and, eventually, his husband.

At this point, I decided that rather than trying to make something happen in the relationship area, I would enjoy the single life. My life had blossomed a great deal in the short space of three years: becoming a homeowner, getting the job with the SBA, and having a son. There was only one missing piece: that all-important creative outlet.

22.

BATMAN BROUGHT ME BACK

I don't know why my involvement in Super Comics and Collectables didn't bring me back to comic fandom. Maybe I didn't have time, juggling two jobs. My return didn't come until a full four years after Super Comics closed its doors.

One day at work at the SBA in the fall of 1990, I heard laughter and some sort of hubbub outside my office. I turned to look through my doorway and saw a dark, caped figure pass by. Did I see what I thought I saw? I poked my head out the door. No, my eyes hadn't deceived me. It was none other than Batman, walking through the government workplace—the Batman of the motion picture, with those molded chest and abdominal muscles. Then it hit me: it was Halloween.

Others in fanciful costumes were roving through other parts of the office. When the Caped Crusader circled around and was moving in my direction, I beckoned him over. "Hey Batman," I said, "where's Robin?"

"He couldn't make it," he said, grinning. "It's a school day."

Now I recognized him: it was my coworker Glenn Moss, sporting an expensive-looking Batman costume. Since the enormous success of Tim Burton's movie, Batman had become a universal folk hero on a scale with Superman. That meant mass marketing, including Batman outfits for adults to wear to Halloween parties.

I told him, "I've been reading and collecting Batman comics since I was eight years old."

He stopped short. "You collect comics? So do I." Glenn and I were about the same age.

I nodded and said, "I was involved in comic fandom in the sixties and early seventies."

"I'm in a comics APA right now," he said. "Have you ever heard of *X-apa*? It's all about the X-Men characters and comics."

I hadn't forgotten that "APA" was fan jargon for "amateur press alliance." "No," I said, "but I used to be in *Capa-alpha*."

"Oh, sure. I know some people in *Capa-alpha*."

"Now? It's still going?"

"Yeah, and there are some other APAs."

"Hang on. Could you get me a current *Capa-alpha* roster? Maybe I'll recognize some of the members' names."

A few days later, I was perusing the list of names and addresses of those in the APA. At least a half dozen were familiar. One name in particular jumped out at me: Jeff Gelb. In 1965, Jeff was the first fan (other than Richard Shields) to contribute to one of my amateur publications. Since he grew up in Rochester, New York, 280 miles from Pittsburgh, we never met in person, but Jeff and I exchanged letters and collaborated on a couple of comic strips for the fanzine *Bombshell*. If anyone on the roster would remember me, it would be Jeff.

His address listing was c/o *Radio and Records,* a music-industry newspaper where he was working. I got his office phone number from directory assistance and called him. Jeff seemed as pleased to talk with me as I was with him. I hadn't realized how ready I was for a connection with someone from the good old days of fandom. Having gone through a fair amount of angst in the past two decades, I looked back on my experiences as a fanzine publisher and participant in comic fandom as some of the happiest times in my life. Now that I was more settled and reading comics again, there was nothing stopping me from returning to Fandomland. Talking with Jeff got my sense of wonder mojo going again.

Jeff began sending me his monthly *Capa-alpha* contributions called *Men of Mystery,* named after his best-known fanzine of the 1960s. Through the first half of 1991, I read his zine, and we talked more on the phone. My enthusiasm grew. I joined the waiting list to become a member of the APA with *Capa-alpha* #321, the July 1991 issue. That got me a sample copy of the new issue.

Looking through it, I found a contribution by member Richard Pryor that reprinted a bunch of old fanzine covers. Ah, the memories those covers brought back! Pryor also published a recent letter from Ronn Foss, which talked about how he was living in rural Missouri and supporting himself with art commissions. After Jeff, Ronn was the fan whom I most wanted to contact. I asked Richard if he had a phone number for Ronn. It turned out Foss didn't have a phone, but Pryor gave me his mailing address.

Ronn Foss Retrospective #1 (January 1992). Art by Foss.

I quickly ascertained that a lot of the fans who were active in fandom of the 1960s were no longer part of the scene. Where had they gone? I wanted to know what such prominent people as Biljo White, G. B. Love, Richard "Grass" Green, and Bill Spicer were up to these days, and to find some way of expressing my appreciation to them for all they'd done for fandom. I decided to see if I could find them and perhaps interview them—for what purpose, I didn't quite know. Also, I wanted to find out if some of them had extra copies of their old fanzines. I had foolishly sold my fanzines (those that hadn't been lost in my apartment fire) years earlier, along with most of my original comic book collection. I didn't yet have access to the internet, so I had to rely on telephones and snail mail to contact these people. I subscribed to *Comic Buyer's Guide* and began scanning its classified ads looking for fanzines for sale. Thus began what amounted to research into early fandom: its origins, its participants, and its publications.

In response to my enthusiastic letter, Ronn Foss responded with an astounding twenty-seven-page typed missive, with illustrations scattered throughout. He answered all my questions, such as what he'd been up to in the intervening years, and he enclosed some of the publications he'd done recently. He was living in an old house in the Ozarks near the small town of West Plains, Missouri. Ronn remembered me, but not nearly as well as I did him, which only stood to reason. Nevertheless, he was obviously delighted and eager to communicate with someone who was, after all, a fan of his stories and art. Since one could contribute to *Capa-alpha* while on the waiting list, I immediately began planning to do a special contribution about him for the APA: a review of his work in fanzines and what he had been up to since then. The resulting publication, my first fanzine since *Sense of Wonder* in 1972, was the sixty-four-page *Ronn Foss Retrospective* in early 1992. I couldn't have afforded to publish something like this even a year or two earlier, but I had passed my second anniversary with the SBA and had gotten another substantial raise.

I was greatly aided by the purchase of an early IBM home desktop computer. I've long since forgotten the model number. I bought it from a friend who was buying a newer, better one. He also sold me a dot-matrix printer. It was a crude beginning, but at least I was computerized, which meant I had a word processor. Being able to make changes without retyping whole documents was an incredible advance. It made my writing much easier.

In 1965, *Super-Heroes Anonymous* #1 had been printed on an early Xerox machine, and the results were unsatisfactory. Photocopiers had come a long way since then, and they were the printing method of choice for many fanzine publishers in the 1990s. The results, when handled skillfully, approximated the look of professional photo-offset printing. It made producing a sharp-looking publication much easier than in the past. True, a sixty-four-page fanzine would cost about three dollars to print each copy, but other fanzines I had in mind would be shorter.

A tinge of sadness emanated from the pages of the *Ronn Foss Retrospective*, which presented a long interview with Ronn and a checklist of his amateur comic strips, as well as many examples of his art. Back in the day, his self-portraits in the fanzines made him look like a young, confident Hugh Hefner. In reality, he was a rather shy, unmotivated fellow who was now eking out a living doing fetish drawings to the specifications of two or three clients for their private collections, artwork that would never be seen by anyone else. His rural house was collapsing through neglect and vandalism. He was living in one room that had a woodstove for heat and no running water or phone. He had a car to go into West Plains to shop, but precious little money to spend. When some of his teeth were pulled or fell out, they went unreplaced, so his voice on the cassette tapes we occasionally traded was sibilant and sometimes indistinct. Yet he seemed resigned to his lot and rarely complained about it. His wife, Coreen, had lasted only a year after their move from Illinois to Missouri in 1975 before leaving him. Despite the brave face Ronn put on his situation (extolling the pleasures of "the simple life"), I could tell he was grateful for the communication with me; and I found myself, quite unexpectedly, becoming close friends with him.

He had so little of a material nature to give, and yet his generosity constantly amazed me. One day he sent me a box containing a small but choice stack of vintage fanzines: mint copies of the two issues of *Alter Ego* he had edited in 1963 and 1964 after Jerry Bails passed it on to him, and others such as Mike Vosburg's *Masquerader,* for which Ronn had done the cover; issues of *The Comicollector* from 1962 and 1963; and several more. He also sent a folder with all the pages of his ditto strips, which had been removed from the fanzines where they appeared: original pages of Dimension Man, Little Giant, the Viper, and the Cowl. I'd never seen some of them, so it was like discovering artifacts from an Egyptian tomb.

"Keep all these fanzines and miscellany for your archive, and preserve them," he wrote. "I know you love these things, as I do, and you're better equipped to preserve them than I am."

In addition to sending fifty copies of the *Ronn Foss Retrospective* to be part of the January 1992 mailing of *Capa-alpha,* I printed extras and gave away or sold another fifty or so to the people on my burgeoning mailing list. Ronn began receiving mail from people he hadn't heard from in decades, and some new art commissions. He had been rediscovered. This attention seemed to give him a whole new lease on life. So much of what I had done in my life up to that point had been for myself—often because I was scrabbling for some kind of foothold in the world, which I was finding only now—so it was a nice feeling to do something for someone else.

⚡

Soon I had another reason to think of someone other than myself— not a new boyfriend or partner, but a sister for Jaimeson. In December 1991, my daughter, Tara Jane, was born. This time, the biological mother was Stephanie Seymour. Tara and Jamieson were as different as night and day. I noticed it from the beginning. For example, when I changed Jaimeson's diaper, he would lie there and grin up at me; when I changed Tara, she would restlessly twist this way and that. I called her my "twist-away baby." Indeed, her most salient personality trait in later life was her push for individual identity and independence.

Now our modern family was complete. We hadn't discussed the number of children we would have, but not long after Tara's birth, I decided that two was enough for me. I had "one of each" and no desire for more. (Later, Stephanie had Samantha, a second daughter, with a different father.) Many unexpected things came out of my decision to father two children. One of the nicest was that, in addition to my immediate Schelly family members, I was now a blood member of two different clans, the Joneses and the Seymours.

How my life had changed in a few short years! My weekdays were spent at the SBA, underwriting bond applications and learning more about the surety industry. My weekends were devoted to working on my fannish projects. And, one day a week, on Daddy Day, I would pick up the kids and have them for an evening.

I loved playing with Superman and Spider-Man action figures with young Jaimeson as he got older. Another favorite activity was draping blankets over folding chairs to form a tent, and then, snuggled inside, pretending we were camping out in the woods while telling each other stories. We watched videos sometimes, or I read to them. I lost count of the number of times I read about Donald Duck's sailboat to Jaimeson, or about Barbie saving the dolphins to Tara. Much to my chagrin, action figures aside, I could never interest the kids in comic books. Animated cartoons, yes, but not comic books. Now, with the benefit of computer-generated effects, the movie and TV worlds were increasingly able to produce the kind of imaginative imagery that had been one of comics' main attractions for me as a boy.

Jaimeson's sister Tara was born on December 19, 1991.

N

When I stepped out of the Alaska Airlines baggage claim area of the San Diego International Airport into a warm summer day, I felt a rush of adrenaline. I was attending the 1992 San Diego Comic-Con, my first major con since the 1973 New York Comic Art Convention. I was looking forward to meeting Jeff Gelb in person. We had decided to share a hotel room to save money. When Jeff showed up that evening, I welcomed him into the room and found him to be just as funny, knowledgeable, and warm in person as he was over the phone. We gabbed about comics and what we were looking for at the con. Then he tutored me a bit on the history of the San Diego Comic-Con.

It had been founded in 1970 by a group that included Shel Dorf, Richard Alf, and Ken Krueger, and it had steadily grown in the ensuing decades. For many years it was held at the El Cortez Hotel, but it finally became too large and relocated to the San Diego Convention Center. When the dominant New York Comicon faded after the death of its leader, Phil Seuling, the rapidly growing San Diego con became the number one convention in the country.

Upon entering the convention hall the next morning, I was stunned by the tableau spread before me. The enormous room was packed with booths from wall to wall. It would have seemed overwhelming except that the first booth in my line of sight was that of Bud Plant Comic Art. That link to my first comics con was reassuring. I also had Jeff as a guide to help me get oriented in the enormous convention center.

My main objective in 1973 had been to show my portfolio to representatives from DC Comics. This time, apart from shopping for old comic books and checking out all the other merchandise on display (posters, T-shirts, toys, souvenirs, etc.), I wanted to meet as many participants in 1960s and 1970s fandom as I could find. Some of them had moved into the professional ranks, even to the highest levels. Paul Levitz had started as a teenager editing the fanzines *Et Cetera* and *The Comic*

Reader, and then he rose through the ranks at DC Comics as a writer and editor to become DC's executive vice president and publisher.

Early on, I made a beeline to the *Comic Buyer's Guide* booth to meet its editors, Don and Maggie Thompson. Shortly before the con, Jeff and I had sold them on a series of columns under the heading "Fandom's Founders," and we wanted to interview them for one of those columns. Crowds of fans around the *CBG* booth kept them busy, but Jeff and I were finally able to sit down with them in a quiet place and record a conversation. I told them the story of how Don had written me a critical letter about my fanzine *Fantasy Forum* in 1966 and how I had taken that to heart. He didn't remember the incident but was pleased I had reacted the way I did. "Most people paid no attention when I wrote letters like that," he said. "Or they got mad." After the interview, the four of us posed for a group photo. I'm glad I pushed us to do this at that time. Don died in his sleep in early 1994, before I had occasion to return to the San Diego shindig.

With Maggie and Don Thompson, and Jeff Gelb, at the 1992 San Diego Comic-Con.

With Jim Shooter, 1992. Photo by Jeff Gelb.

At one point, I spotted Jim Shooter at a booth. He'd had a high-profile career after his early years at DC, serving as editor-in-chief of Marvel Comics from the late 1970s to 1987. Then, with the help of investors, my former boyhood acquaintance founded a comic book company called Valiant, which became quite successful for a while. I didn't know he had been ousted from that company a few weeks earlier and was probably going through a lot of turmoil at this time. Since I had lost most of my hair (it started going when I was twenty-five), I had to introduce myself to Jim, or he wouldn't have recognized me. He posed with me for a photograph, and we exchanged a few words. When I sensed he wasn't interested in talking about old times, I thanked him and moved on.

Not long afterward, I learned that Jim had written the first story with an explicit depiction of gays in a mainstream comic, in *The Hulk!* magazine #23 (1980). The scene of Bruce Banner taking a shower at the YMCA and being accosted and threatened with rape by two young men was heavily criticized by both fans and professionals. In Andy Mangels's article "Out of the Closet and into the Comics" in the comics-oriented periodical *Amazing Heroes* #143 (1988), comics artist Mike Grell is quoted as saying, "The Hulk story was badly done and so blatantly homophobic that I think everybody with a brain in his head who read it was embarrassed by it. I was embarrassed to be working in an industry that would allow something like that to see print in the first place." Nearly all the professionals interviewed by Mangels echoed this view. Howard Cruse, the gay comics creator whom I met in 1982, said, "I found it hard to believe that anybody could be so out of touch that they didn't realize—with the unusual experience of having a gay character—that to have them turn out to be dangerous rapists was so destructive. It was like if the only time comics showed a black person he was looting a store. If you have that image to the exclusion of all other images, it only confirms peoples' worst prejudices."

Bad-ass superhero Northstar openly declares his sexuality, a milestone for Marvel Comics, in *Alpha Flight* #106 (1992). Story by Scott Lobdell, art by Mark Pacella and Dan Panosian. ™ and © Marvel Characters, Inc.

Although gay characters occasionally appeared as supporting characters in comics from DC, Eclipse, and others later in the 1980s, a key event occurred in Marvel's *Alpha Flight* #106, published in early 1992: team member Northstar explicitly stated, "I am gay." John Byrne, who had created Northstar in 1979, maintained that the character had been intended to be gay all along, but he'd only been able to hint at it due to editor-in-chief Jim Shooter's policy against having openly gay characters, and the limitations imposed by the

Comics Code Authority. But Jim was no longer at Marvel, and the Comics Code had loosened up a great deal, so writer Scott Lobdell was free to have Northstar make his declaration. It was great fodder for the "Gays in Comics" panel at the 1992 convention, which had been a part of the San Diego con's programming since 1988. (Scott Lobdell was one of six on the panel, which was moderated by Andy Mangels.) So times were changing, it seemed.

Saturday morning began with the *Capa-alpha* breakfast at the Clarion Hotel. Anyone who had ever been a member of the APA was invited. I got to meet folks such as Tony Isabella, Jim Korkis, Anthony Tollin, Dwight Decker, and Rich Morrissey. I felt like I fit right in, even though I had been away from fandom for so long.

This convention was also the occasion when I met Roy Thomas, who had brought Conan and *Star Wars* to comic books, and went on to write for DC after leaving Marvel in the late 1970s. Much as I enjoyed and admired Roy's comic book writing, I wanted to meet him to discuss his role in early fandom as the editor of *Alter Ego*. As with the Thompsons, it wasn't easy getting his attention. He was beleaguered everywhere he went by fans—me being one of them—but finally, between his appearances on panels and signings at this or that booth, I was able to introduce myself and offer him a copy of my latest amateur publication: *The History of the Amateur Comic Strip*, a tribute to the comics that had appeared in such small-press publications as *Fantasy Illustrated, Star-Studded Comics,* and *Alter Ego.*

As he paged through the zine, Roy instantly got what I was doing and made it clear that he would support my efforts. He had to be somewhere else, so we talked for no more than five minutes, but it was a meeting that would turn out to be one of the most pivotal in my life. He agreed that we should make contact through the mail, and he scribbled his address on my con program. As I watched him being swallowed up by the crowd, I was elated. With Roy on my side, I knew my historical research would accelerate.

N

The convention more than lived up to my expectations, but I had yet to experience my most exciting moment on the convention floor. The ground was laid for this moment beginning in 1968 when Jack Kirby, then the biggest name in the comic book field, moved from New York to California. He was a guest of honor at the first San Diego con in 1970 and at all those that followed, providing a great box-office draw for the event. He was always mobbed at the convention by autograph seekers and well-wishers, as is befitting one of the true gods of comics. In 1992, Kirby was in attendance once again, and the con held a seventy-fifth birthday party for him. My encounter with Kirby occurred in a rather unexpected way.

As I was wandering, I noticed Kirby standing by himself at the end of a near-empty aisle. He seemed to be a little uncertain, as if he was either waiting for someone or trying to decide where he would go next. The con was about to close for the day, and the crowd had thinned out, which was the only reason why no one seemed to notice him.

This, I thought, is my big chance to meet him. Here's my best recollection of our conversation: Gulping a little, I walked up to him and delivered the phrases he had doubtless heard thousands of times before: "Hello Mr. Kirby. I'm a big fan of your work." I reached out my hand. He seemed a little distracted but he shook hands with me.

"Thank you," he mumbled.

"I'm sure you don't remember, but you kindly sent me an original sketch of Captain America back in 1965, when I wrote you a fan letter. I still have that sketch, and I treasure it."

Now he was focusing on me. "I'm glad you liked it."

I ventured, "I love everything you've done, but the FF is my favorite. I especially liked 'The Origin of Doctor Doom!' in the second *Fantastic Four* annual. Victor von Doom is such an interesting character."

A bemused, slightly impish expression came over Kirby's face. "Yes, Doom was a fascinating fellow. He had his own point of view, and his own problems, which most people don't realize." He spoke as if Doctor Doom existed in the real world.

"He was competitive with Reed Richards …" I managed.

"Yes, but do you know what his real problem was?"

I shook my head.

"He was a perfectionist." Kirby's smile was working, and he had a twinkle in his eye, almost as if he was pulling my leg.

"So …" I was trying to get Jack's point. "If you're a perfectionist … and you have a scarred face … then you'd be angry?"

"Yes, because you'd feel like the scars would prevent you from getting the admiration that you deserved," he said. "But Doom wouldn't accept his fate. He wanted to overcome it."

I wasn't sure I understood his point, but I didn't care. Jack Kirby had just shared an insight into one of his characters with me. At that point, another fan or two had come up to listen. "These characters do exist, you know," Kirby said.

"In your mind," I said, "they must be very real to you."

"No, they actually exist," he responded. "I know them intimately."

How to respond to that? I don't think I did. When I hesitated, others started asking him things, so I caught his eye, smiled, and moved away. I was so awestruck to be talking to him, I didn't even think of asking for his autograph. But I already had it on that Cap sketch he'd done for me a quarter of a century before.

Over the course of the con, Jeff Gelb and I cemented our friendship. Apart from his regular gig at *Radio & Records*, Jeff coedited (with his friend Michael Garrett) the *Hot Blood* paperback book series of erotic horror stories, sometimes writing a story himself. His knowledge of fandom and publishing made him a perfect wing man and sounding board. More than that, we had a shared history in fandom, enjoyed each other's personalities, and shared many interests beyond comic books. In short, we had the makings of, as Humphrey Bogart put it at the end of *Casablanca,* a "beautiful friendship."

⚡

When I got home, I was greeted with sobering news. Dee Trageser had written to tell me that Dick had passed away after a protracted battle with lung cancer. I knew he had been diagnosed with the disease and was going through treatment, so this news wasn't entirely unexpected. Still, it was saddening.

With the passage of time, one realizes that not everyone lives to a ripe old age, or even to a nearly ripe age. Some key players in 1960s fandom had passed away before I reentered fandom. I would never be able to meet or interview such people as Larry Herndon (editor of *Star-Studded Comics*), Rick Durrell (a prominent collector), or Phil Seuling. Realizing that many of the original fans were getting older added urgency to my efforts to reach out to them.

Fandom had a huge effect on the comics industry itself by launching comic book conventions that brought fans and pros together and by providing a training ground for a new wave of comics-aware writers and artists who came to the fore in the 1970s (Bernie Wrightson, Frank Miller, Len Wein, Marv Wolfman). When newsstand distribution of comic books began crumbling, members of fandom created new distribution modes that led to mainstream comic books being sold through comic book specialty shops. I was determined that those enthusiastic, even visionary fans should receive the recognition they richly deserved. Fandom needed to be reminded of its roots.

Plus, I wanted to recapture the magic of that halcyon era for myself. As a thirteen-year-old, I wouldn't have known what to say if I'd met the Big Name Fans, who were often in their late teens or twenties. Now, as an adult, I could approach them as an equal. Just as the comic book professionals were surprised and delighted when fans came knocking on their doors because they had toiled in anonymity with no expectation of recognition, so the fans from those early days—many of them no longer active in fandom—were surprised and pleased when I contacted them.

I skipped the San Diego convention in 1993 for financial reasons, but I would make it the following year. In the interim, my fan activity increased exponentially. I was like the proverbial whirling dervish, seeking out more fan contacts, contributing to *Capa-alpha,* and publishing more fanzines, such as one devoted exclusively to telling the story of the Alley Tally Party of March 1964 (when nineteen comics fans got together at the Detroit home of Jerry Bails).

At the same time, I was on a crash course to learn as much as I could about the history of comic books themselves. Such information had been relatively rudimentary during my original period of fan activity, but it had progressed a great deal in the ensuing years. Now I soaked up the history of the medium wherever I could find it. I devoured articles in Bob Overstreet's *Comic Book Price Guide* (which included multiple text features each year) and *Comic Buyer's Guide*, and in such books as the *Smithsonian Book of Comic-Book Comics*, edited by Michael Barrier and Martin Williams, *The Encyclopedia of American Comics* by Ron Goulart, and *The Art of Will Eisner* by Cat Yronwode and Denis Kitchen. I also read numerous interviews with veteran comics writers and artists conducted by Gary Groth and others in the pages of *The Comics Journal*. (Gary and I had a laugh when he recently found a letter I'd written him in 1970 in which I said, "I don't think you have the necessary skill at interviewing.")

As a result of my contacts and research, and in reaction to my new fanzines, I began receiving all manner of fascinating relics of the past. Often, fans would send me odd things such as old correspondence and newspaper clippings, along with their own written reminiscences. Biljo White gave me the original ditto masters for his Eye strips. Mike Tuohey sent me material that had been prepared for an issue of his zine *Super Hero* that was never published. Bernie Bubnis shocked me when he sent one of the rare metal buttons that were given out at the 1964 New York Comicon. Former fanzine publishers sometimes sent copies of their old fanzines. One day, a large box arrived from Ellen (formerly Al) Kuhfeld, which contained a donation of several dozen fanzines from the 1960s.

Sometime in 1993, I decided to formally christen my growing collection of material from fandom's past the Comic Fandom Archives. The idea was that I would collect and preserve such material and would eventually bequeath it to a university library (like those at Ohio State or Michigan State, which both had large comic art collections). In a notice I sent to everyone on my growing mailing list, I pledged that I would never sell any fanzines that were donated to the archive. Of course, I spent a good deal of my own money buying vintage fanzines. By 1994, I'd purchased dozens more. My fanzine holdings soon numbered in excess of one thousand and continued to grow.

Labors of Love (1994), a history of the most notable amateur comics of the classic fanzines of the 1960s. Hamster Press.

The fun of fandom had truly taken over. I was a fanzine publisher again! I was writing editorials, doing artwork, pasting things up, and making copies. In some ways, it was like I was that fifteen-year-old kid again, producing issues of *Incognito* and other zines. People seemed to be genuinely excited about and appreciative of what I was doing. In spring 1994, I produced my most ambitious, elaborate fanzine yet, an expansion of my rudimentary *History of the Amateur Comic Strip,* called *Labors of Love: The Classic Comic Strips of the 1960s Fanzines.* It was a sixty-six-page publication with 144 illustrations from the pages of the original fanzines. The text ran to about twenty thousand words, the longest piece I'd done in years. It helped me hone my rusty writing skills. This one went back to press twice. Bud Plant liked it enough that he ordered a hundred copies to sell to his mail-order customers. Of the 350 or so copies that eventually saw print, about a third of them were given away to contributors, and the rest were sold at either retail or wholesale prices. I had to charge for them because of the costs of printing and mailing. I wasn't making a profit, but I was breaking even, which was all that mattered.

Obviously, my pent-up desire for a creative outlet—to write and publish—was the reason for this explosion of activity. I had been languishing for years, having almost given up my writing dream for lack of a direction. Now, in writing about the history of comic fandom, a subject for which I had real passion, I had found a way to channel that energy. I not only loved my subject matter, but I had the right credentials. I had been there and knew what I was talking about. My approach felt authentic because I'd been a part of the original scene.

Then it came to me: I could write an entire book on the history of comic fandom. The idea hadn't crossed my mind when I reentered fandom, but now it was a no-brainer. The logic of it—the fact that I was uniquely placed and qualified to write it—was so compelling that it was almost as if it already existed. I had already made many of the contacts I would need for such an endeavor, and I'd done much of the research. I could incorporate material from my fanzine-format publications, giving me a head start on the writing. Once I saw it in my head, there was no turning back.

Hence, my decision to attend the 1994 San Diego Comic-Con had a specific purpose: to meet more people, find new sources of information, and see if any publishers found my book idea interesting. But I knew I needed to have a complete manuscript before I could formally approach a publisher.

23.

THE GOLDEN AGE OF COMIC FANDOM

My dream of writing books had never died. Now I had something to write about, something that no one else (as far as I knew) had thought of doing. Jeff Gelb thought it was a great idea, as did the few others whom I consulted. However, none of the publishers I approached at the 1994 San Diego Comic-Con seemed overly excited about putting out such a book. Still, my confidence remained high. When I got home, I cleared my desk, turned on the computer, and began work on an outline for a book with the working title *The History of Comic Fandom*. I still have that initial three page outline, printed on my primitive dot-matrix printer.

I started drafting the book in October, a process that would continue for the next five or six months. It wasn't much different from writing *Harry Langdon* in 1980, except that with *Harry Langdon*, I'd had too little information; with *The History of Comic Fandom*, I had too much.

I had to sift through a mountain of material—hundreds of fanzines, interviews, and letters—and figure out a way to organize it. The goal was to make it read like a story, not a collection of facts or wandering digressions. I still have notes with exhortations such as "Important to emphasize 'storytelling' to avoid book becoming a list of names, zine titles, and numbers." I decided my story would start in about 1960 and end in 1972 or 1973. It would tell fandom's origin, identify its founders and supporting players, and explain how it grew into an ongoing phenomenon. There would be details of the early comics conventions and stories about the ways comics were bought, sold, and traded, leading up to the publication of Bob Overstreet's first *Comic Book Price Guide* in 1970. My initial outline broke it down into fourteen chapters. The finished book had only twelve chapters and a postscript.

I moved my computer to a small side desk, which allowed me to use my massive, door-sized table to spread out the photos, fanzines, and artwork as I organized them according to the chapters I was writing. Again I must sing the praises of word processing, which may be the main reason why I was able to work a full-time job and still take only six months to finish such a complex project. Even so, it challenged me like nothing else I'd worked on before. I was putting my abilities as a historian, writer, and book designer to the test. The manuscript relied heavily on the history of fandom as revealed in the pages of the fanzines of that era.

Photos came from Don Glut, Biljo White, Ronn Foss, and many others. Chuck Moss sent an incredible shot of the fans at the Alley Tally party, as well as a number of other high-quality photos. If only there had been someone, even one person, who had taken photos at the first New York Comicon in July 1964. (To this date, I've never seen a photo of the con taken inside the Workman's Circle hall, where it was held.)

As it was progressing, I corresponded about the book with EC fan John Benson, who urged me to begin with a chapter on comic fandom of the 1950s. That was before my time, but I recognized the importance of EC fandom (and the fandom that followed the death of EC comics in the late 1950s), so with his help I added that information, as well as a bit about the science fiction fanzines that carried comics material in the 1930s and 1940s.

I spoke to many people on the phone (too many to tape and transcribe), although now I wish I had recorded my conversations with Barry Bauman, Biljo White, and others who would soon pass away. I interviewed Fantagraphics publisher Gary Groth in person at a Seattle Thai restaurant, the first time we met in person. Jeff was always close by with encouragement. It wasn't easy, but I had my concept firmly in mind, and my determination never faltered. I was on fire.

To establish my theme, I composed an opening page for the book to set the scene, somewhat like the narrator of Thornton Wilder's *Our Town* does at the beginning of the play:

> This book is a "time machine"... and you are about to take an amazing journey. The Golden Age of comics had ended, and the wild and wonderful world of EC had come and gone, too. But with the onset of the Second Heroic Age, a new breed of comic book fans arose. And those fans had a dream. A dream of a "fandom" they could call their own. A place where fans of comic art—especially the costumed characters who were enjoying a renaissance—could share their hobby with others of like mind.
>
> As the new fan movement grew, the hobby of comic book collecting came into its own. A flurry of fanzines criss-crossed the country and circled the globe, bringing articles, artwork, and ads to a diverse and multitalented audience of eager readers. It was a remarkable time. Excitement was in the air. Every trip to the mailbox brought palpitations, for who knew what wonders awaited?

My theme boiled down to this: the early days of fandom were special because they were a spontaneous expression of love for comic books and strips, and because nearly all of the fanzines were labors of love that weren't done for profit. When the profit motive took over, some of the magic went out of fandom.

I knew I needed a stronger title. *The History of Comic Fandom* was kind of generic, but I hadn't come up with anything better. In early 1995, I met a writer-artist in the Seattle comics community named Nils Osmar, and we became friends. He taught classes in cartooning and had self-published some comic books. We'd get together for breakfast at Julia's, a popular café, and discuss our projects. Although we were about the same age, Nils hadn't been involved in early fandom, but my book interested him. At one point he said something like: "It sounds like fandom in the 1960s was kind of like the Golden Age of comics was for the comics industry, a special time when it was being born." I agreed, and I started thinking, *Yeah, a golden age of fandom*. Eureka! Thanks to Nils, I came up with what I felt was the perfect title: *The Golden Age of Comic Fandom*. This title didn't merely avoid the "bland" problem; it actually encapsulated the whole concept of the book. Those kinds of titles are hard to come by, and I'm glad to have the opportunity to give him the credit for his part in helping name the book.

When I finished the first draft, which would go through much refining in the weeks to come, I sent the manuscript to the most likely publishers. I was confident but nervous, like anyone with a good idea for a book. Would they "get it"? They had to!

They didn't. Or if they did, they didn't believe there was a large enough readership for it. Most publishers, I learned, weren't interested in a book unless they thought it would sell at least two or three thousand copies. I didn't know what sort of sales potential it would have, but it seemed to me that it could sell two thousand copies. After all, it would be the only book written about the people who had laid the foundation for the entire hobby and comics scene that existed in 1995.

I quickly rejected the idea of offering it to Scarecrow Press. True, they printed short-run books, but they made up for the low circulation by charging an extra-high price. In addition, they weren't equipped to publish a book with a complex mix of art and photographs, visual components that would be absolutely integral to the book as I envisioned it.

I couldn't believe it. An idea that was completely original and that would have obvious appeal to a substantial (if admittedly limited) group of readers wasn't enough to interest even the specialty publishers in the comics field itself. It didn't take long for me to realize that, once again, I had run up against a brick wall.

I was sick of being told "no" in my life by the powers that be.

No, you can't have a career in the arts.

No, you can't love the person you want.

No, you can't have children.

No, your book isn't worth publishing.

To paraphrase the words of Howard Beale (played by Peter Finch) in the movie *Network*, I was mad as hell, and I wasn't going to take it anymore!

I hadn't come this far to have my hopes dashed. Yes, I wanted to do the book for myself, but also I was adamant that the founders of comic fandom get the recognition they deserved for all they had given the hobby and the comics medium itself.

The struggle to get published is something I share with countless other writers. Especially before the rise of digital publishing in the late 1990s, many resorted to vanity press services, where, at great expense, they "hired" a company to publish their books. One could hardly call such authors professional, published writers when they sold a few copies to friends and family and were left with garages full of unsold books. To my mind, writing books that *sold*—that people willingly paid coin of the realm to read—separated the dreamers from the professionals. I knew I could and would be able to sell a substantial number of copies of the book. I just had to get it into print.

With that conviction, I decided to turn my fanzine hobby into an actual publishing company. *The Golden Age of Comic Fandom* would be the company's first book. As Will Eisner once said, "When you don't have access to markets, you have to create them yourself … or try to." Whatever it took, whatever the obstacles, I wasn't going to let anything stop me.

I decided to call my company Hamster Press, the tongue-in-cheek name I'd used on my amateur publications since the 1970s. It wasn't exactly a name that would impress anyone, but I didn't want to invite scorn by calling it Worldwide Publications or Galactic Press. Hamster Press was nicely self-deprecating. Also, by continuing to use a name I'd employed

Hamster press insignia, 1995.

in my amateur publications, I was letting people know I was doing this as a labor of love, out of "fannish spirit," not with the idea of reaping big profits (although I would happily take them if my book became a runaway hit). In the spring of 1995, Hamster Press became a true-blue, honest-to-gosh business enterprise, licensed by the state of Washington, with its own bank account and post office box.

None of the professional printers would produce a book by a fledgling publisher on credit. Being a mortgage holder on a modest income meant I had almost no savings, so I didn't have the cash up front for production and printing costs. How to come up with the printer's required advance payment? I had requested bids for printing one thousand, fifteen hundred, and two thousand copies. When the bids came in, I realized that the cash-up-front requirement meant I would have to be content with a modest first printing, and I could do a second printing if the first one sold out. The lowest bid for one thousand copies (the smallest print run that offset book printers usually did) came from Whitehall Printing in Naples, Florida.

Early fundraising advertisement for *The Golden Age of Comic Fandom*, showing my original cover concept (which proved unworkable).

Even with the lowest possible print run, I didn't have enough for the advance payment. I fell back on the same technique I'd used in my old fanzine days: raising money for printing by collecting advance orders. I knew from the sales of *Labors of Love* that there would be at least 250 hardcore fans who would definitely want the book. The dilemma: many of them, perhaps as many as a hundred, had contributed to my research in various substantive ways. In a sense, the book was a group effort. Each of the contributors deserved to receive a complimentary copy of a book that he or she had helped make possible. But if I did that, I would not only eliminate 100 certain customers; I would also be out of pocket for the cost of packaging and postage to send them their books. After a great deal of thought, I decided honesty was the best policy. I sent out a special form letter to that group explaining the situation, and I offered them a five-dollar discount from the $11.95 cover price. It was a compromise that honored their contribution but still helped raise money for the costs involved. The people in the group accepted this proposal all around (only one person groused), and nearly all sent checks. A few even sent full price, just to support the project.

I decided to make a virtue out of the low print run by deeming it a special limited edition, signed and numbered by yours truly. This was possible because I didn't pursue distribution through Diamond Comics, the largest distributor; dealing with them was more than I could handle at that juncture. This meant that all printed copies of the book would be shipped to me in Seattle. Then I would send out the small amounts ordered by Bud Plant, Capital City, and other distributors. Hence, I would have the opportunity to sign and number each copy.

I don't remember how much I accumulated in advance orders, but if I had to add any of my own funds to come up with the cashier's check for the printer, it wasn't much. Now my task was to create the camera-ready pages by the age-old method of pasting up the text, artwork, and photos (screened by a local specialty house) onto pages that the printer would photograph, one by one, and use to burn the printing plates. However, Whitehall Printing, like most professional printers by that time, required that the cover be given to them in digital form. No paste-ups with overlays for blue, red, and yellow, as the old photo-offset fanzines had done. Digital? Uh-oh. Who did I know who could, and would, do a digital cover for me?

Comic book artist and old-time fanzine publisher Mike Vosburg had drawn a beautiful frontispiece for the book. I phoned him and asked if he knew how to create a digital cover. I had a mock-up version—a mishmash of various fan photos, with space for the title in the center—but didn't have the knowledge or software to take it to completion. Mike had little experience with Photoshop, but he was learning, and he gamely agreed to take a stab at it.

I wanted to have the book out in time for the 1995 San Diego convention. Therefore, I geared up to have everything done and sent to the printer in early May. At more or less the last minute, Roy Thomas wrote an introduction for the book, which meant I would be able to use his name in advertising and on the cover to help convince the undecided that it was a quality product. (He also proofed the manuscript and made a number of good suggestions.) In due course, I sent all 144 pasted-up pages in a FedEx box to the printer. I would have Mike send the cover directly to the printer, once I approved his work. As my deadline approached I got anxious because I hadn't yet received Mike's cover, so I called him to find out what was happening. He said, "I'm sending the cover today, but there are some problems that happened after I scanned your paste-up. To get the best results, I would have needed to scan each photo separately, and I wouldn't know how to manipulate that many images in a single document. Take a look at the printout. Maybe it'll be okay; that's up to you."

When I opened the overnight envelope from Mike, I was horrified. He'd done the cover as requested by scanning the pasted-up cover and creating a nice logo for the center. But the photos looked awful due to what I soon learned was called the moiré effect—a distortion that occurs when you rescan prescreened photographs. No, this cover absolutely wouldn't do. What's more, when Mike agreed to give it a try, he didn't know I was sending the guts of the book to the printer without asking them to hold until the cover was ready. They had proceeded to send me proofs, which I approved, and the book was set in their printing schedule for a couple of days hence. They needed the cover right away. Emergency!

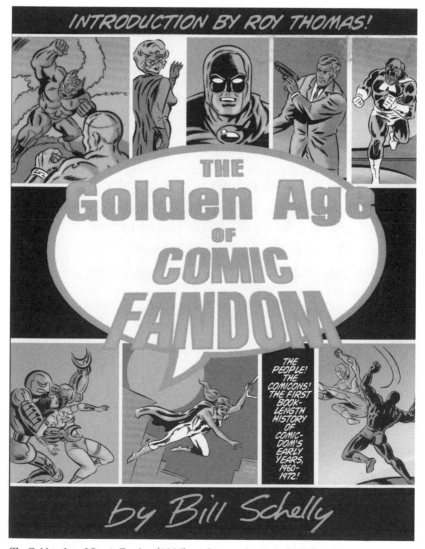

The Golden Age of Comic Fandom (1995), with cover design by Nils Osmar.

It was a problem that had to be solved immediately. Then I realized I knew someone in Seattle who might be able to save me: Nils Osmar. He was experienced with Photoshop. I called and asked if he could help, and he said "Sure, come on over." When I got there later that day, he had already sketched an idea for the cover, using an assortment of generic superheroes. It looked good to me, so I gave him the logo I had already created and the verbiage that had to appear on the cover, and he got to work. I didn't realize he wasn't feeling well.

"I was coming down with the flu the day you called to ask if I could help," Nils told me recently. "I felt then like I had to either get sick or pull out of it to do the cover. I pulled out of it and never did get sick, probably because it was fun working on the cover." The next day (Nils is fast), he had finished his first pass at it. It looked good: slick, professional, colorful. Not what I had had in mind, but perfectly workable and attractive. It was better than my initial idea. All that remained was for Nils to work up the spine and back cover, which he did posthaste. Within three days, I had my cover, and Nils had—and has—my eternal thanks.

Printers work fast too. Within a couple of weeks, a stack of boxes appeared on my doorstep. I opened one and pulled out a fresh, glossy copy of my new book, a consummation devoutly to be wished. The Langdon book seemed like a distant memory. To me, at forty-five years old, this felt like my first book, a kind of miracle.

The details of the distribution of the copies aren't important, and there isn't room to include even a fraction of the letters I received in response to *The Golden Age of Comic Fandom*. Since I didn't yet have email (that was still, for me, a year away), people sent letters by snail mail. I got dozens and dozens of letters, which confirmed that the book had made a big impact on those readers. It has gone on to become a reference in countless books on the history of comics and the hobby of comic book collecting. Clearly, the book was needed.

The reviews were almost entirely positive. In *Comic Buyer's Guide*, Maggie Thompson wrote that it was "accurate and entertainingly anecdotal. Devotees of the field of comic collecting: you've got to have this." In his catalog, Bud Plant enthused, "Schelly has taken a complex chain of sequential and overlapping events and made sense of them, as well as providing a good read. Great stuff!"

The impressive state-of-the-art convention center in San Diego in 1995. Inside, I was proudly selling my new book. Photos by Jeff Gelb.

To be sure, the book had a few detractors. While she liked it in general, Cat Yronwode wrote in her "Fit to Print" column in *Comic Buyer's Guide* that its heavy emphasis on the fanzines made it "more like a history of the mimeo and ditto fanzines" than a history of fandom in general. Some complained, rightfully so, that it gave little attention to the hotbeds of fan activity other than those in the Midwest, New York, or California.

I brought copies of *The Golden Age of Comic Fandom* to the 1995 San Diego fan event, newly christened Comic-Con International: San Diego, and shared a small table with Nils, who was selling his *Photo-Reality Comics*. I also brought copies of *Labors of Love,* but *The Golden Age of Comic Fandom* was front and center. Most of the people who came by and bought the book were, predictably, older fans who had participated in fandom in the 1960s and 1970s, some of whose names I recognized. They often shared stories of their experiences of the old days, and I had a great time talking with them. My only regret is that I was away from the table for one particular sale. When I slid back into my chair, Nils showed me a check from Archie Goodwin. Goodwin was an important writer and editor who had worked for years at both Marvel and DC comics. Less well known was his role in EC fandom in the late 1950s, doing the covers for most issues of *Hoohah!,* the greatest EC fanzine. I would have loved talking to him about those times, but it was not to be. He passed away three years later at the age of sixty.

Selling the book at the convention was an exhilarating experience, topped off when an unaccompanied Stan Lee wandered into the
vicinity. I waved him over and said, "Have you seen my book, Stan?"

He must have had a chance to look through it earlier, because he
grinned and exclaimed: "That's a wonderful book!" With the impri-
matur of Stan Lee's seal of approval, I went home a happy man.

24.

HAMSTER PRESS

The Golden Age of Comic Fandom touched a nerve. Soon all one thousand signed and numbered copies sold out. I even sold numbers 1,001 and 1,002 because there had been a slight overage from the printer.

As I was considering going back to press, readers not only wrote letters of comment but sent additional material from the early years of fandom: photographs, fanzines, convention programs, newspaper articles, and information of all types. I had tapped many contacts and sources to write the book, yet now many more came forward after the fact. Also, there were corrections and suggestions for specific changes, which made me aware that the book had numerous imperfections. Hence, instead of printing more copies of the book right away, I decided to publish a revised and expanded edition. That meant rewriting the copy and producing a new set of paste-ups for the entire book, all of which would take some time.

The publication of *The Golden Age of Comic Fandom* was an ecstatic experience that seemed to instantly heal old hurts. After all the years of feeling helpless and frustrated in my efforts to find creative fulfillment, I now felt empowered as never before. With a little help from my friends, I'd made it happen despite all obstacles.

The first Hamster Press book primed the pump for more. Even before the first one had sold out, I embarked on a book that reprinted the best of the comic strips created for the classic fanzines. Before I had proceeded very far with it, I got a big surprise: my fandom history book was nominated for a Will Eisner Comics Industry Award for Best Comics-Related Book of 1995!

The Eisner Awards are more or less the Oscars of the comics field. A blue-ribbon committee makes the nominations, which are then voted on by all parts of the professional comic book industry: writers, artists, other creators, publishers, editors, retailers, and distributors throughout the U.S. and Canada. There are categories for all types of comic books, as well as graphic novels, archival collections, and comics-related books. I had submitted mine for consideration, and the members of the nominating committee apparently felt it was award-worthy. I didn't think it was likely to win, but I went to the ceremony at the San Diego con in 1996 and had the experience of seeing Nils's book cover projected on a giant screen before the enormous crowd. I also had the experience of not winning the award. (The winner was *Alex Toth*, a book by Manuel Auad that celebrated the career of the brilliant comics artist.) Still, getting nominated gave me a shot in the arm and a sense of validation. Plus, I would always be the author of an Eisner Award–nominated book, which would be handy in promoting my work.

By far the most memorable experience I had at that con, which had ballooned in size to thirty-six thousand attendees, was having lunch with Roy Thomas, Julius Schwartz, and Gil Kane. Neither Schwartz nor Kane remembered me from the 1973 New York Comic Art Convention, when Julie had rejected me from the DC New Talent Program, and Gil had semi-offered me a job. It was also the occasion when I met Roy's wife and sometime writing partner Dann, who joined us in a fancy restaurant at the Hyatt Regency Hotel near the convention center. (I remember whispering to Roy, "Who's the redhead?")

Gil had battled cancer, and while he was optimistic about the future, his appearance showed the effects of his illness. However, his ability as a fascinating raconteur was undiminished, and we all listened happily to his stories of working in comics in the 1940s and in the animation business in the 1980s, and many other things. It seemed he had a story or inside knowledge about every area of the comics business.

At one point we were talking about Charlton comics, the low-rung publisher of some of the worst comics ever published (as well as some good ones). I said, "What always puzzled me was their hot-rod comics. I mean, was there really a readership for hot-rod comics? It was nuts."

Gil looked up and replied, "Ah, m'lad, let me explain how they came to be. I met the man who invented them, and he told me ..." From there Gil was off on yet another funny, informative story, holding us spellbound as he had throughout the lunch. I wish I could remember all the things he talked about. One topic was his rueful recounting of the time he went to pitch a project when he was quite ill, and the young hotshots in the room looked at him like he was a bug that had crawled out from under a rock. He didn't blame them. "I was wearing a truly awful toupee because my hair had all fallen out from chemotherapy, and I looked like some kind of weird gnome from Frankenstein's laboratory," he said. There was much laughter at that luncheon. I'm sure Julie and Roy interjected comments, maybe told their own stories, but the floor, as always, belonged to Gil.

Like many millions of other people in America and around the world, I experienced the sea change that came after I hooked my home computer up to the internet. It happened for me in 1996. I wasn't supposed to use my internet access at work for personal purposes, so even getting clunky dial-up modem access at home ushered in major changes in my life. For a burgeoning historian and researcher, the internet opened up vast sources of information and gave a solo publisher who was constantly looking for ways to promote his books a much greater reach.

I threw myself into completing work on a collection of the best amateur comic strips from the photo-offset fanzines of the 1960s, such as *Fantasy Illustrated, Star-Studded Comics, Alter Ego,* and *Odd,* a humor zine. *Fandom's Finest Comics,* as it was titled, consisted of complete comic strips, the better to show off wonderful work by the best of the amateur writers and artists whom I continued to admire. It reprinted "The Origin of the Eclipse!" by Drury Moroz and Ronn

Foss; "The Life Battery" by Eando Binder (a pseudonym that Marvel Family scripter Otto Binder used for his science fiction writing), Bill Spicer, and Landon Chesney; an adaptation of an authorized Edgar Rice Burroughs Tarzan tale, "The End of Buckawai" by Bill Spicer and Harry Habblitz; and many other stories.

After *The Golden Age of Comic Fandom* was a success, I followed with *Fandom's Finest Comics* in 1997. Cover designed by Nils Osmar. ™ and © respective copyright holders.

My last attempt at creating my own complete comics story (both script and art) using India ink had been in my *Assembled Man* chapter in *Sense of Wonder* #10 in 1971. I decided to see whether the passage of years would yield a better result, now that I'd gained a certain amount of patience that I lacked when I was younger. As a tribute to Dick Trageser, I adapted his prose story "Skimmer's at the Museum!," an Immortal Corpse tale that appeared in the first issue of *Sense of Wonder* in 1967, which would be published as a special feature in *Fandom's Finest Comics*. All the stories of the character had been in text form, and I figured it was about time for him to shamble into graphic story existence. I still had my old drawing board and some drawing equipment from my days as a draftsman at Boeing. A quick trip to the art store for some Strathmore drawing paper, ink, brushes, and pens, and I was all set to go.

While I've always been pretty good with a pencil, I had my usual difficulty with the inking. The result was on the stiff side, but it was better than anything I'd managed before—below professional quality, but a step forward for me.

In the spring of 1997, *Fandom's Finest Comics* saw print, sporting a cover composed of images from the book's interior, designed by Nils Osmar and me. It's obvious that the cover design is an homage to the *Giant Superman Annual* #1, from the title logo to each of the characters being shown in a separate box. This time, I decided to print 2,200 copies, which meant that the upfront payment to the printer would be higher than on the earlier book. Despite soliciting advance orders, which were healthy, I came up short. Just one thing to do: sell some of my old comics, which I had acquired after leaving Super Comics. I didn't have many, but I gathered nearly all of the ones from the 1940s and gave them to a fan who auctioned them off for me. In short order, I had enough money for the desired cashier's check. Giving up some nice copies of *World's Finest Comics* and *Batman* from the 1940s was tough, but I chose to see it as my comics once again helping me achieve my dreams.

Pages 1 and 6 of "Skimmer's at the Museum!," my adaptation of Dick Trageser's prose story from *Sense of Wonder* #1 (1967). Art by yours truly.

The mid-1990s were a tumultuous time for the comics industry. The early part of the decade had seen the rise of newcomer Image Comics, as well as an influx of people only interested in trying to make a killing by buying huge quantities of certain new comic books for resale. The speculator market boom, when a few comic books sold in record numbers, soon collapsed, leading to the demise of a raft of publishers. First Comics, Eclipse, Comico, Malibu, Defiant, Continuity, and others died, and circulations of the remaining publishers' comics plummeted. Two-thirds of all comic book specialty stores closed.

For my part, while I was concerned about what this meant for the future of the medium, I had increasingly turned my attention from new comics to those of the past. I found that I enjoyed reading Silver Age comics, and I took more and more of an interest in comics from the Golden Age. My purchases of new comics declined as I spent more of my hobby dollars on reprints, especially the DC Archive Edition books, deluxe hardbacks that were reprinting classic stories from DC comics of the past, from the late 1930s through the 1960s.

I took Jaimeson to see *Batman and Robin* (1997), the last of the cycle of Batman films that Tim Burton had begun. I was unimpressed, but my son, then seven years old, loved it. I didn't have any luck getting him or his sister interested in reading comic books, but I was thrilled that they both loved the Marx Brothers. They begged me to watch *Duck Soup* over and over again. My cinematic highlight of 1997 was *Titanic*.

As for romance in the 1990s, there's not much to say. I dated from time to time and was open to the possibility of love, but I was careful not to jump too quickly after having done so with Larry. At the age of forty-six in 1997, I had grown accustomed to living alone, and I wouldn't give it up except for something that felt like real love. For the most part, I was okay with the single life, and I was probably better suited for it than a lot of people. Dating took a back seat to work, family, friends, and the many creative projects that blossomed after *The Golden Age of Comic Fandom*.

As a member of *Capa-alpha,* I did several covers in the 1990s,
including this tribute to Adam Strange and Alanna for its fortieth
anniversary edition (March 1998). Characters ™ and © DC Comics.

A print run of 2,200 copies turned out to be way more copies
than I needed of *Fandom's Finest Comics.* I had to rent a storage facility for the extra cartons. I'd overestimated partly because I didn't
realize that after the initial month or two of sales, almost everyone
who wanted a copy—at least, those who kept up with what was
being published about comics—had one. Then sales dropped to a
trickle. This time, I offered the book through Diamond. Their purchase order was for slightly over six hundred copies. I sold about
another five hundred through other distributors or directly through
Hamster Press. These sales brought in enough to cover the book's
costs, but I was stuck with nine hundred extra copies. Many were
eventually consigned to the local recycling center. This extent of

overprinting meant, of course, that I'd sold more of my old comics than necessary to finance it.

Over time, my friendship with Roy Thomas developed. He and Dann were living on a forty-acre estate in South Carolina, tending an assortment of llamas, birds, and other beasts. Although he was always busy with writing assignments, he found time to answer my letters. In early 1997, I proposed that he and I collaborate on a book reprinting the best of *Alter Ego,* the classic fanzine. There had been 11 issues, all but one published in the 1960s. The issues that included Roy's "One Man's Family" and "Bestest League of America" were out of print and hard to find. We launched into production on the heels of *Fandom's Finest Comics,* and we were well on the way to completing it when we had a chance to meet in person again.

N

The 1997 Fandom Reunion began after I had attended the San Diego con for two years in a row, and I was looking for a change. Wouldn't it be nice, I thought, to go to another of the major cons in 1997, and perhaps meet some members of 1960s fandom who rarely or never make it to the California event?

Then another thought occurred to me. Perhaps this was the year to act on previous suggestions for a reunion of old-time comics fans, many of whom were located in the Midwest. A number of them had contributed to my projects. I got in touch with Jim Rossow, Grass Green, and Maggie Thompson. Once I ascertained that they already planned to attend the Chicago Con (which had recently been bought by the *Wizard* folks) scheduled for July 4–6, 1997, and were enthusiastic about the possibility of a full-blown fandom reunion, I decided I would head to the Windy City for my summer comics convention experience and see if I could get more old-time fans to come—if not to the con itself, then to a reunion party held nearby.

Within about two weeks, the plan was hatched. Jerry and Jean Bails could make it, and Roy and Dann Thomas had already planned to come. When long-time Chicago fan artist Russ Maheras (perhaps best known for his many excellent cover illustrations for *The Buyer's Guide to Comic Fandom* and *Comic Buyer's Guide*) offered to find a restaurant for a proposed luncheon affair, the die was cast. It was already spring when I sent out the hastily designed invitations via snail mail and the internet: "Come one, come all to Fandom Reunion 1997!"

Although I sent invitations to forty likely attendees, everyone was encouraged to spread the word. It wasn't long before I began hearing from other folks whose names were happily added to the list of confirmed attendees. Russ had chosen the Pine Grove, a restaurant near the convention site. We didn't know how many would come, but the banquet was set up to accommodate twenty to thirty people.

This Chicago con must have been in a transitional phase, because unlike the year before or after, which had more than twenty thousand attendees, this one attracted only about five thousand. I didn't mind, and I enjoyed a more relaxed experience at the con. On day one, I spent time chatting with Tim Corrigan and R. C. Harvey while strolling among the airy, lightly populated aisles. Paramount in my mind was the reunion the next day.

The 1997 Fandom Reunion at the Pine Grove restaurant in Chicago. Left to right: Jerry Bails, Bob Beerbohm, Mark Edmunds, Roy Thomas, Bob Butts, Ron Massengill, Grass Green, Jerry Ordway, Mike Tuohey, Russ Maheras, and Howard Keltner. Photo by Dann Thomas.

Dann Thomas, Bill Schelly, and Maggie Thompson at the reunion. Photo by Russ Maheras.

Saturday arrived. On the way to the site in Russ's car, I reflected how I had never dreamed as a kid that I would ever get to meet in person such Big Name Fans as Jerry Bails, the proverbial "father of fandom," and Howard Keltner, publisher of *Star-Studded Comics.* The adrenaline was pumping as I entered the place. Some invitees were already there in the restaurant's banquet area. Booths for seating were arranged along the walls, and a U-shaped configuration of tables occupied the center of the room. Soon the room was filled with thirty jabbering, smiling comics fans, illuminated by photo flashes that were almost strobelike at times. Russ Maheras saw to it that the event was recorded for posterity with his camera, and I did the same during the latter part of the event.

I passed around a book to collect everyone's signature while I shook hands and introduced myself around. Like me, many who had known each other strictly through the fanzines or correspondence were now pressing the flesh. I watched Grass Green meet his frequent collaborator Howard Keltner for the first time. After *Star-Studded* was discontinued in 1972, Green taught Keltner how to switch from pen to brush to achieve a more fluid inking style. An undercurrent of strong emotion was apparent to all involved, and not just between those two. Other than three wives of participants, Maggie Thompson was the only woman present, but she was used to that. She was reunited with old friends from the Midwest: Jim Rossow, Bob Butts, and Mike Tuohey. Comics dealer Bob Beerbohm was there, as were Mike Tiefenbacher, Dwight Decker, and Tony Isabella. DC artist Jerry Ordway attended, as did underground comix creator Jay Lynch.

Jerry Bails hadn't seen many of his old friends from Midwestern fandom since the Alley Tally party. Roy Thomas was also shaking hands with people he hadn't seen in thirty-plus years. I made the strongest connection with Bails. For some reason, I'd had the impression that he was a brainy, rather cold individual, and I was delighted to find him a warm, friendly, even gregarious fellow, who was genuinely humble about his contributions to fandom. Later, at the hotel, I had the chance to show him my rough layouts for the upcoming Hamster Press book, *Alter Ego: The Best of the Legendary Fanzine,* which would be published later that year. "These look great, Bill," he said. "Thanks, Dad," I joked.

Jerry laughed and said, "I feel almost like you're my son, carrying on the work I did, decades ago." In later emails, we continued joking about our father-son connection. One couldn't choose a better father figure in fandom.

The reunion was a rousing success, but another enterprise I learned about at that convention had a more far-reaching impact on my life. At some point during the convention, I was having lunch with Roy and Dann Thomas in a restaurant in our hotel. After we'd chatted a moment, I noticed two people I recognized sitting by themselves at a small table, not far away: John and Pam Morrow, publishers of *The Jack Kirby Collector.*

Photo of Jerry Bails, Howard Keltner, and Roy Thomas taken the evening before the Chicago reunion by Dann Thomas.

I turned to Roy and said, "That's John Morrow sitting over there. Do you know him? Should I invite him and Pam over?"

Roy grinned. "We've traded emails but haven't met. Sure."

I caught John's eye, waved, and beckoned. After a moment's hesitation, the two Morrows joined us. They began talking about a new magazine they were planning to publish called *Comic Book Artist.* The earliest print allusion to it was in *The Jack Kirby Collector* #16, the July 1997 issue, where their editorial stated: "We're considering publishing a new, *TJKC*-style zine, with each issue devoted to different comics greats. It'd be spearheaded by *TJKC*'s new associate editor Jon B. Cooke." After shaking hands for the first time, Roy and John revealed that Roy might be a contributing editor to *Comic Book Artist,* perhaps even with a partitioned *Alter Ego* section in the back. This would serve several purposes: it would be a selling point, what with Roy being a well-known comics professional; it would provide an added dimension to the book, since it would feature Roy's interest in comics from the 1940s and 1950s; and it would help editor Cooke fill up his pages with high-quality material.

Soon after this lunch in Chicago, Roy enlisted me as associate editor of his *Alter Ego* section, writing something about the his-

tory of fandom in most issues. Since he and I had developed a strong rapport, I unhesitatingly accepted the gig, which would pay a modest amount. Before our "best of" *Alter Ego* book came out that fall, I was already on board for this exciting revival of the classic fanzine. By the time the first issue came out in the spring of 1998, what started as a sixteen-page section had evolved to have its own flip cover and pages. Thus, the magazine could be displayed on a shelf as either *Comic Book Artist* or *Alter Ego*. The cover of that issue, which appeared the following spring, was a beautiful Hawkman drawing that I'd asked Joe Kubert to do as a birthday gift for Ronn Foss. It was the only thing I brought to the first issue. For me, being officially involved with *Alter Ego* was a dream come true. We had no idea that within a year it would break out into its own separate magazine and that twenty years later it would still be around, passing the 150-issue mark.

The coming-out party for *Comic Book Artist* and *Alter Ego* was held at the 1998 Comic-Con International in San Diego. John Morrow designed a huge banner displaying both covers for the Two-Morrows booth. He also gave me space there to sell copies of *Alter Ego: The Best of the Legendary Comic Fanzine,* my third Hamster Press trade paperback book. It was a convention I would never forget.

Alter Ego returned as a flip section in *Comic Book Artist* magazine, with a cover by Joe Kubert. This was *AE* volume 2, #1. Above: Schelly and Gelb pose in front of the TwoMorrows Publishing banner at the 1998 San Diego con. Photo by John Morrow. Hawkman ™ and © DC Comics.

I was able to share a table with John Broome at a dinner sponsored by the American Association of Comic Book Collectors. Broome had written about half of the stories of the Flash, the Atom, and Green Lantern in the early 1960s. This was the only comics convention Broome ever attended. Will Eisner, whose *A Contract with God* had helped spur the development of the graphic novel in recent times, was at the same table. I reminded Will that we had exchanged a few letters when I wanted to put together a book about him after *Sense of Wonder* #12 in 1973. He looked at me a moment and said, "Oh, yes. The school teacher." What a memory. That was right around the time I was student teaching, so I would have told him about my apparent vocation (which I never pursued).

Alter Ego: The Best of the Legendary Fanzine ended up being nominated for an Eisner award. Roy and I were both at the awards ceremony, but it didn't win. The loss was disappointing, but I figured, well, maybe there will be other opportunities.

Roy and I were pleased that Julius Schwartz was at the convention and agreed to sign copies of the *Alter Ego* book, which sported his introduction. The three of us sat shoulder to shoulder signing the latest Hamster book. During a brief lull, I had a moment to look to my right and appreciate being able to sit on the same side of the table with Roy Thomas, the first man to succeed Stan Lee as editor-in-chief of Marvel Comics, and Julie Schwartz, the man who ushered in the Silver Age of Comics.

It struck me that Julie had played an important role in my life. He was the one who had publicized *The Rocket's Blast-Comicollector* in that *Justice League of America* letter column in 1964, making it possible for me to discover the joys of fandom. And it was Julie, along with Vince Colletta, who had rejected me from DC's Junior Bullpen Project.

Earlier, I'd mentioned that dark day in 1973 to him. "You turned me down for the 'new talent' program," I said with a look of mock tragedy stitched across my face.

Without missing a beat, Julie gently jabbed a finger at my chest and said, "I was *right*, wasn't I?"

Julius Schwartz, Roy Thomas, and yours truly signing copies of *Alter Ego: The Best of the Legendary Comics Fanzine* at Comic-Con International: San Diego in 1998. Photo by Jeff Gelb.

I had to ponder that one for a moment.

On some level—a *cosmic* level, if you will—Julie and Vince had been right. My life, it seemed, had been destined to go in another direction. Howard Siegel's advice had been wise. I might have made it as a professional artist with the right effort and tutelage, but it turned out that I didn't have the passion for art that I had for writing. I was better off doing something else to earn a living. Otherwise, I might have become cynical and could have lost my love for comic books. Eventually, as a writer about fandom and comics history, I would achieve a status I could never have reached in pro comics. With the perspective of time and the advantage of hindsight, I was at peace with the way events had gone.

This, I thought as I signed another copy of the *Alter Ego* book and passed it on to Roy, is the right place for me. How fitting to be sharing it, if only for a moment, with Julie.

25.

THE ART OF BIOGRAPHY

More Hamster Press books followed the *Alter Ego* retrospective. 1998 saw the publication of two: a corrected and expanded version of *The Golden Age of Comic Fandom*, with a new cover by Michael T. Gilbert, and volume 2 of *Fandom's Finest Comics*, with a cover by Jerry Ordway. As the title suggests, the second volume of *Fandom's Finest* collected more of the best comic strips from the fanzines of the 1960s and early 1970s. Hamster Press ended up publishing a total of ten books.

Those books had an unintended effect. Fans in increasing numbers started collecting the old fanzines that the books depicted, discussed, and excerpted, creating a demand that caused prices to rise. Some fans specialized in collecting fanzines with work by certain people who had gone on to important careers in comics or other fields, such as Frank Miller, Gene Simmons, and Stephen King. Others wanted fanzines with art done especially for those issues by such professionals as Steve Ditko, Jack Kirby, and other favorites. Some were (and are) completists who wanted them all, which, depending on how you count, could number as many as four thousand or more. As a result, publications from the 1960s that could be had for $10 in 1995 were sold for ten times as much a few years later. It had never occurred to me that my modest efforts could cause a decisive shift of that nature. I was affected by the higher prices myself when I later tried to plug the gaps in my fanzine archive.

Putting together the reprint anthology books was fun. Each one was special and required a certain amount of creativity. My fandom history work then migrated to the pages of *Alter Ego* magazine in my "Comic Fandom Archive" columns, which appeared in almost every issue. Since I still (as always) wanted to write books, I decided to pen a book-length memoir of my own experiences growing up in fandom. My purpose was to evoke the zeitgeist of the era so fans from later generations would know what it was like to be a part of that formative time. It would be a ground-level look at fandom.

Writing *Sense of Wonder: A Life in Comic Fandom* in 1999 and 2000 (which, in revised form, became part 1 of this book) meant spending a great deal of time thinking about my early life and reconstructing the significant milestones of those years. It also gave me the experience of collaborating with veteran comic book artist Dick Giordano when he agreed to ink my penciled drawing for the book's cover. Now I realized what it took to get my artwork up to a professional level: just have it all inked by Giordano, a true master of the pen and brush! He made me look good.

I asked Howard Cruse, whose graphic novel *Stuck Rubber Baby* won both Eisner and Harvey awards in 1996, if he would consider reading the manuscript for *Sense of Wonder* when it was done and give me a blurb I could use to promote the book—"If you like it, of course," I said. Howard agreed, but after reading it, he wrote that he was disappointed that I didn't reveal my homosexuality in the book. Writing about growing up, he said, was the perfect opportunity to talk about the emergence of my sexual orientation and how I'd coped with it. I responded that I thought it would get in the way of my story about discovering and participating in comic fandom. To myself, I admitted that I wasn't ready. I was out to my friends and family, who were accepting, but broadcasting it to the world at large made me nervous. As I thought about it more, I vowed to be more forthcoming if I ever had a chance to do an expanded version of the book. Despite Howard's disappointment with that aspect of the book, he liked the rest of it enough to give me a nice blurb.

Initial cover sketch and the final cover for the first edition of *Sense of Wonder* (TwoMorrows Publishing, 2001). Pencils: Bill Schelly. Inks: Dick Giordano. Characters ™ and © DC Comics.

Sense of Wonder: A Life in Comic Fandom was published by Two-Morrows Publishing at the end of 2001. I was uncertain what sort of response it would receive. Would people think it was an ultimate act of egotism? Would it sell? John Morrow was taking a bit of a risk with it. I needn't have worried. It sold as well as the best of my Hamster books, and it generated a great deal of mail. One of the most interesting letters came from Marshall Lanz, my boyhood partner in crime.

My earlier attempts to find him had been unsuccessful. Now I learned that Lanz was married and lived part time in Pennsylvania and part time in Florida, and I sent him a copy. He wrote, "I laughed my ass off … when I read about [our] experiences in Pittsburgh. It was great!" He didn't take offense at anything I had written, but he did tell me that "my wife says when the next printing comes out, please tell everyone her husband isn't a high school dropout!" He met his wife-to-be, Jeanne Russell, when they were both getting their college degrees in fine art. When we reconnected, Lanz was running a cottage industry selling his self-designed ceramics, such as pottery, sculpture, and yard art. I was glad he was doing well. We exchanged letters and had a couple of entertaining telephone conversations. In many ways, he hadn't changed. That wicked sense of humor was still there, though perhaps a bit muted. I'm glad I made him a character in the book and was finally able to catch up with him a bit. (He's no longer described as a high school dropout in part 1.)

Predictably, most of the emails and letters came from people who had been in fandom at the time. The main theme of those letters was how reading about my experiences caused them to recall their own. It brought them back to that time in their own lives, which they remembered with great fondness. This taught me an important lesson: an autobiography can go beyond the subject's own story to touch the lives of readers in unexpected ways.

5111 Lantern Hill Drive: The House That Loved Comic Books. Photo taken in 1985.

One of the most unexpected missives came in the form of a letter that took my breath away. It was from a person named Wayne Faucher, who wrote shortly after the book came out. It's worth quoting at length:

> I just got my copy of your outstanding book *Sense of Wonder* and was struck by an odd parallel.
>
> I am currently an inker on a Spider-Man title at Marvel *(Peter Parker, Spider-Man)* after an eight-year stint at DC inking mostly Batman books. Being in comics was not my original intent, however.
>
> I earned my BFA in graphic design from the Rhode Island School of Design in 1983. From there I spent the better part of a decade pursuing that career in Boston, Manhattan, and finally, Pittsburgh. There I took a job as a design director for a marketing firm. I soon discovered that the person I was hired to replace had reconsidered *his* move, and I was out of a job.
>
> There I sat in my newly purchased home with my wife expecting our first child … and no job. Inexplicably, I decided to make a major change in our situation, even though it was not the most opportune of moments. I wanted to be at home with my family. I was tired of leaving for work every day. I had always enjoyed comic books, but hadn't thought of it as a career since I was a kid. Why now? Was the thought of having my own kid somehow rekindling an old dream? Or, was it something else?
>
> I called a friend who was working at a small-press company and was soon inking my first comic. A year later, I was at DC. That was nearly ten years ago, and comic books are still the sole support of my family. I've since moved to Johnstown to be closer to the in-laws (free babysitting), and I enjoy the

benefits of small-town living very much. But I sometimes wonder about that fateful, off-the-wall choice to get into comics in the first place. Was it just circumstance or some echo from the past?

Your book may have finally answered that for me. The house I lived in at the time of this odd turn of events was in a sleepy community outside Pittsburgh called White-hall, on a hilly street called Lantern Hill Drive, in a small brick house with the numbers 5111 on the front. Strange, but true.

How about that for a wild coincidence—that Wayne should choose a career in comic books after moving into my childhood home, the same place where I fell in love with comics in the early 1960s? I've since decided to dub the place The House That Loved Comic Books. Cue *Twilight Zone* music. Fade out.

Sense of Wonder was a transitional book for me. It was a step toward a new direction for my comics-related writing: biography. Some people only want to read analysis and discussion of the work itself, but I'm interested in the person behind the work. How does the life affect the work, and vice versa?

In 2000 there weren't any book-length biographies of comic book writers or artists, what I call "true bios." There were plenty of biographical articles and introductions to reprints, but nothing in depth, like the biographies of Ernest Hemingway or D. W. Griffith. I was discussing this on the phone with Roy Thomas one day. He agreed that there was a lack of such books, and he pointed out that the writers had far fewer articles written about them than the artists. "Someone should write a book about a comic book writer," he said.

"For instance, Otto Binder," I replied. Certainly, the man who was probably the most prolific comic book scribe of the 1940s, and who had cocreated Supergirl, among his many other additions to the Superman mythos, was a worthy subject.

"Yes, Otto Binder or Gardner Fox," Roy said.

"You should write a biography of Otto Binder," I urged. "I'll publish it through Hamster Press, if no other publisher will take it."

Roy demurred. "I don't have time, at least right now, with all my other commitments. Why don't you write it and publish it? I'll help in any way I can."

After hanging up, I considered it. I'd already written about the influence that *Giant Superman Annual* #1 had had on me in 1960, and Binder had written most of those stories. I loved his work on Captain Marvel and the Marvel Family in the 1940s and 1950s. I had also greatly enjoyed his stories of Adam Link, the first sentient robot, whose pulp adventures were reprinted in a paperback book in 1965. It would be an opportunity to tell his story and to chronicle Binder's many kindnesses to fans.

Binder was the type of author with whom I felt another sort of affinity. One of the recurring themes in his stories was the importance of egalitarianism and diversity. The Legion of Super-Heroes had powerful women who were absolutely the equal of the men. He wrote stories of exceptional sensitivity about those who were different. Of Binder's story "The Shyest Boy in Town" in *Superboy* #80, author Michael T. Grost wrote, "It contains a heartfelt plea to leave 'different' youths alone, and to respect their individuality. Such works in the 1950s and 1960s were often coded pleas to not discriminate against gay people; they also were general looks at nonconformism."

I remember reading that comic book when I was eight or nine. At

Publicity shot of Otto Binder, circa 1964. Courtesy of Michael Turek.

that age, I wouldn't have picked up on anything relevant to my nascent sexuality, but I do recall the feeling of warmth and humanity that the story conveyed. That same warmth was also present in many of his stories of the Superman mythos, which was part of the reason I liked them so much. He was my kind of author at that stage in my life, and as an adult too. I decided that, yes, I did want to tell his story. It was the perfect type of long-form project to suit me.

While continuing to write columns and do interviews for *Alter Ego* magazine, I began gathering information about Otto Binder. I gradually filled in the details of his life: his boyhood in Midwestern small towns (like Smallville), his early years as a writer of science fiction (writing the first "I, Robot" story in 1939), and his switch to comic book writing in 1942. I was astonished when I realized that not only had he written more than half of all the stories of the original Captain Marvel and the Marvel Family in the 1940s and 1950s, but he also wrote many early Captain America stories. After the Captain Marvel comics ceased in 1953, Binder switched to DC and became the chief writer of the Superman stories of the mid- to late 1950s. Some of his creations—or, more properly, cocreations, since the artists deserve equal credit—in addition to Supergirl are the Legion of Super-Heroes, Brainiac, Krypto, the bottle city of Kandor, and Lois Lane's sister Lucy Lane. While writing these classic comic book stories, Binder also did straight science writing, including books such as *Planets: Other Worlds of our Solar System* for Golden Press, which millions of children read in the early 1960s. Later in life, he became fascinated with UFOs and wrote about them extensively in magazine articles and a series of popular paperback books. Sadly, he died in 1974 of a heart attack at only sixty-three years old (about the same age as my father when he passed away).

One of the great joys of working on the book was interacting with so many people who had been important in Binder's life. It gave me a legitimate reason to talk to all sorts of interesting people: Michael Uslan, executive producer of all the Batman movies, who, as a teenager, visited Binder in his New Jersey home; Louis Black, pillar of the film and music scene in Austin, Texas, another of Binder's protégés; Richard Lupoff, science fiction and mystery writer who brought Binder into fandom's fold in 1960. I was able to obtain rare photographs of Binder from his close friend Julie Schwartz, and I interviewed Bill Woolfolk, his fellow writer and friend in the comic book field, about spending time with Otto in his home in the 1940s and cofounding the magazine *Space World* with him in 1960. In addition to getting fantastic information for the book, I was getting to know people I'd admired for decades. Jerry Bails and Roy Thomas shared letters Binder had written them in the 1960s and 1970s. I was also able to interview some of his surviving relatives, such as his nieces Bonnie Binder Mundy and Patricia Turek, who were helpful.

When it comes to research, luck is always a factor. This project was blessed with a great deal of it. I discovered that many of Binder's literary papers were in a special collection at the Cushing Library at Texas A&M University. Hal Hall, the collection's curator, told me the collection included a manuscript that looked like some sort of autobiography, titled *Memoirs of a Nobody*. Soon I realized this was an unknown, unpublished book by Binder. Hall arranged for me to receive a copy of it, along with copies of numerous letters to and from Binder's brother Earl from the 1930s, which documented the breakup of their writing partnership. This material was like gold to me. Unfortunately, *Memoirs of a Nobody* turned out not to be an actual autobiography; it was a lightweight book of breezy, humorous commentary on various aspects of daily life, and it revealed few facts about his youth or experiences as a writer. Still, I found some tidbits in it that proved useful.

The second discovery was a tape recording made of a discussion at Binder's home in 1973 when he was visited by three fans: Randy (J. Randolph) Scott, who had made the tape, Tom Fagan, and seventeen-year-old Frank Miller. This discussion was revealing in many ways. For me personally, the opportunity to hear Binder's voice was invaluable. There's so much one can glean from a person's voice and manner of speaking. After listening to him discuss his career with the three attentive fans, I felt as if I had come as close as possible to actually meeting him. I got to hear him speak the name of Mary, his only daughter, who was tragically killed at fourteen by an unlicensed driver. Being a parent, I thought I could understand how awful that must have been for him and his wife, Ione. What would I do if something like that happened to Jaimeson or Tara? It was unthinkable.

✸

The Otto Binder biography was the first book I wrote in my freshly finished basement office, a much larger space than I'd had upstairs. Now I had my Bat-Cave! Somehow, in this customized sanctum, I found my concentration was better. Populated by such totems as my *2001: A Space Odyssey* movie poster, a bookcase with my favorite books, and reproductions of comic art, it was a world that reflected my interests and obsessions. In the PBS TV series *The Power of Myth*, Joseph Campbell extolled the value of having a "sacred place … where you can simply experience and bring forth what you are, and what you might be. This is the place of creative incubation. At first you may find that nothing's happening there, but if you have a sacred place, and use it, and take advantage of it, something will happen." The seventy-eight thousand words of the Binder manuscript flowed easily and quickly. This experience contributed to a growing sense that biographical writing might be my métier. After four or five months of writing sessions, it was done.

Over the years, I'd been in sporadic touch with my high school friend and sweetheart, Barbara Barker. She was living in a house near Sedro-Woolley, a small Washington town seventy miles north of Seattle. I'd solicited her expert editing skills on my *Sense of Wonder* book, and I now recruited her to edit the Binder manuscript. She took me to task for making some condescending comments about Binder's belief in UFO phenomena. "The fact that you don't believe in UFOs isn't relevant in this book," she said. "After all, you're not an expert on such things." I had to agree. Moreover, I didn't want to insult anyone who might be reading the book because they'd heard of his reputation as a writer on that subject. I altered the text accordingly.

Words of Wonder: The Life and Times of Otto Binder was published in late 2003. It was the first hardback book from Hamster Press and my first biography in twenty-one years. I wasn't sure how it would sell, so I printed only 1,200 copies, making it another "limited edition." I didn't want to repeat the mistake I'd made when overprinting *Fandom's Finest Comics*. This time I underestimated demand. It sold out within weeks, forcing latecomers to turn to the collectable marketplace. It wasn't long before the book was selling for twice the cover price.

I didn't submit the book to mainstream newspapers or magazines for review, but the response from the fan press was excellent. I received fewer letters by snail mail than for past books, but twice as many emails. The one that meant the most to me was the response from Binder's niece, Bonnie Mundy, who wrote: "I started reading it shortly after it arrived and discovered that you captured the personalities so well that I was filled with memories and emotions. I can hardly wait to share these memories with my daughters and grandchildren. You have an amazing gift, and I know Otto, Jack, and the clan would be proud of your ability and aptitude to put your words and theirs in print."

I was also surprised and pleased to receive a brief letter dated May 19, 2004, which read:

Dear Bill Schelly:

Thank you for the complimentary copy of your new biography of Otto Binder. I deeply appreciate this because I remember meeting him in New York during the World Science Fiction Convention in 1939 when I was 19 years old; fond memories of a wonderful past.

With much gratitude and thanks,

Ray Bradbury

I had never expected to hear from the great writer of fantasy, science fiction, horror and mystery. Knowing that Bradbury had held my book in his hands and had thought enough of it to respond, when I know he was constantly inundated by complimentary books, meant a lot to me. I saw him in person a couple of months later at the 2005 San Diego convention, on a panel with Julie Schwartz, talking about how he found success by doing what he loved. In that moment, sitting in the front row a few feet from him, I felt a real connection with Bradbury because I knew what he said was true. By writing about the art form and hobby that I loved, I was finding the career as a writer that I had dreamed about all my life.

Of course, there were disappointments. I was keenly aware that there were flaws in *Words of Wonder*. In the layout process, an entire paragraph was accidentally omitted, which caused an embarrassing gap in the text. After Barbara edited it, I'd somehow managed to introduce new grammatical errors. There were also some errors of fact that were brought to my attention. This was mortifying, as I tried hard to pay attention to the details. In fact, the same sort of thing had happened after the publication of each of my earlier books and has occurred with every book I've written since. The lesson, which I'm still struggling to accept, is that there's no such thing as a perfect, error-free book. It doesn't matter how much time you spend, how many people look it over, or anything else you can humanly do. Perfection—especially in the kind of books I write, which convey a lot of facts—is impossible. Not that you shouldn't still aim for it.

I also heard from people who knew Otto Binder, relating anecdotes that would have been wonderful for the book. A neighbor near the Binder home in upstate New York sent photos of the house, which I didn't have. Fans sent copies of letters from Binder, and on and on. As with *The Golden Age of Comic Fandom*, I decided there had to be an expanded and corrected version of *Words of Wonder* someday. I didn't know when or how—I was close to being burned out on self-publishing—but I kept all that new material together, saving it for a time when the opportunity presented itself. (The revised edition was published in 2016, under the new title *Otto Binder: The Life and Work of a Comic Book and Science Fiction Visionary.*)

To a great degree, I have *Alter Ego* to thank for helping me grow beyond being a fandom historian into becoming a historian of comic books themselves. In the process, I made another significant step forward as a writer: I was published by DC Comics.

Some of my friends had written introductions for the DC Archive Editions books, which reprinted classic comics from the past. I thought, "Why can't I get to do some of those?" Hence, when I was at the San Diego convention in 2003, I attended a panel about the Archive books in hopes of introducing myself to Dale Crain, then editor of the series, and offering to write an intro for one of their books. One of the nice things about conventions is that one can often meet participants in small or moderately sized panels afterward.

While Dale was gathering up his notes, I introduced myself as Bill Schelly, associate editor of *Alter Ego,* and asked, "How does one get to write one of the archive introductions?"

He smiled. "I love *Alter Ego.* Here's my card. Why don't you email me, and we'll see?"

I wrote him, and less than two weeks later, Dale got back in touch with me. "I'm in a bind. The guy who was going to write the introduction to the third *Plastic Man Archives* can't do it. I hate to give you such short notice, but could you get it done in a couple of weeks?" He overnighted a package with copies of the stories, and I got to work. Admittedly, I was nervous. This was DC comics. My work had to be first rate. Also, if he liked what I did, it could lead to more. I got it to him within a week. He read it and liked it, and it wasn't long before I received a nice check in payment.

In this way I became a go-to writer when a short deadline loomed for a DC Archives intro. Over a period of nine years, I wrote a dozen introductions for the series. I also wound up doing an intro for

Batman of the Forties, a trade paperback book edited by Bob Green-berger. I still had to pinch myself to make sure I wasn't dreaming. Here I was, in late middle age, writing for DC about characters such as Superman and Batman, the two heroes who had made me a comic book reader in the first place.

N

By 2004, I was eager to give up the role of publisher and sole pro-moter of my books. I wanted my next book to have enough wide-spread appeal that I would be able to interest a publisher who could get it into mainstream bookstores, such as B. Dalton, Borders Books and Music, and Barnes and Noble. Those stores had established a category called "Graphic Novels," which also included books about the history of comics. Yes, I wanted my stuff to be available through comics specialty shops, but I also wanted to reach the mainstream customer who might have been drawn into the field by bookstore hits such as *Maus* or *Sandman.*

I sometimes ask my friends for book suggestions. This time, I asked Bud Plant if he had any ideas for a biography.

"I don't know about a biography, although there'd probably be a great deal of interest in that," he said. "But I know there's never been a good Joe Kubert art book, one that covers his whole career. I'd like to see a book like that, and I'm sure I could sell quite a few."

Joe Kubert's career as a comic book artist and writer spanned almost the entire history of the medium, starting in the early 1940s when he was a teenager and still going strong sixty years later. He was best known for his versions of Hawkman in the 1940s and the 1960s, and for virtually cocreating Sgt. Rock with writer Robert Kanigher. His version of Tarzan was applauded by the most hard-core Edgar Rice Burroughs enthusiasts. He had received every exist-ing award for comic art—the Eisner, Harvey, Inkwell, Inkpot, and National Cartoonists Society awards—and had been inducted into the Will Eisner Comic Book Hall of Fame. People throw around the sobriquet "living legend" a lot, but Joe Kubert was the genuine article. He definitely merited a biography.

On the other hand, did Kubert have name recognition enough to interest a mainstream publisher or to instantly appeal to a bookstore browser? As a comics artist, he had been interviewed and reviewed in many newspapers and even on the odd TV show, especially in connection with the Joe Kubert School, which had been going since 1975. His graphic novel *Fax from Sarajevo* (1996) had won critical acclaim and did well in the bookstore market. But the reality in 2004 was that no comic book creators were household names except for Stan Lee. Even Art Spiegelman, Will Eisner, and Jack Kirby, the next biggest names, were known mainly by comic book and graphic-novel readers (plus, in Spiegelman's case, by readers of *The New Yorker*). I judged that Kubert's name recognition was in the next tier down from them, alongside Wally Wood and a few others. Since I wasn't going to write about Lee, Spiegelman, Eisner, or Kirby for various reasons, Joe Kubert was the best choice possible. It helped that I was a fan and admired his work.

Joe Kubert it was. But would Kubert be willing to help? As always, access to key material is essential. I hoped to interview not just him but his wife and sons, and to be able to use family photographs. For that, I would obviously need his cooperation.

I'd had some contact with Kubert before, and I'd sent him a copy of my Binder book, which he said he read cover to cover and enjoyed. So when I called him in mid-2004, I was optimistic that he would go along with my plan to write a bio about him. I was wrong. He was horrified. Here's the conversation, which is vivid in my memory:

"Not interested," he said. "It would be embarrassing, and besides, my life is very ordinary."

"Ordinary?" I countered. "You've been in the comic book field almost since it began. You're a living legend!"

He laughed that gutty laugh of his. "Oh, come on. Besides, I don't want to spend my time with something like that. I just want to write and draw comics." This was understandable. Although Kubert was in remarkable health for his age, he was seventy-eight years old, and his increasingly valuable time was running out.

Still, I was passionate about Kubert's work, and my gut told me that this was a project that could take me to the next level as a writer. Time seemed to stand still. What I said next would be my last shot at convincing him. Then it came to me, in a moment that will forever be ingrained in my memory:

"But it wouldn't be your book," I said. "It would be mine. All you'd have to do is let me interview you." When it was quiet on his end of the line, I pressed on. "Joe, believe me, *someone* is going to write your biography someday. Since you liked my Binder book so much, why wouldn't you want it to be me?"

Another pause, and he finally said, "Bill, I think I want you working for me. You don't take no for an answer." We both laughed. He agreed to be interviewed for a biography, and he even said it was fine with him if I visited him at his school to do the interview and see the place.

Visiting the Joe Kubert School of Cartoon and Graphic Art (now the Kubert School) in the fall of 2004. Photo by Peter Carlsson.

A few months later, I arrived at Newark International Airport, rented a car, and drove inland to Dover, New Jersey, where Kubert lived. This was harder than it sounds, because I suffer from a low-grade agoraphobia that makes it difficult for me to drive in unfamiliar urban areas. However, I wasn't going to let that stop me. I found my way to a motel in Dover without incident. Joe met me in the lobby, and I experienced his famously firm handshake. That began my two and a half days there.

Everything came off without a hitch. Joe and his wife, Muriel, had me over for dinner in his home, and he even let me photograph the ancient drawing board he'd used as a boy after uncovering it in his basement. We talked for a couple of hours, and I met various people in his world, including his son, Adam, and right-hand man Peter Carlsson. I explored the school and even visited a couple of classrooms. "A lot of people have interviewed me here," Kubert told me, "but you're the only one who wanted to visit a classroom." Joe spent quite a bit of time with me, including two or three more meals, and he let me watch him work at his drawing board on an upcoming book called *Jew Gangster*. When I left, I knew the trip would enable me to write a book that took the reader right to the center of Kubert's life. Even getting lost on the drive back to the airport and almost missing my flight didn't shake my confidence.

Over the phone, I interviewed his army buddy and lifelong friend Bob Bean, who had never talked about Kubert for attribution before; Joe's sister, Roslyn; longtime comic book crony Irwin Hasen; DC Comics colorist Jack Adler; and numerous others who could give me fresh perspectives on Joe's life and work. The book took me two years to finish and another year before I found a publisher. I worked harder on it than any of my earlier books. I had a fantasy of it being published by a major New York firm, but after having some difficulty finding an agent to represent me, I came down to earth and called Gary Groth.

Fantagraphics Books, I knew, produced top-quality books and had a good bookstore presence with comic book compilations of such titles as *Love and Rockets* (Los Bros. Hernandez) and *Eightball* (Daniel Clowes), as well as the series *The Complete Crumb* (Robert Crumb). What I didn't know was that Gary was friends with Joe and had even played racquetball with him a number of times (Kubert played racquetball well into his sixties). They shared a great love of comic art and had the mutual respect of two hard-headed business-men. Gary said, "Sure, send over the manuscript."

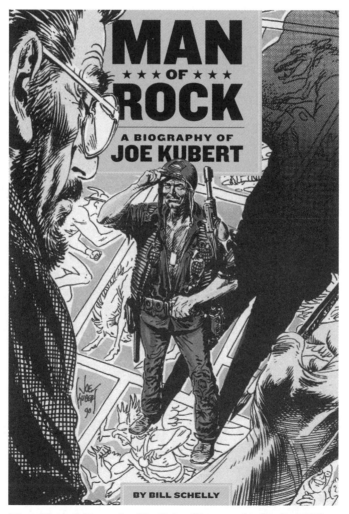

Man of Rock: A Biography of Joe Kubert (Fantagraphic Books, 2008). Art by Joe Kubert. Sgt. Rock ™ and © DC Comics.

"I'll bring it by," I responded. "I live about ten minutes from your office." Ultimately, Fantagraphics published the book, titled *Man of Rock: A Biography of Joe Kubert,* in November 2008.

Fantagraphics Books agreeing to publish the Kubert book represented another significant step for me as a writer. Since I'd returned to fandom, I'd self-published all my books except *Sense of Wonder: A Life in Comic Fandom,* which TwoMorrows published as a sort of spinoff from my regular columns in *Alter Ego.* Fantagraphics, on the other hand, decided to publish my book strictly based on its subject matter and the quality of the manuscript.

The response to *Man of Rock* was gratifying, and it sold reasonably (if not spectacularly) well. It was my first book to appear on the shelves at Barnes and Noble. I received a nice thank-you letter from Joe. All in all, it was a positive experience, and I felt that this book was better written than my prior ones. Perhaps its admiration of Kubert was laid on a bit thick, but it did address shortcomings in his work. The reviews in trade journals and from readers on Amazon. com were good—except for one. An internet reader-reviewer truly disliked the book, and apparently all biographies, and me too. He or she ("Anonymous") ended a rambling, vituperative review with: "When one's own artistic and creative abilities have fallen short, it appears that the fallen can still live vicariously through those who are truly worthy of our attention."

Of course, this is hogwash. Biographies are a legitimate, respected book genre of long standing. The modern biography goes back to James Boswell's celebrated *Life of Samuel Johnson* (1791), and the basic biography form goes back even further, to Plutarch's *Parallel Lives,* written around 80 AD. Biographies are popular because people like to read about the lives of famous, talented, or successful people. They may admire that person and want to learn about what makes them tick or how they achieved what they did. There's nothing easy about writing a good biography. In fact, biographical writing is an art form that's deceptively difficult to do well.

We've all read bad biographies, often about well-known celebrities, that merely stitch material together from public sources: newspaper clippings, previously published interviews, even other books. These forms of celebrity voyeurism may tilt toward this or that sensational angle that gets played up on the cover or in the ads, in a cynical attempt to part the customer from his or her money. Other biographies are well-intentioned but offer nothing new, or perhaps they lack anything but the crudest insight into the person being profiled. You come away from them perhaps learning a few things but without feeling you got to truly know the book's subject.

At the opposite end of the spectrum are biographies that take you so far into their subject's mind and world that they provide something like a channel from the subject to the reader. Good biographies must present new facts, original research, and excerpts from new interviews. And they must be well written. That was the kind of book I wanted to write, a book that exceeds readers' expectations.

Was I, through this project, trying to live vicariously through Joe Kubert or to glorify myself by attaching my name to his? No. I was trying to write the best damn book I could, one that I was proud to share with the world. This wasn't the last time I was determined to raise my game.

26.

JAIMESON'S JOURNEY

After reading the past few chapters, one could have the impression that I did nothing but work at the SBA and write or compile books from 1995 to 2005.

There's no denying that the number of articles, columns, and books I produced during that time was a result of obsessive effort. I would get into a project and then be unable to let it go until it was completed. This happened partly because I had waited so long to get to this place, and I didn't want to take a chance that it would slip through my fingers if I took a break. Nevertheless, throughout those years I did have a private life, although not with a significant other. I was single and fine with it, though I was not unaware of missing the give and take, emotionally and physically, that relationships provide. It's just that I experienced the pure, unconditional love that a parent has for his or her children, and that seemed to fill up most of the empty places.

By the fall of 2004, when I visited the Kubert School, Tara was in the seventh grade and Jaimeson was a freshman at Skyview Junior High in Bothell, Washington. There had been some bumps in the road. The family had undergone a shakeup when their biological parents split up. Renie Jones was now with Nancy Balin, and Stephanie Seymour was with a man named Amana Fisher. However, they were living about a mile apart, and the kids had adjusted to spending school days with Renie and weekends with Stephanie. It worked, and relations between the parents were (mostly) on an even keel. Although Jaimeson and Tara bickered and competed with each other, their bond was strong because they were always together at one house or the other. I was the person who was the biological link between them, and I was glad when everyone agreed they shouldn't be separated.

I saw Jaimeson and Tara once a week like clockwork. I cooked them dinner and sometimes helped them with homework, but mostly I played games and watched their favorite television shows with them, and sometimes we went out for ice cream at the local mall or to movies. I would drive to Bothell, pick them up, and then drive them home at the end of the evening. Plus there were birthday celebrations, family get-togethers, the holidays, and school events. Jaimeson had joined the cross-country running team at school, and Tara was playing drums and other percussion instruments in the junior high symphony. I attended some, if not all, of the meets and performances. Jaimeson even demonstrated a bit of art talent when he created a large drawing of Groucho Marx in art class and did some paintings that showed a strong sense of design and color. Although I was their father, in practice I was more like a loving uncle. As unorthodox as it was, it worked, and they were doing well.

All this is to set the scene for an awful medical diagnosis that hit our family shortly after 2005 arrived. We discovered that Jaimeson had a secret: one of his testicles had enlarged and had become painful. He hid this from us, for reasons he never could explain, until he couldn't any longer. In mid-January, I received a phone call from a tearful Renie. Jaimeson was diagnosed with stage IV testicular cancer and was having surgery to remove the testicle immediately. The cancer was advanced and had spread throughout his body, but it had not yet crossed the "blood barrier," so a cure was still possible. The odds were about 30 percent that he would survive for more than four years. He was fourteen years old.

It's impossible to describe the effect this had on everyone in the family—his moms, his step-parents, me, his aunts and uncles, grand-parents and cousins, and of course his sisters, because Stephanie and Amana had a child named Samantha, whom Jaimeson considered his sister, along with Tara. Anyone who has gone through something like this with a child knows that the entire family "has cancer." As for Jaimeson, he was surprisingly stoic and unfailingly optimistic.

I couldn't help thinking of Otto and Ione Binder, who lost their daughter Mary when she was fourteen. When Jaimeson was diagnosed, I was about the same age Otto was when tragedy struck his family. The difference was that Otto and Ione had their daughter snatched away. There was no illness, no hope, no goodbye. She was alive one moment, gone the next.

We had hope, but the battle ahead looked grueling. We consulted with Dr. Lawrence Einhorn of Indiana University, who had pioneered the optimum chemotherapy for testicular cancer. He was the doctor who had treated Lance Armstrong, who had been cured of testicular cancer even more advanced than Jaimeson's. We were determined our boy would have world-class experts on his team, and he did. Fortunately, Einhorn's chemotherapy cocktail did its job and killed the cancer. However, that was only part of the cure. Then came a series of major surgeries to remove the cancerous growths from around his heart and other parts of his thorax. Every bit of it had to come out. This wrenching, worrying, painful process went on through 2005 and 2006.

Jaimeson Jones in 2007, when he ran cross-country at Bothell High School, shown running in west Seattle's Lincoln Park.

Jaimeson later wrote: "The hospital bed is where immaturity goes to die. It was in those monotonous hours of painful boredom that my mind resorted to thoughts unnatural for someone my age. I suppose such intimate encounters with death will do that to a person. Lying there, heavily medicated, having just been sliced and diced on the operating table, there was nothing else to do. Gone was my teenage invincibility."

How Jaimeson faced it all with such optimism and bravery is a mystery to me. My admiration for him grew to gigantic proportions. What an amazing kid. He made it through, and as soon as he could, he was running with his cross-country team again. Jaimeson graduated with his class in 2008. By then, his support system extended to his teachers, his coaches, and the student body of Bothell High School. All of us were relieved beyond words, even as we were forever changed by the experience.

At the time, I was writing *Man of Rock*. Toward the end of 2006, when Jaimeson was in recovery, I gave a draft of the book to Jerry Bails. After establishing a solid connection at the 1997 Fandom Reunion, we were in frequent contact via email. Since Kubert was Jerry's favorite artist, I figured he would enjoy an advance look at the book. I also knew he was in failing health.

Jerry had some nice things to say about the Kubert manuscript, to which I responded on November 15, 2006:

Dear Jerry,

Thank you for your email, and the kind words you expressed about my work. In my mind, I feel as though I am sort of continuing your work … which, I guess, is why I wanted to send you the finished manuscript, just to show you that it was done.

I loved my father, but as we discussed a few years ago, I think I've looked up to you as my dad too—in terms of the person who inspired me in my activities to report, chronicle, and celebrate the great comic book writers and artists of past and present. And to do it with high standards, intellectual rigor, and a lot of heart.

My best wishes to you always, Dad.

Bill

Jerry wrote back that same day:

Bill

Thank you for the sweet words. As with so many others who have taken up the torch, you have surpassed my puny efforts.

Bestest,

Jerry

Those were his last words to me. I didn't agree that his efforts were puny, but I appreciated the thought. Eight days later, Jerry Bails died.

He passed away on November 23, 2006, apparently of heart failure. A few years earlier, I had drawn Jerry's portrait for a celebration of his seventieth birthday in *Alter Ego*. Now fandom's "father" was gone, and I found myself eulogizing him in the magazine, as did Roy Thomas and many others. My personal debt to Jerry is enormous when I consider what fandom meant to me as a teenager and continues to mean to me as an adult.

Jerry Bails at 70, drawn for an *Alter Ego* cover in 2003.

In 2007, my mother's health took a turn for the worse. She turned eighty that year but had been brought low by an aneurysm that nearly killed her. Mom recovered but remained frail, and it seemed the time was approaching when she couldn't live alone. I stayed with her for a week to help her after shoulder surgery. I was glad we had that time together. After returning home, I took to phoning her once a week, much more often than I had before. We had long talks, many of them lighthearted. She loved the *American Idol* and *Dancing with the Stars* TV shows. I started watching them to give us fodder for conversation. It was fun. But then, one week in May 2008, she complained of odd headaches. A few days later she passed away. I felt this loss a lot more than the loss of my father. Mom had always been there, and while we didn't have the closest relationship, I loved her as one can only love one's mother.

My mother, Joanne Schelly, in her seventies.

Somehow I completed two books in 2007 and 2008. *Man of Rock* was my number one priority, but I'd also decided it was time to update and revise my Harry Langdon biography. In the twenty-five years since Scarecrow Press had published the book, I kept expecting another, better bio to appear. That didn't happen, which left the door open for me to finally make it the book I'd originally envisioned. I located the box with all my Langdon research documents and movie stills, and I started screening his movies again. Kino Video had released the DVD *Harry Langdon … The Forgotten Clown* (2000), with his greatest silent features, and I still had videotapes of many of his other movies (and an old VHS machine that still worked).

Once again, I was beguiled by his Langdon's comedic skill and pantomimic genius. However, this time I realized how much an appreciation of his slow, methodical comedy depended on seeing it as a radical break from the fast-paced comedy of most other silent clowns, such as Harold Lloyd *(Speedy)*. I could understand why modern audiences, who didn't know that context, wouldn't get Langdon. Still, I felt he was worthy of a more complete, better-written biography. Over a period of about nine months, I was able to discover all kinds of new information about his career and life, and I ended up rewriting just about the entire book.

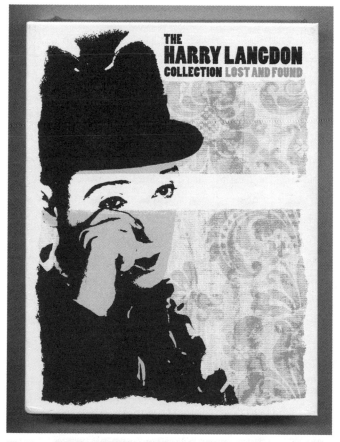

The Harry Langdon Collection: Lost and Found, a DVD set issued in 2007. © All-Day Entertainment.

While I was working on it, David Kalat of All-Day Entertainment tapped me to appear as a talking head in a Langdon documentary. It was to be a special feature on a box set called *The Harry Langdon Collection: Lost and Found*, which collected all of the short silent films Harry did for Mack Sennett, as well as some talkies and other rarities. My part was filmed in Seattle by Nils Osmar, who was a filmmaker as well as a graphic designer and teacher. The box set, now a collector's item, came out in December 2007.

At the San Diego con the following year, I got a kick out of seeing the new edition of my Langdon biography displayed at the McFarland Publishing booth. The title was now *Harry Langdon: His Life and Films.* I told McFarland's representative, Susan Kilby, that I'd just turned in the manuscript for my Joe Kubert biography, so I was considering future projects. She said, "We'd love to look at anything else you'd care to offer."

Later, when Jeff Gelb and I were eating lunch at the Milky Way, a kosher restaurant in Beverly Hills owned and operated by Leah Adler (better known as Steven Spielberg's mother), I wondered if I had another book of fandom history in me. It occurred to me that I could fairly easily write a book consisting of short biographies of some of the most active fans in the 1960s. It would be a way to do something more to honor Jerry, Ronn, Don, Maggie, Roy, and others who had gotten comic fandom started. Jeff and I had briefly written a column called "Fandom's Founders" for *Comics Buyer's Guide,* so the title *Founders of Comic Fandom* rolled easily off my tongue. Gelb liked the idea, and I was off to the races.

Self-publishing had served its purpose for me, but now I was finished with it, and McFarland seemed like the perfect solution for my next book because they specialized in publishing short-run books. I figured there would be a relatively small but hardcore audience for it. They enthusiastically approved the idea, and on the basis of a brief written proposal, they sent me a contract. It was another first: the first time a publisher committed to a book before I had written a single word.

Writing commenced and was well along by the spring of 2009. Compiling ninety biographical profiles proved to be more difficult than I anticipated (no book is ever easy), but I'd learned by this time that if one worked consistently, it would eventually come together.

Life was good. Tara had switched from percussion to the French horn, and she showed real talent in playing the difficult instrument. She was a junior in high school, had grown to five feet eight inches tall, and had long, beautiful blond hair. Her aptitude for higher mathematics emerged, and she was talking about studying engineering in college. Jaimeson was in the midst of his second semester at Washington State University in Pullman, where I had come out of the closet all those years ago. He'd started as an architecture student, but when he realized it didn't suit him, he quickly changed his major to "undeclared." When Barack Obama's presidential campaign ignited his interest in politics, he began thinking about going into political science.

Tara at eighteen.

He had also switched sports, from cross-country running to rowing on the Cougar crew team. It was an inspired choice. Jaimeson thrived as part of a team, and despite his novice standing, he quickly became an integral member of the crew. Photos showed that he was gaining muscle quickly, too. While he was figuring out his ultimate course of study, rowing gave him something to focus on and a social network to participate in.

As part of his cancer follow-up, Jaimeson had periodic blood draws and CT scans, which had all come back negative. Each time, Renie called me to report the news. It had become a routine. Until it wasn't. She called in May of 2009, and I immediately knew something was wrong. Her voice was quavering. She could hardly speak. Her message was chilling in its simplicity: "The cancer is back." I felt the world rock on its axis, and my heart fell to the floor.

Thus began the second phase of Jaimeson's journey, which was much darker and more intense than the first. I was ignorant about what a "recurrence" meant. I thought, okay, they caught it early. Another dose of chemo should clear it up. Then I found out that a recurrence meant the original treatment hadn't effectively obliterated the disease, and although there were more types of treatment, his chances for a real cure were much smaller this time around.

The Cougar crew team was in a competition in the Tacoma area. Most of his family attended to see the team in action. When the race was over and Jaimeson walked by carrying the rowing shell aloft with his teammates, I hardly recognized this muscular young man, seemingly brimming with good health. It broke my heart to see him, at nineteen years old, facing such a daunting struggle. But he had beaten cancer once. Dammit, he could do it again! That was how he felt, and how I tried to feel. But a great fear welled up in me, and in the months that followed, it grew.

Jaimeson put college aside, although the members of the crew team kept in touch and did everything they could to support him in his time of need. Despite grueling, high-dose chemotherapy (which had many awful side effects), the cancer could not be stopped. Renie carried much of the burden, as did Stephanie. Renie's partner, Nancy, and other family members helped a lot. I can't speak to what they were feeling inside, except that I know it was an enormously difficult, horrendous time for all. Although Jaimeson again remained optimistic, as did his girlfriend, Sara Jezerski, everyone else's hopes faded and then fled completely—although few of us would admit it, even to ourselves. As 2009 turned into 2010, the strategy became one of slowing the cancer, which was now in his lungs, as much as possible, and quickly making plans so that not a day of Jaimeson's life would be wasted. No one called it his "bucket list," but that's what it was.

In February, Jaimeson flew to Europe with Tara, Sara, and his cousin Jules, for three weeks. They had a marvelous time being tourists, staying in youth hostels, and meeting the locals. Not long after they returned, Jaimeson and I left for a father-son trip to New York City and Washington, DC. Although we visited the Statue of Liberty and wandered around Times Square, our main reason for going to New York was to be in the studio audience for *The Daily Show* with Jon Stewart and *The Colbert Report* with Stephen Colbert. Actually, we were special guests of both shows.

Fandom made this possible. Those were Jaimeson's favorite television shows, and they also happened to be the favorite shows of animation and comic book writer Mark Evanier, who had worked in television. I got in touch with Mark, explained the situation, and asked if he could suggest how we could get tickets and perhaps meet Stewart or Colbert. I expected a little helpful advice. What I got from Mark was a *fait accompli:* email addresses to representatives of each show so I could solidify plans for us to visit, meet the stars, and even have special backstage tours of the theaters where the shows were filmed. Through his contacts, Mark had arranged everything.

Sister and brother, somewhere in Europe, February 2010.

Thanks to doors opened by Mark Evanier, Jaimeson and I were given backstage tours and met Jon Stewart *(The Daily Show)* and Stephen Colbert *(The Colbert Report)*.

Jaimeson had the time of his life meeting his idols, posing for photos with them, and poking around backstage. We each received swag bags of T-shirts, hats, and other items from both shows. After the Colbert show, we went for some New York pizza. Jaimeson was grinning ear to ear, and I thought, *This is one happy young man.* We met up with my fandom friend John Benson, who took us to the Museum of Natural History and for a brief walk in Central Park. It was a beautiful day. The trees were blossoming.

The trip to Washington, DC, was nearly as thrilling. After Senator Patty Murray met Jaimeson in Seattle, she cleared the way for a tour of the Capitol building. Even the pages who conducted the tour were in awe when we walked out onto the floor of the empty U.S. Senate chamber. "We never get to come here," they marveled in hushed tones.

It did my heart good when Jaimeson moved into Sara's apartment a few blocks away from my house. He and Sara were in love. They walked over on Father's Day, and we ate burgers off my barbecue. It was a lovely but bittersweet occasion because I knew his time was growing short. Although Mark arranged for both of us to be guests of Comic-Con International in July 2010, Jaimeson wasn't up to it. I went to accept the Bill Finger Award for Otto Binder, an award for comic book writers who hadn't received a great deal of recognition for their fine work. I was happy to do it, but my mind and heart were elsewhere.

It seemed the only place I found solace was in my writing. During my regular workday at the Small Business Administration, there were too many distractions for me to really concentrate. Concentration was the key. If I could narrow my focus to the words on the screen

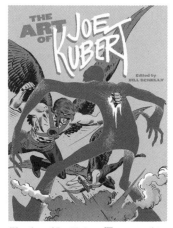

The Art of Joe Kubert (Fantagraphics Books, 2011). Art by Joe Kubert. Hawkman ™ and © DC Comics.

before me and finding the best way to translate my ideas into those abstract symbols, the cares of the world receded for a time. Not only that, but such concentration gets you high. It's the same principle as meditating on a mantra. Instead of turning to alcohol to numb my fears or to tranquilizers of some sort (legal or illegal), I made writing my drug of choice. I focused on writing the text for a coffee-table book titled *The Art of Joe Kubert*. Unlike drugs, the creative high is a clean, clear, intensely human euphoria. This method of coping hearkened back to the way I'd gotten through some tough times in my youth by focusing on creating fanzines rather than on my teenage troubles.

Sometimes I wonder how I slept those last months. It helped that I had my writing during the day. But at night, thinking about Jaimeson and all he was going through—he would never admit that his fight was nearly over—took me to places inside that I'd never known before and hope never to know again. It seemed that the universe had sneered at my parental pretensions. When I'd had a son, I was confident I could be a more supportive parent than my own had been. Instead, I brought a child into the world who was fated to suffer and die young.

On October 7, 2010, Jaimeson breathed his last, with Renie holding his hand and the rest of us nearby. He was no longer conscious when the moment came. His journey on this earth was over.

✦

Our family has never been the same after losing Jaimeson. How could it be? We had walked hand in hand with him. Now we had to find a way to heal, a way to go on. It was difficult for all of us. It was especially tough on Tara, the person who had spent more actual time with Jaimeson over the years than anyone else. She had dropped out of her freshman year in college to have as much quality time with her brother as possible.

We had a wonderful celebration of his life with about two hundred people present: family, friends, teachers, coaches, fellow team members, and a newspaper reporter or two. It was now the beginning of our journey without that brave, staunch, beautiful young man.

As for me, my family and friends in Seattle helped me make it through. Renie and I had become closer than ever after spending so much time together during Jaimeson's illness, much of it in hospital rooms. Fandom, as always, was there for me. Jeff flew up and spent a weekend with me a few days after Jaimeson passed.

I was never more thankful for the friends and activities of comic fandom than I was at this time. I don't know how I could have survived it otherwise. Fandom gave me a sense of stability and continuity, a place where I belonged and that continued to give me opportunities to express myself in print. The message was clear: *You have a reason to go on. There's more for you to do.*

27.

FANDOM'S FIFTIETH BIRTHDAY

While carrying a deep and abiding grief over Jaimeson's passing, I welcomed the diversion of drafting a new book. It was a volume in the *American Comic Book Chronicles* series from TwoMorrows Publishing. Mine would cover comics of the 1950s. I also began organizing another fandom reunion, this time on the West Coast.

In my essay "A Brief History of Comic Fandom" for the *Comic Buyer's Guide 1996 Annual,* I wrote: "The appearance of *Alter Ego* #1 in 1961 is often cited as the moment modern comic fandom was born, because it was sent free to the readers in DC letter columns, as well as to addresses Jerry found in [the fanzine] *Xero* and other fanzines, in a concerted effort to instigate such a movement."

Often cited by whom? No one but me, as far as I know. Truth is, I was the only one promulgating the idea, although no one challenged the notion. That essay was updated and reprinted in my book *Founders of Comic Fandom* when it was published by McFarland in early 2010, again giving March 1961 as the date comicdom was born.

The organizers of Comic-Con International: San Diego apparently latched on to this notion. At the 2010 event, I heard that the con committee had decided to make the fiftieth anniversary of fandom one of its major themes in 2011, thereby creating a perfect opportunity for another fandom reunion. In accordance with this theme, the con planned to invite as its guests of honor fan writer Richard Kyle, *Comic Art* coeditor Maggie Thompson, *Xero*'s progenitors Dick and Pat Lupoff, *Alter Ego* coeditor Roy Thomas, and Jean Bails on behalf of her late husband Jerry, the founder of *Alter Ego.* I knew this group would form an excellent nucleus for a special gathering. (I was also invited as a special guest.)

Accordingly, I sent out an email to my mailing list touting the idea of a fiftieth-anniversary reunion, urging members of fandom from those early years to make a special effort to attend. In mid-November 2010, I emailed noted fanzine collector Aaron Caplan and told him of my intention to hold an informal fandom reunion at the upcoming convention, perhaps in one of the hotels. I knew that Aaron, who came to Comic-Con most years, had been in touch with lots of old-time fans in his quest for vintage fanzines, and he could help contribute more names and contact information for an invitation list. He enthusiastically pitched in.

Where to hold it? The fandom reunion in Chicago in 1997 took place in a restaurant. That worked for a gathering of thirty-three people, but this one would undoubtedly be bigger, and a restaurant didn't seem practical. A meeting room in a hotel was a possibility, but I didn't relish trying to make arrangements from afar. It was Jeff Gelb who said, "Why don't you see if the con will give you a room in the convention center?" Good old Jeff. In February, I asked Gary Sassaman, a friend who was on the con committee, whether the powers that be would supply a room for the reunion. He passed my idea along to Jackie Estrada, who handled such things. The official word from Jackie came at the end of March in 2011: she had successfully elicited the convention's support for a private reception/party on Saturday night at the event. Now the reunion would be a part of Comic-Con, which I thought was all to the good. Jackie took on the responsibility of hosting the party, decorating the room, providing food, and maintaining the invitation list. Anyone could attend, but they had to register in advance so she would know how much food to order and how big the room should be.

Once the venue and date were set, I sent out an official group email invitation asking for RSVPs and answering a list of anticipated questions. Numerous RSVPs began arriving, which I compiled and sent to Jackie. (She, of course, was also sending out invitations.) Understandably, the expense and other difficulties caused many to opt out. For some, the staggering size of Comic-Con was more than they could handle. But there were also those who enthusiastically ratified the idea and vowed to make the extra effort to be there. Already I was looking forward to the fourth week in July. Anticipation began to build.

The excitement was palpable as people began queuing up to the registration table outside room 28DE in the San Diego Convention Center. It was 8:15 p.m. on Saturday, July 23, 2011. The party celebrating the fiftieth anniversary of comic fandom was about to commence.

Fandom Reunion invitation (designed by Gary Sassaman) and commemorative button (designed by Aaron Caplan) that includes small images of the fanzines *Comic Art* #1, *Alter Ego* #1, and *Xero* #1. ™ and © respective copyright holders.

Displays at the fandom reunion meet-and-greet in the San Diego Convention Center. Photos by David Armstrong.

Jackie had installed a couple of volunteers at a registration table outside the room. Each attendee was handed a program with photographs of the convention's special guests for the event. They also were asked to sign the guest book, and they received a commemorative button designed (and paid for) by Aaron Caplan. Jackie gave each a lanyard with a souvenir card proclaiming "Comic Fandom 50th Anniversary," designed by Gary Sassaman.

Upon entering the room, the first sensation one encountered was the aroma of hot food. The con had paid for a buffet that included a taco station, a bruschetta and flatbread station, grilled marinated vegetables, and a variety of pastries, crackers, and cheeses, plus coffee and other beverages. There was even a large sheet cake with a replica of Gary's design on it.

David Armstrong had created several large, fancy standee displays with original artwork and enlargements of photos of many of fandom's founders (some of whom were no longer around) that were placed around the room. They were elaborate, professional-quality displays with special lighting so they could be read even though the overhead lights in the room were dimmed. Greg Koudoulian and friends had also put together a display in tribute to the late Shel Dorf, a Comic-Con cofounder, and there was a large display of vintage fanzines from Jackie Estrada's personal collection for anyone to pick up and look through. Small tables and chairs were scattered about for those who ate or just wanted to get off their feet.

Fanzines from reunion organizer Jackie Estrada were on display. Photo by Bob Cosgrove. Photo of Jackie at the event by Batton Lash.

But the major thing one noticed was the cacophony in a room full of high-spirited, happy fans greeting old friends, meeting people they had only known though the mail or cyberspace, posing for photographs, discussing the displays, munching on the food, and generally having a good time. For me this was a chance to meet many fans—often readers of my books—in person. I was too keyed-up to eat because I wanted to at least say hello to everyone there.

One thing didn't happen, by design: I had made it a point to confirm that there would be no platform or microphone, no speakers, no interruptions for thank-yous, no introductions of special guests. There was no showboating of any sort. True to fandom tradition, it was an entirely egalitarian affair. Yes, there was the moment when the event temporarily focused on the cutting of the enormous sheet cake, and when Mike Tuohey presented Roy Thomas with his original copy of *Alter Ego* #1. This was accompanied by many photo flashes as Caplan, Gelb, Maheras, Armstrong, and others recorded the moment for posterity. But it passed quickly, and everyone returned to visiting, laughing, posing for still more photos (flashes were in evidence throughout), and enjoying a celebration of the movement that had brought us together way back when—indeed, a movement that had provided the impetus for the San Diego con itself and the reunion we were enjoying.

Bill G. Wilson *(The Collector)* and Gary Groth *(Fantastic Fanzine)* sat side by side in a famous photograph from the 1969 New York comics convention, when each was about 15. They recreated the moment at the Fandom Reunion. Today, Bill and his wife Beth own their graphic art company, and Gary owns Fantagraphics Books. Photo by Russ Maheras.

Roughly 150 fans filled the room and created quite a cacophony! Photo by Aaron Caplan.

Near the fanzine display, one could look at "the way we were" in a giant blowup of a group photo of those who attended the banquet at the 1969 New York convention, with Gary Groth and Bill G. Wilson as young teenagers sitting side by side in the front row. Now Gary and Bill posed for photos next to their boyhood images.

It was great to see Johnny Chambers get a chance to visit with George R. R. Martin. Johnny, who was perhaps best known for his Little Green Dinosaur cartoon character, had become George's first publisher when he published a Martin story in his fanzine *Ymir* in 1964. Martin's *Game of Thrones* had recently completed its first smash-hit season on HBO, and he had become as big a celebrity as a writer can be. Johnny and George were meeting in person for the first time.

Left to right: Gene Henderson, Richard Alf, Dave Scroggy, Rose Scroggy, Paul Sammon, Clayton Moore, unidentified attendee, Denis Kitchen, and Greg Koudoulian. Photo by Bill G. Wilson.

I took a moment to stand back and marvel at the event itself, and I was grateful for the memories that arose as I noticed certain fans in the room. Memories of receiving the contribution to *Super-Heroes Anonymous* from Jeff Gelb ... meeting Bill G. Wilson at the house of Marshall Lanz ... receiving a cover for *Fantasy Forum* from Alan Hutchinson, who was at the reunion with pal Gary Brown ... poring over issues of *Star-Studded Comics* with art by Buddy Saunders ... having my ideas about comic books expanded by the essays of Richard Kyle in *Graphic Story Magazine*. Here they were, together in one room.

There were more recent memories attached to others in the room, such as receiving Roy Thomas's introduction for *The Golden Age of Comic Fandom*, which helped launch Hamster Press ... having Russ Maheras pitch in to make the 1997 fandom reunion possible ... and hearing from Mark Evanier that all the arrangements had been made for Jaimeson to have some of his wishes come true.

These things and more caused me to realize, again, what a blessing fandom had been in my life. It had been a source of empowerment, making it possible for me to become a writer of books, something I'd dreamed about since I was nine. Now, as I found a way to go on after my son's death, it was a source of healing.

I gabbed nonstop with fans, sometimes straining to be heard above the noise. The reunion, which attracted about 150 people, lasted only a few hours, but by the time it was over, my voice was shot. The only thing

I didn't talk about was my next project, which I had only begun researching in earnest a few days before the convention. It would be my most ambitious book yet, one that I hoped would be my magnum opus.

28

MAD ABOUT HARVEY

Gary Groth never told me what he thought of my writing in *Man of Rock*. He'd merely said he thought it was "well researched" and "factually accurate." Like a lot of professionals in his position, he seems to feel that agreeing to publish a book is compliment enough. However, something happened in April of 2011 that gave me a better idea of what he thought of my work.

We were sitting in his office, him behind his perpetually paper-laden, messy desk, and me lolling in his "guest chair," a cracked vinyl affair that always had to be cleared of debris before one could sit in it. *The Art of Joe Kubert* was at the printer. We were batting around book ideas.

"Have you read the new Kurtzman book by Kitchen and Buhle?" he asked, nodding toward a copy of *The Art of Harvey Kurtzman* (Abrams, 2009) that sat on top of a stack of books nearby. It was the same sort of book as *The Art of Joe Kubert:* oversized, with the emphasis on artwork in full color, and a text of about forty-five thousand words. I said I had, and I thought that as a biography, it was incomplete, largely because the text said little about the last third of Kurtzman's life. Groth felt the Kitchen-Buhle text didn't do Kurtzman justice. "There's room for a better, really good Kurtzman biography," he said.

This hung in the air for a while, until I realized he was suggesting it as a possible project for me. "That would be a *huge* challenge!" I blurted.

"Exactly," Groth responded. That he apparently thought I was capable of writing a book worthy of Harvey Kurtzman, the brilliant writer and cartoonist who had created *Mad,* was the type of compliment that meant more to me than any other. Gary read literature; he knew who James Boswell was and what good biography was, so if I took on something like this, the bar would be high. However, I was ready for a big challenge, and that's what I told him.

Harvey Kurtzman in the 1970s. Photo © by E. B. Boatner. "Superduperman!" by Kurtzman and Wallace Wood from *Mad* #4 (1953). ™ and © William M. Gaines, Agent, Inc.

"Well, then," he said, smiling, "give it some thought."

Thought? I'd been a fan of Kurtzman's work since before I knew his name, back in the early 1960s when I was reading those paperback books that reprinted stories from the early comic book issues of *Mad*. As related earlier, I first encountered the name Harvey Kurtzman in 1966, when Lanz and I discovered those issues of *Playboy* with *Little Annie Fanny*. A couple of years later, when EC fandom was on the rise with the publication of the fanzine *Squa Tront*, I learned that Kurtzman had not only created *Mad*, but he had also been the writer and editor of the EC war comics. Once I read a couple of those, I began poring over every copy of *Two-Fisted Tales* and *Frontline Combat* I could get my hands on. I loved them so much that I tried to imitate Kurtzman's innovative storytelling techniques in a comic strip for my fanzine *Sense of Wonder* in 1972. Now I had the chance to write a book about the man who had invented, written, and designed so many great comics I'd loved since I was a boy. But there were practical matters to be considered.

As I've already pointed out, writing a book about someone takes more than just the desire to do it. It also takes access to the material—the good stuff. Kurtzman had passed away in 1993. Would his family agree to let me interview them? Would they help with photographs? Would I be able to delve into his papers and art files? There was also the fact that John Benson, one of my best friends in fandom, was a writer who happened to be the premier *Mad* scholar and one of the two or three fans most knowledgeable about Kurtzman's career.

I'd corresponded briefly with Benson before I dropped out of fandom in 1974, but our real friendship was formed twenty years later, when I was writing *The Golden Age of Comic Fandom*. John and I also shared a love of cinema, and that's when we became regular correspondents. For this proposed project, Benson could be a tremendous source of information and guidance, since he had known and interviewed Kurtzman, knew Harvey's wife, Adele, and also knew and had worked with Denis Kitchen, the agent for the Kurtzman

Estate. But would he feel I was encroaching on his territory? Did he, for example, plan to write his own Kurtzman biography?

"Hell no!" he exclaimed, when I got him on the phone. "I'd never take on a project like that."

I said, "Then will you help me if I go ahead with Gary's suggestion? And do you think Adele Kurtzman will talk to me?" We mulled this over, but he readily offered his help if I chose to go forward. Benson is one of the most intelligent, perceptive comic-art aficionados I've ever known, and he would be more than a source of information; he would be an advisor who could guide me in all sorts of ways.

After hanging up with Benson, I got back in touch with Gary and told him I would do the book if Adele would talk to me. She was eighty-five years old, so I felt it was imperative that I get in touch with her as soon as possible. Nevertheless, I needed to prepare before I made the call. You have to know your subject before you know which questions to ask. Although I was a Kurtzman fan, there was a lot about him I had yet to learn. I spent a couple of months reading everything I could on the man and his work, including the numerous interviews he'd given, and I sketched out a basic outline of his life. Fortunately, Adele did talk to me, and so did all three of Harvey's daughters, Meredith, Liz, and Nellie. My initial conversation with Adele occurred on July 5, 2011.

In a way, everything that had happened since my return to fandom—and, really, since my childhood—had been preparation for writing this book. I marshaled all of my sources of information, all of my contacts, and all my own inner resources, because it was clear from the start that this was my most ambitious project ever. It was an opportunity to show what I could do. It would be a lot of work, but more than that, I had to raise my game to do anything like justice to my subject.

Toward that end, I did things that might sound silly or extreme, but I believe they helped. In order to maximize my mental capacity, I took supplements (with B12 and other vitamins) designed to enhance brain power. I also got back on my treadmill and began getting regular exercise, which I knew from experience helped with mental clarity as well as physical endurance. I read some excellent biographies just to study the form and to see how other writers handled various issues. But probably the most dramatic thing that helped me write the book was retiring from my job at the SBA.

In the summer of 2011, I passed my twenty-second anniversary working for the federal agency. I'd initially intended to stay until I was sixty-five, or in more recent years, until I was sixty-two, when I could get Social Security to augment my government pension. Changes in the agency in the past year had made the job much less enjoyable than in the past. In fact, the job had become almost unbearable due to policies coming down from our superiors in Washington, DC. I would be sixty in November. One day, when I was talking to my financial advisor about my job, I said, "I don't know how much longer I can hold on."

She responded with what turned out to be magic words: "Maybe you can retire at sixty. Send me your latest financial information, and I'll crunch the numbers." Given that I live a modest lifestyle, it turned out that I *could* retire at the end of 2011! That and the agency's timely buyout offer (a lump-sum payment as an inducement to get older workers to retire) cemented my decision. So, after spending my spare time doing telephone interviews and other research on Kurtzman, and outlining the book, I began writing in earnest on New Year's Day of 2012, my first day as (gasp) a full-time writer. It sure took the sting out of turning sixty.

Being able to write every day, putting my best brain power and my prime-time energy into it, made a huge difference in the quality of my work. I also found it easier to think in greater depth and with greater specificity. When writing about a creative individual, one must find interesting ways to describe the work and to explain what's special about it. Ideas are as important in nonfiction writing as they are in fiction, and many of them involve making connections and pointing out juxtapositions of facts that make a point and illuminate the reader. To quote the noted journalist and author Norman Cousins, "A book is like a piece of rope; it takes on meaning only in connection with the things it holds together."

So far I've discussed the inspiration behind the book, but a great deal of nonfiction writing takes perspiration, too. By that I mean gathering facts. I had to track down every existing interview with Harvey Kurtzman and with his colleagues and best friends, such as Al Jaffee, Arnold Roth, William M. Gaines, Harry Chester, Hugh Hefner, Robert Crumb, Gloria Steinem, Willy Elder, and so on. I also had to gather and read as many comics and magazines by Kurtzman as I could get my hands on. I collected a complete set of his *Help!* magazine from the 1960s. One of his fans and correspondents late in life was Jacques Dutrey, a French fan who had compiled a complete index of every piece of creative work that Kurtzman had done in his life. He shared it with me, saving me a tremendous amount of work. Sadly, Jacques, who helped in many other ways, didn't live to see the book published. He died of cancer while I was working on the final draft.

Gathering everything together was no mean feat, and it was a continual process that only stopped when the manuscript was finished. Yet the existing information could only be a starting point for additional research. My goal was to write as close to a definitive biography of Kurtzman as I could, so it was incumbent on me to find out new information, new facts, unknown or unpublished interviews—anything to create a complete portrait of the man, his creative methods, and the basic events of his life, from birth to death. It had to have things in it that even a dyed-in-the-wool Kurtzman fanatic didn't know. Most importantly, I knew I had to get the absolute truth about the creation of *Mad* (and who came up with the title) and why Kurtzman left *Mad* after just twenty-eight issues. Without answering those two key questions satisfactorily, the book couldn't be definitive.

As I learned more about Kurtzman's life, I was better able to formulate questions to fill in the gaps when I talked to Al Jaffee, Arnold Roth, Drew Friedman, Jack Davis, and many others who had collaborated with him. They opened up to me because I could point them to my other books available online and assure them I already had a publisher. Once I established that basic credibility and was able to show that I'd done my research, I found that every one of them was eager to talk about their work or friendship with Harvey. Kurtzman was a creative genius and a charismatic leader, a pied piper whom others willingly followed, even when some of the post-*Mad* projects weren't very successful from a financial standpoint. Everyone wanted to talk about Harvey. I just had to ask a few questions, and they were off to the races.

When Kurtzman left *Mad* in 1956, he did so to create a new, slick satire magazine for Hugh Hefner, the publisher of *Playboy*. Another key question about Kurtzman's career had to be answered: why Hefner pulled the plug on *Trump* magazine after just two issues. I contacted Hefner's public relations people and asked to interview him about Kurtzman and *Trump*. There was a little back-and-forth to establish my credentials and confirm that I had a publisher, and then—bingo. Hefner agreed to talk to me, but only if I kept it short, to a half hour or so. We ended up talking for about forty-five minutes. I was nervous as hell. It's hard to convey to young people today just how important and influential *Playboy* was from the 1950s to the 1980s.

Hefner, who was eighty-five, was candid, mentally sharp, and able to sum up his thoughts well. What he told me during that phone call answered my questions about the demise of *Trump* and has now become the final word on the subject. (My publisher wouldn't appreciate it if I gave the answer away here.)

As to the question of access to Harvey Kurtzman's personal papers, I have both Denis Kitchen and John Benson to thank for that. As agent for the estate, Kitchen had taken possession of all of Kurtzman's records, correspondence, contracts, and similar materials. Would he allow me to visit and look through them? It turned out that wasn't necessary, since John Benson lived within reasonable proximity to Kitchen's home in Massachusetts, where the records were then stored, and he was willing to go through them for me. The five hundred or so digital photos Benson sent me of highlights of those papers proved to be a treasure trove of information, especially about the Kurtzman lawsuit against Gaines for royalties promised on the early *Mad* paperback books. As you can tell, my access to key material proved almost unlimited, something I partially chalk up to having paid my dues on earlier books. Still, I was extraordinarily lucky. As a publisher, Gary Groth had forged friendships with Robert Crumb and other key people who contributed to the book partly because they knew he wouldn't publish it unless it was good.

Still, this huge amount of material had to be edited and shaped into a readable book. That was my challenge through 2012, 2013, and much of 2014. Through each of the first three drafts, the word count kept increasing until it hit 220,000 words, double the word count of *Man of Rock*. I became alarmed. After doing some rough figuring, it looked like the book might run as much as 750 pages. When, I thought, had I ever read a book that long or longer? Only two instances came to mind: Vincent Bugliosi's *Reclaiming History: The Assassination of President John F. Kennedy*, 1,648 pages about the assassination of President Kennedy (and I skimmed a lot of it); and volume 1 of Mark Lewisohn's *Tune In: The Beatles: All These Years*, the first of his projected Beatles trilogy, which runs 944 pages. As fascinating as Kurtzman's career was, and as profound an effect on American and world culture as *Mad* had, it was asking too much of potential customers to buy and read a version of his life story that ran 750 pages. I decided to make cuts—and to be fairly ruthless about it. I went through and eliminated anything that was nice to know but not absolutely necessary, and I substituted paraphrasing for certain lengthy quotes from various sources. By the time I was done, the book was thirty thousand words shorter. As someone later said, "That's a whole book." As is almost always the case, cutting made the book better. It would still be long—it ended up, with endnotes and index, running 642 pages. The question was, how many people want to know this much about Harvey Kurtzman?

With Gary Groth on the Harvey Kurtzman panel at Comic-Con International: San Diego in 2015. The Kurtzman book cover was designed by Keeli McCarthy.

We soon found out. *Harvey Kurtzman: The Man Who Created* Mad *and Revolutionized Humor in America* (the "revolutionized" part came from Groth) quickly became my best-selling book when it was published in 2015, easily topping the sales of everything else I'd written before—by a wide margin. I couldn't have been prouder when I walked into the Fantagraphics office and held the book in my hands for the first time. The staff crowded around, and even Gary (who has "seen it all") seemed genuinely excited about it. The cover, designed by Keeli McCarthy, featuring one of E. B. Boatner's best Kurtzman photos, was perfect. Later, when I found it staring out at me from a shelf in Barnes and Noble, I just about burst with pride. It almost didn't matter what anybody else thought of it. I knew what a long road I'd traveled to get to the point where I could take advantage of such a great writing opportunity and show what I could do. It's by no means a perfect book, but I gave it my all.

⚡

Fandom brought me many friends, but my love life was one area that fandom hadn't fixed. Then something happened. It involved Mario Vitale, the fan in Rhode Island whom I fell in love with back in the summer of 1973. Things had ended badly between us, and I'd felt terrible about it. It was a cornerstone event in my life, one that shaped my attitude about romance and relationships for all the years that followed. I compared anyone who came along to Mario, and they all fell short. From time to time, I wondered how things had worked out for him. I toyed with the idea of contacting him, but I was hesitant because I felt I had let him down so badly. Many (maybe most) of the people who were my friends at an earlier time haven't been interested in getting back in touch when I found them years later. My memories of the intense love I felt for Mario in 1973 were precious to me. An unpleasant encounter now could taint those memories.

Finally, in 2015, when my Harvey Kurtzman book was published, I decided to see if Mario was on Facebook. He was! I sent him a message saying I'd been writing books and asking if I could send him my latest "for old times' sake." He replied affirmatively and gave me his address. I was relieved that he seemed friendly, if reserved. I inscribed a copy of the book ("What a long strange trip it's been …") and sent it off. He responded with a nice thank-you and a few other brief comments, which at least helped me feel like he was okay with being back in touch. I more or less forgot about it until I heard from him a full year later. "Amid the demands of life," he wrote in May 2016, "I have only now got to reading it, and I thank you again for sending it. What an astounding work your Kurtzman book is! How do you do it? It is an extraordinary work in its detail and erudition! And so highly readable and engaging!"

I wrote that I would soon begin expanding my *Sense of Wonder* memoir. Would it be all right if I included our meeting back in 1973? He responded that he would probably be fine with it, but could I send him the original book to give him an idea of what we were talking about? This led to more messages through Facebook, ending with us exchanging some memories of things we did on that visit way back when, like seeing the movie *The Paper Chase* together. Then he wrote, "All that aside, being with you was the best part and I remember that vividly and always have. And always will." That led me to suggest, gingerly, if we could switch to email communication where we could write at greater length. That began a correspondence that surprised both of us.

Actually, it overwhelmed us. After reconstructing our memories of that amazing nine-day meeting after the 1973 New York Comic Art Convention (I'd always wondered what happened to my con T-shirt, which Mario now told me he'd found under his bed after I left), we embarked on catching up on our lives and interests, and—lo and behold, I found my old feelings of love for him rekindled, and he confessed to similar feelings for me. All the things that had drawn me to him as a correspondent when I was in high school and college were still there.

He had gone on to study literature as a graduate student, but, like me, he hadn't been able to find a job in his field of choice. Instead, he embarked on a successful career in financial services, much as I had at the SBA. (He wasn't yet retired.) Now, all these years later, we were both still in one piece and both still loved comics, movies, books, fine art, music, and … each other.

Harvey Kurtzman: The Man Who Created Mad received excellent reviews, the best of all my books. Steven Hiller of *Atlantic* magazine wrote, "Schelly's exhaustive biography makes [it] exceptionally clear that Kurtzman … was the Matt Groening/Jon Stewart/Tina Fey of his day, giving Kurtzman a hero's welcome into the pantheon of American cultural pioneers." On his Facebook page, film director Terry Gilliam told his followers, "A wonderful book about Harvey Kurtzman, my mentor, who taught me most of what I know about humour, has just been published. Read. Enjoy." It was selected by *Playboy* as its Book of the Month for May 2015, and it received a nice notice in *Rolling Stone* magazine. However, one review was especially meaningful to me. It came from comics writer and journalist S. C. Ringgenberg, who wrote, "This recent biography of Harvey Kurtzman will probably stand as the definitive biography of one of America's most influential humorists and cartoonists. Schelly, a longtime comics fan and historian, has really outdone himself with this volume. What really struck me as a reader, however, is the quality of Schelly's writing. There are long stretches of exposition that could have been dry, but Schelly manages to make the entire book an engaging reading experience." I had worked hard on improving my writing, so it meant a lot to me that someone noticed.

The Kurtzman biography was nominated for a Will Eisner Comics Industry Award for best comics-related book of 2015. The other nominees were heavyweights: *King of the Comics: One Hundred Years of King Features Syndicate,* edited by Dean Mullaney; *Only What's Necessary: Charles M. Schulz and the Art of Peanuts* by Chip Kidd and Geoff Spear; *Out of Line: The Art of Jules Feiffer* by Martha Fay; and *Will Eisner: Champion of the Graphic Novel* by Paul Levitz. I had been at the award ceremonies when I didn't win in 1996 and 1998, so I didn't go to Comic-Con in July to hear the announcement of the winner. I didn't want to jinx it.

After being nominated twice before in the 1990s, it was gratifying to finally win a Will Eisner Comics Industry Award for *Harvey Kurtzman: The Man Who Created* Mad *and Revolutionized Humor in America* as Best Comics-Related Book of 2015. Photo at the Eisner Award ceremony by Rob Salkowitz.

On the big night, July 22, I was home. The Eisner awards were hosted by John Barrowman, but they weren't streaming a live broadcast, so Mario and I went to Facebook. At exactly 9:00 p.m., a Facebook friend posted his congratulations and a photo of the big screen in the auditorium in San Diego, where the awards were held, with my book being shown as the winner. I could hardly believe it.

"I won!!" I messaged Mario.

"I expected it all along!" he wrote.

What are the odds that I could celebrate winning the Eisner Award within days of reuniting with the long-lost love of my life?

Nevertheless, I swear with my hand on my *Fantastic Four Omnibus,* this is exactly how it happened.

29.

LOVE STREET

In 2016, when I started writing this expanded version of *Sense of Wonder,* I celebrated my twenty-fifth year back in comic fandom. I shudder to think how much poorer my life would have been if I hadn't returned to the fold in 1990.

Turning sixty-five years old doesn't seem as daunting as I thought it would. I'm in good health and doing what I love on a daily basis. I feel like the same person inside that I was when I was fifteen or twenty-five, except that I'm happier now and have a great deal more experience to help me deal with life's inevitable problems.

I was a late bloomer. One day, fellow comics historian Michelle Nolan said after reading *Man of Rock,* "If you'd started writing when you were younger, Bill, you could have been a really fine writer." After we both burst into laughter (because it hadn't come out quite the way she meant it), I had to say that I have no regrets about being a late bloomer. It's never too late to start. Frank McCourt didn't publish his first book—*Angela's Ashes,* which won a Pulitzer Prize—until he was sixty-six. Norman Maclean was seventy-four when he published his only novel, the best-selling *A River Runs Through It.* So, Michelle, who knows? Maybe there's still time for me to become "a really fine writer."

A family member recently asked, "Have you ever thought of doing a book on something or someone beyond comic books, which could be a bigger deal?" My response was, "Sometimes, but I already have what I want. It's just a matter of scale." My writing career is modest, but with all the satisfactions and many fewer hassles than bigger writers have.

There's a virtue in doing one thing and doing it well. That's how one excels. And I'm still trying to improve my work and go beyond my limitations. One can always be smarter, funnier, more skillful—or so I believe.

Next, I researched and wrote the biography *John Stanley: Giving Life to Little Lulu.* The project gave me the great pleasure of reading most of Stanley's ceaselessly clever Little Lulu stories, as well as his tales of Nancy and Sluggo, Melvin Monster, and many other characters. Other book opportunities have come my way since winning the Eisner Award, but, if the day arrives when they dry up, I'll go back to self-publishing in some form. I write. That's what I do. I'll find some way to do that until I can't any more.

One issue that arose was what to do with my Comic Fandom Archive, established in the early 1990s to gather, utilize, and preserve material from and about the history of comic fandom: all the fanzines, artwork, recordings, photographs, correspondence, and other ephemera, which will be a treasure trove for people studying popular culture in the future. Thus, I was delighted when, in the course of discussing other matters with Karen Green of Columbia University Libraries, a mere mention of my archive led to a discussion on that subject. Before long, we agreed that Columbia would set up a special collection for both the archive for and my own literary papers. In the past year or so, I've begun getting those papers (and other materials) in order, preparing for the time when I'm ready to surrender them to Columbia. It's a great feeling to know they will be preserved for posterity.

John Stanley: Giving Life to Little Lulu (Fantagraphics, 2017). Cover designed by Keeli McCarthy.

As for the state of gay characters in comic books, it seems like it's finally happening in a big way. It's nice to know that there are comic books that acknowledge and even celebrate the existence of LGBTQ and other gender and sexually nonconforming people in the world. Northstar married Kyle in *Astonishing X-Men* #51 in 2012, the same year X-Man Bobby Drake (Iceman) came out. Kevin Keller is pretty well established as an ongoing character in the Archie-verse, as is Batwoman (rebooted as a lesbian in 2006) in Gotham City. Comics outside of the superhero realm, such as Japanese *yaoi*, are replete with gay love stories for teenage girls. The list goes on.

When asked what comics books I read these days, I'll admit to being greatly interested in those of the past. That's part of being a comics historian, but it's also because, as someone once said (I don't know who), everyone's "golden age of comics" is when they were ten years old. For me, that means comics from the Silver Age. I periodically reread the Stan Lee–Steve Ditko issues of *Amazing Spider-Man* and Jack Kirby's tremendous Inhumans-Galactus saga in *Fantastic Four*. Still, subsequent decades brought abiding favorites, such as the politically incorrect work of Robert Crumb, the Alan Moore–written issues of *Saga of the Swamp Thing*, the beauty of Craig Thompson's graphic novel *Blankets*, the dazzling expansion of the blind hero's origin in *Daredevil: Man Without Fear* by Frank Miller and John Romita Jr., and the raw, unflinching graphic novel about the Nazi death camps in World War II, *Yossel: April 19, 1943*, by Joe Kubert. As we've discovered over the years, any kind of story can be told in comics form. It's a magical medium with a language all its own. The possibilities are infinite.

Looking back over the past sixty-five years, I realize that, beyond my very existence, I owe so much to my birth family, the Schellys and the Winns. And I'm unendingly grateful for my new families, the Joneses and the Seymours, and to my daughter, Tara. And to her brother Jaimeson, who gave us all so much in his brief twenty years, and who continues to live in our hearts.

When someone is single, friends are so important. From Dick Trageser to Barbara Barker, Bob Sanborn, and Jim Malek in Idaho, and Ed Brooks, John Teegarden, Dale Nash, and Jim Holt (among many others) in Seattle, I've been fortunate in finding interesting, intelligent, loving, and supportive friends. Each one has been pivotal in my life, and I hope I've given back some measure in return.

Mine has truly been a life in comic fandom, since the years when I foolishly strayed have now faded into insignificance. Fandom is merely an aggregation of fans with a common interest—in this case, a shared love of comic art. As I look back, I remember Marshall Lanz's fun-loving ways, Ronn Foss's generosity, John Benson's sage advice, Roy Thomas's help on many projects, Gary Groth's faith in me, and Jeff Gelb's unwavering support. I couldn't have a truer, more loyal friend than Jeff.

Am I single now? Not really. Mario and I live a continent apart, so it's going to take some figuring and patience to see how our relationship develops. But in my heart, and in his, we are together. We like to say we live together on Love Street.

Writer at work. Photo by Tina Bradley.

When people ask me how I've been able to write so many books, I tell them it's because each one was a labor of love. I can still hear Ray Bradbury's impassioned, emotional, high-pitched voice urging each one of the thousand fans in the room at Comic-Con International to "Love what you do and do what you love," adding, "Imagination should be the center of your life."

Don't ever lose your sense of wonder. I did, for a while. But with the help of family, friends, and fandom, I was able to find it again. Otherwise, as Albert Einstein wisely said, "He to whom this emotion is a stranger, who can no longer pause to wonder and stand rapt in awe, is as good as dead."

As far as I can recall, my sense of wonder took flight with a small act of kindness: when, as a boy, my father told me I could pick out a comic book at the train station, and I chose *Giant Superman Annual* #1. He could have remained firm in his insistence that I put it back and instead choose one that only cost ten cents, like the ones my brothers had chosen. But he looked into my eyes, saw how much I wanted it, and plunked down a quarter. Thanks, Dad.

INDEX

A

Able-Man Book Store, 108
Academy of Comic Book Fans and Collectors, 105, 182
Action Comics, 26, 45
Action Hero, 99, 102, 127, 130
Adam Link, 353
Adams, Neal, 42
Adler, Jack, 363
Adler, Leah, 374
Adventure Comics, 26, 121, 122
Adventures of Superman, 19–20
Agee, James, 257, 258
AIDS, 268
Albee, Edward, 168
Alex Toth, 330
Alf, Richard, 304, 389
Allen, Irwin, 76
Alley Tally Party, 102, 312, 318, 341
All-Star Comics, 50
Alpha Flight, 307
Alter Ego, 49, 50, 51, 53, 67, 71, 74, 82, 83, 97, 183, 302, 308, 331, 338, 342–43, 348, 359, 365, 371, 383, 384, 385, 388
Alter Ego: The Best of the Legendary Fanzine, 341, 342, 343, 344, 345
Amazing Heroes, 306
Amazing Spider-Man, 38–41, 48, 407
Amazing Spider-Man Annual, 43–45, 68
American Association of Comic Book Collectors, 344
American Civil Liberties Union (ACLU), 175
American Comic Book Chronicles series, 383
The American Dream, 168
American Zoetrope, 270
Angela's Ashes, 405
Anthro, 140
Apex Treasury of Underground Comics, 248, 249
Arbunich, Marty, 53

Archie Comics, 63
Armstrong, David, 387, 388
Armstrong, Lance, 369
Arnold, Busy, 184
The Art of Harvey Kurtzman, 391
The Art of Joe Kubert, 379, 380, 391
The Art of Will Eisner, 312
The Assembled Man, 161, 164, 167, 168–72, 173, 174, 175, 181, 184, 190, 201, 205, 333
Asterisk, 146
Astonishing X-Men, 407
The Atom, 344
At the Mountains of Madness, 217
Auad, Manuel, 330

B

Bails, Jean, 338, 383
Bails, Jerry, 50–51, 90, 103, 105, 158, 182, 183, 302, 312, 338, 339, 340, 341, 355, 370–71
Balin, Nancy, 367, 377
Bancroft, Anne, 147
Bar, Ken, 222
Barker, Barbara, 137, 139, 143, 157, 165, 253, 356, 358, 408
Barrier, Michael, 312
Barrowman, John, 403
Bat Lash, 140
Batman, 20–21, 22, 26, 27–28, 42, 53, 76, 90, 158–59, 179, 215, 218, 226, 227, 277, 297, 360
Batman (comic), 21, 26, 195, 277, 333
Batman (film), 292–94, 297
Batman (TV show), 76–77, 294
Batman and Robin (film), 336
Batman Annual, 28–29
Batmania, 49, 50, 53, 70, 72, 88
Batman of the Forties, 360
Batwoman, 407
Bauman, Barry, 318

Bean, Bob, 363
Beck, C. C., 67, 195, 218, 233–35
Beerbohm, Bob, 339, 341
Beetlejuice, 294
Benson, John, 318, 379, 393–94, 397, 408
Berry, D. Bruce, 151, 155
Bibby, Dave, 145, 151
Binder, Eando, 332
Binder, Earl, 355
Binder, Ione, 369
Binder, Otto, 51, 67, 332, 352–59, 369, 379
Birch, D. J., 25
Biro, Charles, 163
Black, Bill, 198
Black, Louis, 354
Blackhawk, 82, 83
Blackhawk, 26
Blackjack, 125
Blankets, 407
Blue Beetle, 63
Blue Mountain Rock Festival, 175, 190, 191
Boatner, E. B., 400
Bodé, Vaughn, 183, 218, 231
The Boeing Company, 254, 262, 272, 275, 333
Bogart, Humphrey, 148, 310
Bombshell, 110, 130, 298
Borasio, Diana, 256, 260, 263, 265, 267, 270
Boswell, James, 365, 392
Bradbury, Ray, 357–58, 409
Bridgeman, George, 124
Brimstone, 123–24, 142–43, 178
Brooks, Ed, 267, 408
Broome, John, 344
Broom-Hilda, 225
The Brothers Mad, 115
Brown, Gary, 95, 126–27, 390
Brownlow, Kevin, 256, 259
Bruce Wayne, 27, 79
Bubnis, Bernie, 312
Buckler, Richard, 110–11, 195, 198
Bugliosi, Vincent, 398
Buhle, Paul, 391
Burroughs, Edgar Rice, 163, 332, 360
Burton, Tim, 293, 294, 297, 336
Butts, Bob, 339, 341
The Buyer's Guide to Comic Fandom, 184, 199, 339
Byrne, John, 307

C

Campbell, Joseph, 356
Capa-alpha, 158–59, 187, 250, 298–99, 300,
    302, 308, 311, 337

Caplan, Aaron, 384, 385, 386, 388
Capra, Frank, 258, 261–62
Captain America, 42, 66–67, 90, 140, 186,
    309, 354
Captain America, 48, 140
Captain Ego, 87
Captain Marvel, 51, 67, 218, 233, 234, 353, 354
Captain Marvel Adventures, 51, 67
Captain Marvel Junior, 51
Cardy, Nick, 140
Carlsson, Peter, 363
Casey, Coreen, 102, 145, 182, 301
Chambers, Johnny, 389
Chaplin, Charlie, 256, 257, 258, 263
Charlton Comics, 63, 231, 330–31
Cheech Wizard, 231
Cherokee Bookstore, 108
Chesney, Landon, 87, 88, 332
Chester, Harry, 396
Chicago Con, 338, 339
Chiller Theater, 161
Chit-Chat, 52–53
Cinema Books, 255
Clark, William, 134
Clark Kent, 11, 13, 27
Cloak and Dagger, 130, 131
Clowes, Daniel, 364
Cockrum, Dave, 193, 248
Coddington, Walt, 105
Colbert, Steven, 377, 378
The Colbert Report, 377, 378
The Collector, 125, 130
Colletta, Vince, 224, 226–28, 344–45
Come with Me, 157, 271–72
Comic Art, 97, 102, 383, 385
Comic Book Artist, 342–43
Comic Book Price Guide, 183, 223, 312, 318
Comic Buyer's Guide, 300, 305, 312, 326, 327,
    339, 374, 383
Comic Comments, 95
Comic-Con International: San Diego, 327,
    343–45, 379, 383, 384–85, 399, 409
Comic Crusader, 183
Comic fandom
    adults in, 103–4
    conventions, 125–26, 311
    FIAWOL vs. FIJAGH, 101
    fiftieth anniversary of, 383–90
    lure of, 100–101, 103
    origins of, 50, 59, 383
    race and, 102
    research on, 196–97
    women in, 102

Comic Fandom Archives, 312–13, 406
Comic Feature, 125
Comiclub, 85, 111
Comico, 336
The Comicollector, 47, 302
The Comic Reader, 71, 183, 200, 232, 304–5
Comics Code, 45, 52, 103, 196, 308
The Comics Journal, 312
Comic World, 61
Comique, 187–89
The Complete Crumb, 364
Conan the Barbarian, 163, 308
Construction Bonding and Management
  Services, 284, 291
Continuity, 336
A Contract with God, 198, 344
Cooke, Jon B., 342
Copner, Michael, 260, 261
Coppola, Francis, 270–71
Corrigan, Tim, 339
Cousins, Norman, 395
The Cowl, 87, 302
Crain, Dale, 359
The Creeper, 140
Creepy, 104, 116, 221
Crime Does Not Pay, 153
Crisis on Infinite Earths, 277
Crumb, Robert, 248, 364, 396, 398, 407
Cruse, Howard, 269–70, 307, 348

D

The Daily Show, 377, 378
The Dangling Conversation, 130
Daredevil, 42–43, 90, 407
The Dark Knight Returns, 282, 283
Davis, Jack, 396
DC Archive Editions, 336, 359
DC Comics, 12, 26, 38, 42, 45–46, 50, 90, 121,
  122, 125, 126, 140, 187, 201, 227, 233, 304,
  305, 307, 359–60. *See also* Junior Bullpen
  Project
DCTC (DC Trade Center), 105
The DCTC Bulletin, 106, 107, 109, 125,
  130
Decker, Dwight, 308, 341
Defiant, 336
Detective Comics, 20, 26
DeWald, Wayne, 95
Diamond Comics, 323, 337
Dick Grayson, 27–28
Differo, 130
Dimension Man, 302

Ditko, Steve, 38, 41, 43, 44, 45, 61, 67, 68, 69,
  70–71, 75, 107, 140, 155–56, 184, 191–93,
  197–98, 347, 407
Doctor Doom, 309–10
Doctor Solar, 63
Doctor Strange, 42, 67, 69, 71, 74–75, 140
Donald Duck, 303
Dorf, Shel, 304, 387
DuBay, Bill, 53, 61, 79, 221, 223, 228–29
Durrell, Rick, 311
Dutrey, Jacques, 396
Dyke, Rod, 247–48

E

Earthquake Comics, 73, 130
EC, 51–52, 96, 153, 177, 178, 196, 318, 319,
  327, 393
Eclipse, 307, 336
Edmunds, Mark, 339
Eerie, 104, 116, 221
Eightball, 364
Einhorn, Lawrence, 369
Einstein, Albert, 4, 409
Eisenstein, Gabe, 85, 111
Eisner, Will, 92–93, 100, 151, 154, 163, 184,
  195, 197, 198, 312, 321, 344, 361
Eisner Awards, 329–30, 344, 402–3
Elder, Will, 115, 116, 396
Elfman, Danny, 294
The Encyclopedia of American Comics, 312
Enterprise, 130
Erwin, Lee, 256
Esser, David J., 105–6, 111, 125, 126
Estrada, Jackie, 384, 385, 386, 387
Et Cetera, 304
Evanier, Mark, 377, 378, 390
Ewbank, Tom, 292
The Eye, 47, 48, 50, 61, 62, 312
The Eye, 61
The Eyrie, 129–30, 157

F

Fagan, Tom, 218, 355
Famous Monsters of Filmland, 221
Fandom Reunion
  1997, 338–42, 370, 390
  2011, 383–90
Fandom's Agent, 154
Fandom's Finest Comics, 331–35, 337–38,
  347, 357
Fantagraphics Books, 363–65, 379, 388, 400

Fantastic Four, 107
Fantastic Four, 41, 46, 309, 407
Fantasy Fandom Crossroads, 73, 125
Fantasy Forum, 95–98, 305, 390
Fantasy Illustrated, 88, 163, 308, 331
Fantasy Magazine, 50
Fantucchio, John, 61, 158, 163
Faucher, Wayne, 351–52
Fax from Sarajevo, 361
Fay, Martha, 402
Feiffer, Jules, 20, 90, 274
Feldstein, Al, 153
Fighting Hero Comics, 47, 50
Film Comment, 259
Films in Review, 259
The Films of Alfred Hitchcock, 148
Finch, Peter, 321
Finn, Richard, 284
First Comics, 336
Fisher, Amana, 367, 368
Fisher, Tom, 127, 151–54, 184–85, 198
Fix, Nicholas, 284, 291
Flash, 63, 90, 344
Flash, 26, 46, 50
Flash Gordon, 142, 241
Fleming, Ian, 72, 89, 129, 130
Flotsam, 178
Fly-Man, 63
For Boys Only, 75
The Forbush Gazette, 106, 107, 109, 130, 178
Forever People, 187
Foss, Ronn, 87, 88, 97, 98–99, 102, 127, 142,
    145, 146, 158, 181–82, 190, 193, 238, 299,
    300–302, 318, 331–32, 343, 408
Founders of Comic Fandom, 374, 383
The Fountainhead, 155
Fox, Gardner, 353
Frankenstein, 161, 164
Frazetta, Frank, 116, 138, 193, 220
Fredrik, Nathalie, 148
Friedman, Drew, 396
Frontline Combat, 186, 393
Furst, Anton, 294

G

Gafford, Carl, 224
Gaines, William M., 218, 220, 396, 397
Gambaccini, Paul, 182
Game of Thrones, 389
Garrett, Michael, 310
Gay Comix, 269–70
Gelb, Jeff, 68, 107, 209, 298, 304, 305, 310,
    317, 343, 374, 381, 384, 388, 390, 408

Gemignani, Margaret, 102
Get Smart, 76
Giant-Size X-Men, 248
Giant Superman Annual, 8–14, 15, 16, 19, 26,
    45, 51, 244, 333, 353, 409
Gilbert, Michael T., 347
Gilliam, Terry, 402
Giordano, Dick, 348, 349
Glacier Park, 173
Glut, Don, 318
Golden Age Collectables, 247–48, 277
The Golden Age of Comic Fandom, 317–30, 347,
    358, 390, 393
Golden Horseshoe, 244–45, 250
Golden Press, 354
Gold Key, 38, 46, 63
Goodwin, Archie, 327
Gosh Wow!, 183
Goulart, Ron, 312
The Graduate, 147–48, 157
The Graphic Art Collector, 109
Graphic Story Magazine, 163–64, 390
Graphic Story World, 200
The Great Comic Book Heroes, 20, 90–91, 274
The Great Movie Comedians, 258
Green, Karen, 406
Green, Richard "Grass," 87, 88, 102, 300, 338,
    339, 340
Green Arrow, 21, 53, 79, 158
Greenberger, Bob, 360
Greene, Don, 165
Green Lantern, 90, 220, 344
Green Lantern, 26, 46, 50
Greim, Martin, 183
Grell, Mike, 307
Grost, Michael T., 353
Groth, Gary, 312, 318, 363, 388, 389, 391–93,
    394, 398, 399, 400, 408
Gruenwald, Mark, 218, 222, 223
Guidebook to Comic Fandom, 59
Gulacy, Paul, 248
Guthrie, Arlo, 141

H

Habblitz, Harry, 332
Hall, Hal, 355
Hamilton, Donald, 129
Hamster Press, 159–60, 321–22, 329, 337, 341,
    343, 347, 353, 357, 390
Hanley, Alan, 186, 218, 231
Hanna-Barbera Productions, 78
Hardy Boys, 30
Harrington, Eva, 143, 154

Harrison, Ernie, 137, 138, 148
Harry Langdon, 258–66, 272, 317, 372–74
Harvard Exit, 255–56
Harvey, R. C., 339
Harvey Comics, 92, 93
Harvey Kurtzman, 391–403
Hasen, Irwin, 363
Hawk and Dove, 140
Hawkman, 90, 360
Heath, Russ, 218
Hefner, Hugh, 396, 397
Heinlein, Robert A., 134, 135, 141–42
"Heisenberg Alley," 151–54, 184
Held, Claude, 90
Help!, 396
Henderson, Gene, 389
Henry, Buck, 147
Henry, Stan, 269
Heritage, 241
Herndon, Larry, 109, 142, 181, 191–93, 311
Herriman, George, 274
Herring, Dave, 88, 109
Hiller, Steven, 402
Hinton, S. E., 271
The History of the Amateur Comic Strip, 308, 314
Hitchcock, Alfred, 148, 255, 270
Hitchcock/Truffaut, 148
Hoffman, Dustin, 147
Hogarth, Burne, 218
Hollywood and the Academy Awards, 148
Holt, Jim, 255–56, 287–88, 289, 408
Hoohah!, 327
Horror Comics of the 1950s, 186–87
Hot Blood, 310
Hot Wheels, 187, 190
House of Mystery, 201
House of Secrets, 201
Howard, Robert E., 163
Howard, Sherman, 99, 102, 127, 128, 142
Howard, Wayne, 102, 127
The Hulk, 140
The Hulk!, 306–7
The Human Torch, 90
Huston, John, 201
Hutchinson, Alan, 64, 95, 96, 106, 107, 390

I

Iceman, 407
Image Comics, 336
The Immortal Corpse, 53–57, 64–66, 77, 96,
   98–99, 127, 158, 273, 333, 334–35
Incognito, 74, 79, 81, 82, 88, 89, 95, 97, 117,
   173–74, 175

Infantino, Carmine, 140
Iron Man, 41, 126, 140
The Irving Forbush Gazette, 106, 107, 109,
   130, 178
Isabella, Tony, 223, 224, 308, 341

J

The Jack Kirby Collector, 341, 342
Jackson, Fred, 102
Jaffee, Al, 396
James Bond, 72–73, 76, 89, 129, 146
Janson, Klaus, 282
Jennings, Robert, 97
Jew Gangster, 363
Jezerski, Sara, 377, 379
Jimmy Olsen, 20, 75, 125, 209–10
Joe Kubert School, 361, 362, 363
Johnson, Steve and Dave, 146
John Stanley: Giving Life to Little Lulu, 406
Jones, Jaimeson Carl, 295–96, 303, 336,
   367–70, 375–81, 390, 407
Jones, Jeff, 218
Jones, Maureen "Renie," 290, 294–96, 367,
   368, 376, 377, 380, 381
J'onn J'onzz, 21
Jonny Quest, 78–79
Journey into Mystery, 41
Junior Bullpen Project, 212–17, 219, 223–24,
   226–28, 237, 344
Justice League of America, 50
Justice League of America, 26, 46, 47, 92, 344
Justice Society of America, 50

K

Kalat, David, 374
Kaluta, Mike, 201, 213
Kane, Bob, 218, 226
Kane, Gil, 220, 231–33, 236, 237, 330–31
Kanigher, Robert, 140, 360
Keaton, Buster, 255, 256, 257, 258, 264
Keaton, Michael, 293, 294
Keltner, Howard, 339, 340, 341
Kennedy, John F., 114, 134, 398
Kerr, Walter, 256, 258, 262
Kevin Keller, 407
Kidd, Chip, 402
Kilby, Susan, 374
King, Stephen, 347
King of the Comics, 402
Kirby, Jack, 38, 42, 61, 66–67, 70, 122, 140,
   187, 190, 235, 309–10, 347, 361, 407
Kitchen, Denis, 312, 389, 391, 393, 397

Klein, Gene, 146
Kohoutek, Mark, 278–84
Kohoutek, Tom, 275–76, 278–80, 282–84
Komik Heroz of the Future, 71
Korkis, Jim, 308
Koudoulian, Greg, 387, 389
Krazy Kat, 274
Krenkel, Roy G., 195, 198
Krueger, Ken, 304
Kubert, Adam, 363
Kubert, Joe, 140, 343, 360–66, 370, 374, 379,
     380, 407
Kubert, Muriel, 363
Kubert, Roslyn, 363
Kuhfield, Ellen, 312
Kurtzman, Adele, 393, 394
Kurtzman, Harvey, 114–16, 186, 391–403
Kyle, Richard, 104, 143, 164, 184, 195, 200,
     383, 390

L

Labors of Love, 313, 314, 323, 327
Langdon, Harry, 256, 257–66, 269, 372–74
Langdon, Mabel, 259–61, 264
Lanz, Kay, 84, 86, 91, 107, 126, 176, 177,
     179–80
Lanz, Marshall, 81–88, 90, 91–94, 98, 105 14,
     116, 118–19, 125–26, 134, 135, 141, 145,
     176–79, 238, 349–50, 390, 393, 408
Layton, Rod, 247
Lee, Stan, 38, 41, 42, 44, 45, 67, 122, 183, 218,
     328, 344, 361, 407
Legion of Super-Heroes, 121, 122, 209, 353, 354
Levitz, Paul, 304, 402
Lewis, Meriwether, 134
Lewisohn, Mark, 398
"The Life You Save May Be Your Own,"
     201–2, 205
Lightning Man, 85
Lillian, Guy H., 186
Little Annie Fanny, 114, 115, 116, 393
Little Giant, 302
Little Green Dinosaur, 389
Little Lulu, 406
The Lives and Times of Archy and Mehitabel,
     274
Lloyd, Harold, 256, 257, 258, 373
Lobdell, Scott, 307, 308
Lois Lane, 10, 20, 27, 75
Lois Lane, 26
Long Pants, 256, 259
Loomis, Andrew, 124
Looney Tunes, 8

Lost in Space, 76
Love, G. B., 60, 101, 102, 163, 200, 235, 300
Love and Rockets, 364
Lovecraft, H. P., 217, 236
Lupoff, Pat, 383
Lupoff, Richard, 355, 383
Lynch, Jay, 341

M

Maclean, Norman, 405
Mad magazine, 114–16, 218, 392–93, 396,
     397, 398
The Mad Reader, 115
Magnum Opus, 142
Maheras, Russ, 339, 340, 388, 390
Malek, James, 261, 408
Malibu, 336
Maltin, Leonard, 258, 259, 270
The Man from O.R.G.Y., 129
The Man from U.N.C.L.E., 76, 129
Mangels, Andy, 306–7, 308
Man of Rock, 364–65, 370, 372, 391, 398,
     405
Man of Steel, 282
Marceau, Marcel, 263
Mark, Ted, 129
Marquis, Don, 274
Martin, George R. R., 389
Marvel Comics, 38, 41–42, 45, 46, 47, 50,
     66–67, 79, 103–4, 107, 122, 140, 183, 187,
     222, 231, 281, 306, 307–8, 344
Marvel Family, 51, 67, 353, 354
Marx Brothers, 336
Masquerader, 302
Massengill, Ron, 339
Master Comics, 51
Master of Kung Fu, 248
Master of Sound, 73
Mastroserio, Rocke, 193
Matt Helm, 129
Matthews, Gordon, 186
McCarthy, Keeli, 399, 400, 406
McCourt, Frank, 405
McFarland Publishing, 374, 383
Memoirs of a Nobody, 355
Men of Mystery, 298
Metzger, George, 183
Miller, Frank, 282, 311, 347, 355, 407
Miller, Raymond, 47, 61, 91–94, 109, 127, 154,
     158, 184–85, 198, 238
Mister Miracle, 187
Mitchell, Ken, 90
Moench, Doug, 248

Monroe, Marilyn, 146–47
Moore, Alan, 407
Moore, Clayton, 389
Moroz, Drury, 331
Morrissey, Rich, 308
Morrow, John, 341–42, 343, 349
Morrow, Pam, 341–42
Moss, Chuck, 318
Moss, Glenn, 297–98
Mr. A, 155–56, 191–93, 197
Mullaney, Dean, 402
Mundy, Bonnie Binder, 355, 357
Murray, Patty, 379
Myers, Russell, 225

N

The Name above the Title, 258
Nash, Dale, 268–69, 408
National Periodical Publications, 12
NBC Saturday Night at the Movies, 146–47
Network, 321
New Gods, 187
Newton, Don, 163, 193, 195, 198–99, 238
New York Comic Art Convention, 212–13,
    218–26, 231–36, 330, 401
Nichols, Mike, 147
Nicholson, Jack, 293, 294
Nick Carter, 129
Nick Fury, Agent of S.H.I.E.L.D., 218, 221
Nixon, Richard, 114
Nolan, Michelle, 405
Northern Pacific Railroad, 15, 16, 18, 64, 69,
    73, 79, 83, 107, 108, 109, 111, 113–14, 132,
    214, 273
Northstar, 307–8, 407
Nostalgia Press, 186

O

Obama, Barack, 375
O'Brian Gang, 187–91, 200
O'Connor, Flannery, 201
Odd, 331
Ogle, Stephanie, 255
O'Neil, Dennis, 42
Only What's Necessary, 402
On the Drawing Board, 183
Ordway, Jerry, 339, 341, 347
Osmar, Nils, 319–20, 325, 326, 327, 330, 332,
    333, 374
*Otto Binder: The Life and Work of a Comic Book
    and Science Fiction Visionary,* 359
Our Army at War, 140

Out of Line, 402
The Outsiders, 271
Overstreet, Bob, 183, 223, 312, 318

P

Pacella, Mark, 307
Pacific Marine Schwabacher, 246
Palumbo, Dennis, 125, 126
Pan, 73
Pandora, 102, 145
The Panel Art Examiner, 109, 130–31
Panosian, Dan, 307
The Parade's Gone By, 256
Patten, Fred, 186
Perrin, Steve, 97
Perry, George, 148
Pete Ross, 26, 27
Peter Parker, 41, 43, 209
The Phantom, 63
Photoplay, 259
Photo-Reality Comics, 327
Pitt, Stanley, 198, 200
Planets: Other Worlds of Our Solar System, 354
Plant, Bud, 200, 218, 221, 223, 304, 314, 323,
    326, 360
Plastic Man, 90, 95, 96
Plastic Man Archives, 359
Playboy, 114, 115, 116, 393, 397, 402
Plush, Perry, 277, 280, 282
Plutarch, 365
Potter, Doug, 99, 109, 128
The Power of Myth, 356
Powers, Wayne, 262
Pryor, Richard, 299
Psycho, 148

Q

Quality Comics, 184

R

Race Royal, 77–79, 89
Rand, Ayn, 155
RBCC (Rocket's Blast-Comicollector), 47,
    48, 50, 55, 59, 60–61, 67, 81, 89–90, 91,
    101, 102, 105, 163, 184, 195, 199, 200,
    235, 344
Reclaiming History, 398
Reeve, Christopher, 294
Richardson, Frank Howard, 75
Richard Stern, 129–30, 157
Ringgenberg, S. C., 402

"Rites of Man," 185, 186, 197

A River Runs Through It, 405

Robin, 20–21, 22, 26, 27–28, 216, 277

Robinson, Chuck, II, 187

Roche, Anthony, 151

Rogers, Chuck, 125

Rogers, Jimmy, 158

Rogofsky, Howard, 90

Rohauer, Raymond, 264, 265–66

Rohde, Stephen P., 264, 265

Romeo and Juliet, 174

Romita, John, 107, 407

Ronn Foss Retrospective, 299, 300–301, 302

Rossiter, Jeannie, 241

Rossow, Jim, 338, 341

Roth, Arnold, 396

Russell, Jeanne, 349

Rutherford, Tony, 110–11, 128

Ryan, John T., 195, 198

S

Saga of the Swamp Thing, 407

Saha, Heidi, 231

Sammon, Paul, 389

Sanborn, Bob, 137–38, 143, 165, 185, 186, 408

Sanctum, 73, 146

Sanders, Butch, 42

San Diego Comic-Con, 304–10, 311, 315, 317, 324, 327, 330

Sassaman, Gary, 384, 385, 387

Saunders, Buddy, 61, 97, 390

Savage, Mark, Jr., 128

Scarecrow Press, 264–66, 271, 320, 372

Schelly, Bill. *See also individual publications, characters, and employers*
  birth of, 18
  childhood of, 6–17, 19–36
  in junior high school, 37, 60, 71–72
  in high school, 132, 136–39, 143–44, 148–49, 157, 158
  in college, 149, 165–68, 174–75, 202, 206, 212, 214
  moves to Seattle, 243–44
  at Super Comics and Collectables, 278–84
  buys house, 287–89
  retires, 395
  creativity and, 30–33, 35–36, 75–76, 253, 314
  as father, 294–96, 302–3, 367–70, 375–81, 407
  personality of, 32

  romantic relationships of, 144, 157, 165, 241–43, 289–91, 296, 336, 400–403, 408
  sexual orientation of, 2, 43, 116–18, 144, 207–11

Schelly, Carl (father), 6, 7–8, 10, 11, 15, 16, 17, 18–19, 23, 26, 31, 34, 55, 68, 75, 76, 107, 133–35, 142, 148–49, 214, 246–47, 273

Schelly, Charles and Helena (grandparents), 18

Schelly, Dave (brother), 6, 7, 8, 16, 18, 24, 25, 33, 133–35, 142, 160, 173

Schelly, Joanne Winn (mother), 6, 7–8, 11, 12, 15, 17, 18–19, 25, 47–48, 68, 72–73, 75, 81, 84, 121, 133–35, 136, 142, 144, 246, 247, 272, 372

Schelly, Steve (brother), 6, 7, 8, 16, 18, 23, 24, 114, 133–35, 142, 202, 204, 205

Schwaberow, Mickey, 142

Schwartz, Julius, 46, 47, 50, 92, 224, 227–28, 234, 330, 344–45, 355, 358

Science Fiction and Comic Association (SFCA), 47

Scott, Randy, 355

Scroggy, Dave, 389

Scroggy, Rose, 389

Seattle Counseling Service (SCS), 267–68

Second Genesis, 280, 281, 284

Secret Agent, 76

Secret Six, 140

Seduction of the Innocent, 195

Sekowsky, Mike, 92

Sennett, Mack, 374

Sense of Wonder
  naming of, 98
  #1, 98–100, 111–13
  #2, 122–23, 126–29, 130
  #3, 142, 143
  #4, 143
  #5, 151–55
  #6, 155–57, 193, 334
  #7, 157–58
  #10, 175, 178, 184, 333
  #11, 184–87, 191–93, 197–98
  #12, 195, 198–200, 208, 221, 228–29, 270

Sense of Wonder: A Life in Comic Fandom, 348–52, 356, 365, 401

Seuling, Phil, 90, 218, 221, 304, 311

Seymour, Stephanie, 262, 290, 294, 296, 302–3, 367, 368, 377

Seymour, Tara Jane, 302–3, 367–68, 375, 377, 380, 407

Sgt. Rock, 140, 360

The Shadow, 63, 64

The Shadow, 213

Shakespeare, William, 174
Shanklin, Richard, 200
Shazam!, 212–13, 233–34
Shelley, Mary W., 161, 172
Shelly's Leg, 245, 250
Shields, Richard, 46–47, 48, 51–52, 55–57, 60, 81, 298
Shoenfeld, Robert, 183
Shooter, Eleanor, 122
Shooter, Jim, 121–25, 126, 128, 142–43, 238, 306, 307–8
Shooter, Kenneth, 121, 122
Shor, Norman, 53
Showcase, 140
Shroud, 131
Siegel, Howard, 234–36, 237, 238, 243, 345
A Sign for Cain, 196
The Silent Clowns, 256
Silver Surfer, 73
Simmons, Gene, 146, 347
Simon, Joe, 67
Simon and Garfunkel, 147
Slam-Bang, 61
Slide, Anthony, 264, 265
Small Business Administration (SBA), 291–92, 297, 300, 303, 379, 395, 402
Smith's Frozen Foods, 160–61, 168
Smithsonian Book of Comic-Book Comics, 312
The Snow-Man, 68, 69, 70, 117–18
Son of Vulcan, 63
Space World, 355
The Speakeasy, 187
Spear, Geoff, 402
Speer, Gary, 174–75, 191, 250–51
Spicer, Bill, 163–64, 300, 332
Spider-Man, 38–41, 42, 43–45, 71, 107, 231, 277, 303
Spiegelman, Art, 361
The Spirit, 90, 92–93, 100, 151, 198
The Spirit, 92, 93, 104, 151, 184
Sprang, Dick, 21
Springsteen, Bruce, 251–52
Squa Tront, 393
Stanley, John, 406
Star Brite, 73
Starlin, Jim, 61
Star Rangers, 127, 128, 142, 215
Star-Studded Comics, 61, 88, 97, 142, 181, 191, 308, 311, 331, 340, 390
Star Wars, 308
Steinem, Gloria, 396
Steranko, Jim, 218, 221
Stewart, Jon, 377, 378

Stonewall riot, 160, 208, 211
Stranger in a Strange Land, 134, 135, 141–42, 161
Strange Tales, 41, 75
Strange Tales Annual, 38
Strnad, Jan S., 186
The Strong Man, 256, 258, 259
Stuck Rubber Baby, 348
Sub-Mariner, 90
Sub-Mariner, 90
Summers, Larry, 290–91, 295, 296, 336
Superboy, 26, 27, 210
Superboy, 26, 210, 353
Super Comics and Collectables, 278–84, 297
Supergirl, 13, 277, 353, 354
Super Hero, 312
Super-Heroes Anonymous, 52–57, 62–70, 95, 301, 390
Superman, 8–15, 19–20, 22, 26, 27, 75, 90, 215, 277, 303, 353, 354, 360
Superman (comic), 26, 45, 46
Superman (film), 294
Superman's Pal Jimmy Olsen, 26, 187, 209
Surety Insurance Services, 275–76, 282, 284
Swamp Thing, 277
Swan, Curt, 75, 122

T

Tales from the Crypt, 51
Tales of Suspense, 41
Tarzan, 103, 332, 360
Teegarden, John, 269, 408
Teenage Mutant Ninja Turtles, 282
Thailing, Bill, 90, 218
Thomas, Dann, 330, 338, 340, 341
Thomas, Roy, 50, 51, 79, 82, 105, 183, 308, 324, 330, 338, 339, 341–42, 344, 345, 352, 355, 371, 383, 388, 390, 408
Thompson, Craig, 407
Thompson, Don, 97–98, 238, 305
Thompson, Maggie, 97, 102, 305, 326, 338, 340, 341, 383
Thor, 41, 73
T.H.U.N.D.E.R. Agents, 63
Tiefenbacher, Mike, 341
Timely Comics, 47, 90
Tollin, Anthony, 224, 308
Tommy Tomorrow, 21
Toth, Alex, 169, 187, 190
Tower Comics, 63
Trageser, Dee, 273, 274, 310, 333, 334
Trageser, Dick, 63–65, 77, 96, 97, 98, 99, 114, 116, 127, 146, 237–38, 272–74, 310–11, 408

Truffaut, François, 148
Trump, 397
Tune In, 398
Tuohey, Mike, 312, 339, 341, 388
Turek, Patricia, 355
Two-Fisted Tales, 393
TwoMorrows Publishing, 343, 349, 365, 383
Twylite, 100, 127

U

University of Idaho, 149, 165–68, 174–75, 190, 202
Usagi Yojimbo, 282
Uslan, Michael, 354

V

Valiant, 306
Van Hise, James, 163, 200
Varley, Lynn, 282
The Viper, 302
Vitale, Mario (pseudonym), 146, 208, 214, 236, 241–43, 250, 290, 400–403, 408
Voice of Comicdom, 88, 131
Vosburg, Mike, 302, 324
Voyage to the Bottom of the Sea, 76

W

Walczak, Larry, 125
Waldroop, Matt, 127
Walker, Alan, 71
Walt Disney, 8, 38
Warren, James, 116, 198, 218, 221, 223, 231
Warren Publishing, 228, 237
Washington State University, 210–11, 375
Watchmen, 282, 283
Webb, Charles, 147, 157
Wehrle, Joseph, 200
Wein, Len, 248, 311
Weingroff, Rick, 97
Weird Science, 51
Weisinger, Mort, 27, 122, 125, 143
Weiss, Alan, 61, 88, 201
Wertham, Frederic, 27, 195–97

Whale, James, 161
White, Biljo, 53, 61, 83, 87, 88, 182, 300, 312, 318
Whitehall Printing, 322, 323
Whiz Comics, 51, 90
Who's Who in Comic Fandom, 50–51
Wilbur-Ellis, 262, 266, 272, 276, 290
Wilder, Thornton, 319
Wildey, Doug, 78
Will Eisner, 402
Williams, Martin, 312
Willingham, Calder, 147
Wilson, Bill G., 125, 126, 388, 389, 390
Winn, Russ and Gladys, 18, 19
Wise Blood, 201
witzend, 155
Wolfman, Marv, 311
Woman's Century Club, 255
Wonderment, 131
Wonder Woman, 90
Wood, Wally, 155, 361, 392
Woolfolk, William, 67, 355
Woolley, Chuck, 154
Words of Wonder, 357–59
The World of Fanzines, 197
World's Finest, 21, 26, 333
Wow Comics, 51
Wrightson, Bernie, 201, 311

X

Xal-Kor the Human Cat, 87
X-apa, 298
Xero, 383, 385
X-Men, 248, 298

Y

Yancy Street Journal, 49, 50, 53, 79, 107
Yarmak, 198–99
Ymir, 389
Yossel: April 19, 1943, 407
Yronwode, Cat, 312, 327

Z

Zanadu Comics, 277–78, 280

ABOUT THE AUTHOR

 Bill Schelly has been chronicling and adding to the pop-culture fringes since the mid-1960s. He became widely known in the comics community thanks to his popular fanzine *Sense of Wonder* (1967–1972). He began researching the history of comic book fandom in 1991, resulting in his book *The Golden Age of Comic Fandom* (1995). In 1998, he became associate editor of *Alter Ego* magazine.

Schelly has written several biographies of film and comics artists, including comedian Harry Langdon and artist Joe Kubert. His *American Comic Book Chronicles: The 1950s* (2013) was nominated for a Harvey Award. He recently authored *Harvey Kurtzman: The Man Who Created* Mad *and Revolutionized Humor in America* (2015), which received the Will Eisner Comics Industry Award in 2016 for Best Comics-Related Book. Schelly has also received an Inkpot Award from Comic-Con International: San Diego. In 2017, Fantagraphics published his book, *John Stanley: Giving Life to Little Lulu.*

About North Atlantic Books

North Atlantic Books (NAB) is an independent, nonprofit publisher committed to a bold exploration of the relationships between mind, body, spirit, and nature. Founded in 1974, NAB aims to nurture a holistic view of the arts, sciences, humanities, and healing. To make a donation or to learn more about our books, authors, events, and newsletter, please visit www.northatlanticbooks.com.

North Atlantic Books is the publishing arm of the Society for the Study of Native Arts and Sciences, a 501(c)(3) nonprofit educational organization that promotes cross-cultural perspectives linking scientific, social, and artistic fields. To learn how you can support us, please visit our website.